The Urban Book Series

The Urban Book Series is a resource for urban studies and geography research worldwide. It provides a unique and innovative resource for the latest developments in the field, nurturing a comprehensive and encompassing publication venue for urban studies, urban geography, planning and regional development.

The series publishes peer-reviewed volumes related to urbanization, sustainability, urban environments, sustainable urbanism, governance, globalization, urban and sustainable development, spatial and area studies, urban management, transport systems, urban infrastructure, urban dynamics, green cities and urban landscapes. It also invites research which documents urbanization processes and urban dynamics on a national, regional and local level, welcoming case studies, as well as comparative and applied research.

The series will appeal to urbanists, geographers, planners, engineers, architects, policy makers, and to all of those interested in a wide-ranging overview of contemporary urban studies and innovations in the field. It accepts monographs, edited volumes and textbooks.

Indexed by Scopus.

WU Siegfried Zhiqiang

The AI City

Springer

WU Siegfried Zhiqiang
Shanghai, China

ISSN 2365-757X ISSN 2365-7588 (electronic)
The Urban Book Series
ISBN 978-981-96-2559-8 ISBN 978-981-96-2560-4 (eBook)
https://doi.org/10.1007/978-981-96-2560-4

This Springer imprint is published by the registered company Springer Nature Singapore Pte Ltd.
The registered company address is: 152 Beach Road, #21-01/04 Gateway East, Singapore 189721, Singapore

Foreword

The Chinese Academy of Engineering conducted a strategic assessment of the development of next-generation artificial intelligence (AI) in China and concluded that AI research in China should advance not only in five key directions—big data intelligence, swarm intelligence, cross-media intelligence, human-machine hybrid augmented intelligence, and autonomous intelligence—but also in applications such as smart cities, intelligent manufacturing, and smart healthcare. This book represents a distillation of the research findings from the urban applications subproject under the Chinese Academy of Engineering's research project, "Development Strategy for China's Artificial Intelligence 2.0."

In 2012, China introduced the Pilot Management Measures for Smart Cities. Since then, the country has gradually explored the construction of smart cities nationwide and successively launched a series of national-level strategic policies. These policies proposed more forward-looking and systematic national urbanization strategies, along with strategic guidance for advancing related scientific and technological fields. This approach has progressively facilitated the development of smart urbanization, transitioning from pilot projects to maturity and from superficial to deeper levels of implementation.

Today, artificial intelligence (AI) technology has begun to integrate into various dimensions of smart city development, including planning, design, construction, and operation, as well as the operational dimensions of production, living, ecology, and management. While people have developed a preliminary understanding of AI-driven cities, there remains a need for systematic construction of their connotations, characteristics, elements, key technologies, and driving forces for development.

"The AI City" presents a theoretical framework for AI-driven cities, consisting of three main components: core architecture, scenario systems, and technology systems. Through 15 chapters, it systematically introduces the concept of AI-driven cities, elaborates on the theoretical foundation of the evolution from smart cities to AI-driven cities, and explores the technological frontiers, core objectives, and key components of such cities. The book also features a wealth of practical case studies that illustrate the integration of AI technologies with urban planning, governance, and various urban scenarios, showcasing China's innovative approaches and unique characteristics in urban intelligence development. It offers a framework to guide future research and practice in AI-driven cities and serves as an essential reference for practitioners, policymakers, scholars, and students in urban governance, smart urban transformation, and urban planning and development.

Hangzhou, China
November 2022

PAN Yunhe
Member and Former Executive Vice
Academician of the Chinese Academy
of Engineering
Professor at Zhejiang University

Preface

Many of you might be familiar with the concept of the "City Brain." Through long-term observation, we have discovered that if all the operational information of a city were centralized into a single "City Brain," it could lead to the issue of an "overburdened brain." To address this, we embarked on an entirely new exploration by selecting a 2-square-kilometer experimental area to simulate how an AI model could learn to operate in coordination with a real city. The goal is for AI to understand how a social community organizes, collaborates, and acts, thereby forming a multi-brain collective intelligence model that goes beyond a single brain. I call this new model the "City Multi-Brain."

We have completed the first CIMAI system based on the multi-brain structure, adopting a multi-level, distributed, and cross-business architecture. This system forms an efficiently functioning intelligent decision-making network that includes a main brain, auxiliary brains, sub-brains, and terminal brains. Certain decisions can bypass the main brain and provide direct feedback, significantly improving decision-making efficiency—marking a historic innovation in AI models.

The multi-brain structure involves diverse stakeholders, including strategic city decision-makers (such as the municipal Party secretary and mayor), department managers (various municipal commissions and bureaus), investors and developers (entrepreneurs and real estate developers), operations managers (responsible for the day-to-day operations of urban functions, such as school principals, store managers, and business executives), employees, and visitors. On the AI city simulation platform, we constructed six key stakeholder models to simulate and learn how different actors perceive, judge, and make decisions individually while interacting as a group within the same urban space. This ensures balanced development and sustained benefits for all parties.

On the AI city simulation platform, we also proposed the "composite board theoretical model", designed to support the self-organization, self-operation, self-growth, and self-coordination of these six stakeholders across nine AI scenarios. These scenarios encompass various domains, including employment, living, finance, education, healthcare, and safety. This collaborative model ensures sustainable and balanced urban development across multiple sectors.

We discovered that once AI cities breakthrough to learn from urban social communities and adopt innovative models, enabling information exchange and predicting others' decisions across systems on a unified spatial platform, a remarkable synergy emerges. This synergy allows for complementary strengths and weaknesses among various stakeholders.

In the domains of resilience, sustainability, and intelligence, we have conducted a series of multi-objective, multi-stakeholder simulations across different scenarios. Time and again, we have been moved by the progress achieved through the collaborative learning of the "AI City Multi-Stakeholder Multi-Brain System."

The multi-brain model we have explored, evolving from AI learning urban group collaboration to the first application of the multi-brain architecture in urban experiments, confirms that smart cities have transcended the stage of simulating a single social brain and entered a new era of multi-brain learning and collaboration.

We believe this not only brings innovation to the AI city model but also proposes a more advanced intelligent framework for multi-stakeholder collaboration and urban management. This breakthrough represents a significant innovation in AI models, deeply influenced by the Chinese Academy of Engineering's AI 2.0 project.

In 2007, during the preparation for the World Expo, the Tongji University team collaborated with IBM to jointly propose the internal architecture and a series of fundamental concepts for smart cities. The World Expo even featured a dedicated thematic pavilion, the "City-Being Pavilion," to convey the idea that a city is not only a complex living organism but also an intelligent being. This intelligence, supported by big data and digital technologies, positions the city as an intelligent life form. Following the Expo, the concept of the city as an intelligent being gained global recognition and dissemination.

With the rapid rise of artificial intelligence, a new wave of integration between AI technologies and the urban intelligence process has emerged. This marks the latest and highest peak in the 8000-year history of urban construction, while also posing significant challenges and risks. Therefore, the concept of the "Artificial Intelligence City" (AI City) must first establish clear goals, ensure that technology serves a greater good, and remain true to its original purpose: using technology to enhance the quality of urban life rather than exacerbating inequality and opacity.

The second key aspect we propose for AI City is that it should not function merely as a governing brain but should enable people at all levels to become part of the city's brain—what we call the concept of the "multi-brain." A city should embody democratic plurality and integrated intelligence, representing the collective intelligence of an intelligent urban life form. This is the essence of urban wisdom and the future trajectory of urban development.

The future of AI cities hinges critically on ensuring fundamental safety measures as AI is integrated into urban environments. Issues such as pandemics, epidemics, urban flooding, and fires remain challenges that humanity aspires to overcome but has yet to fully address. With AI technologies, there is an opportunity to explore and create safer cities, paving the way for innovative solutions to these persistent problems.

Another critical application of AI lies in supporting vulnerable groups. For instance, AI can provide life care support for elderly individuals living alone, assist people with disabilities in overcoming daily challenges, ensure a safer and more enriching childhood for children, and offer employment, healthcare, and cultural learning opportunities to large numbers of migrants with AI assistance. Moreover, countless other vulnerable individuals stand to benefit from AI empowerment, making it a vital tool for promoting inclusivity and equity in society.

In the exploration of AI city scenarios, the architecture of numerous new technologies and the sharing and segmentation of digital storage remain significant unresolved challenges. Balancing the protection of individual privacy and digital security with ensuring the efficient operation of the overall system presents critical technical and ethical issues that must be addressed in the future.

The arrival of AI cities is inevitable, bringing benefits to a broader population. Open discussions on the ethical use of technology and breakthroughs in technical challenges are essential as we collectively explore ways to integrate AI with urban life, creating a future that is more prosperous and enriched for all.

Shanghai, China
December 2022

WU Siegfried Zhiqiang
Member of Chinese Academy of Engineering
German National Academy of Science and Engineering
The Royal Swedish Academy of Engineering Sciences
Professor at Tongji University

Acknowledgements **Research and Planning Design Team Members**: WU Siegfried Zhiqiang, GAN Wei, YANG Ting, MA Chunqing, LI Shuran, LIU Xiaochang, LI Mohan, LIU Zhiyu, ZHOU Mimi, HAN Jing, ZHAO Gang, QIAO Renlu, ZHAO Shuang, RONG Liying.

Contributors and Illustrators: GAN Wei, MA Chunqing, HEI Jinghao, LI Shuran, LIU Xiaochang, LI Mohan, LIU Zhiyu, ZHOU Mimi, HAN Jing, ZHAO Gang, QIAO Renlu, Qingrui Minyag JIANG, ZHAO Shuang, RONG Liying, XU Haowen, HE Zhen, XU Xiaodong, LIANG Jing, LIU Zhenyuan, JIANG Limin, ZHOU Shiqi, FENG Fan, LU Feidong, SHA Yutian, HE Rui, WEN Xiaoyi, YAN Juan, WU Yuwei, LI Lan, JIA Weiyi, CHEN Zeyin, ZHU Yumo, SUN Mingli, YANG Shujie, MA Qicheng, QI Yue, XU Huikun, YANG Jingyi, JIN Tianji, ZHANG Xiuning, WANG Ziqi, WANG Lun, ZHANG Guobin, HUANG Xiaoyu, YUAN Xiaoqiu.

Competing Interests The author has no competing interests to declare that are relevant to the content of this manuscript.

Contents

Chapter 1
The Development of the Smart City

Abstract Since IBM introduced the concept of a "smart Earth" in 2008, smart cities have progressively emerged as a global priority. The United States has supported the development of smart grids and intelligent transportation systems through governmental funding; European nations such as the United Kingdom and the Netherlands have focused on constructing sustainable and intelligent urban environments; while in Asia, countries like South Korea, Japan, and Singapore have initiated their respective smart city initiatives. With the rapid pace of urbanization in China, smart cities have been recognized as an innovative model to enhance urban governance. Since 2012, China has embarked on pilot projects and promoted smart city construction. Major cities such as Beijing, Shanghai, Guangzhou, and Shenzhen have achieved significant progress in areas like intelligent transportation and smart healthcare. However, challenges remain, including inadequate data sharing and suboptimal interdepartmental collaboration.

Keywords Smart city · Global development · Urbanization · Data sharing

1.1 The Concept of the Smart City

"Smart cities" have become a global focal point in the field, with the concept of "smart Earth" introduced by IBM in 2008 gaining recognition from the US government as an important strategy to address economic crises. In collaboration with IBM, Professor Wu Zhiqiang proposed the concept of "smart city (see Fig. 1.1) and established the Tongji University-IBM Smart City Research Center in 2010. The US National Intelligence Council's Global Trends 2030 report released in December 2012 identified information technology as one of the four most influential categories for global economic development, with "smart city" being a key component within this category.

Z. WU, *The AI City*, The Urban Book Series,
https://doi.org/10.1007/978-981-96-2560-4_1

Fig. 1.1 IBM's future smart city architecture

1.1.1 Early Adoption of Smart City Initiatives in the US

The US government promotes the construction of smart cities through financial funds, and guides enterprises to invest in scientific research in related fields to encourage innovation. The construction of information infrastructure, smart grid, smart transportation, and smart medical care is the focus of the current smart city construction in the United States. To promote smart cities, the US government plans to invest more than $160 million in federal research funding to support more than 25 new technology collaborations to help solve critical challenges at the grassroots level. These key challenges include easing traffic congestion, fighting crime, boosting economic growth, tackling climate change, and providing city services.

1.1.2 Leader of "Smart Cities" Practice in the Europe

The United Kingdom, the Netherlands, Sweden, Denmark, Spain, France, and other countries have started early in actively promoting the construction of smart cities. The European Vision 2020 proposes building a smart, sustainable, and inclusive Europe, with smart cities as an important part of the process, hoping to maximize the potential of current infrastructure and capital through the construction of smart cities, and developing new products and services that adapt to social and environmental challenges.

1.1.3 Strategic Implementation Across Asia-Pacific Nations

As early as 2004, South Korea and Japan launched the U-Korea and U-Japan national strategic plans. Singapore has made remarkable achievements in the construction of smart cities with its "Smart Island Plan" (IT 2000) in 1992 and "Infocomm 21" in 2000.

1.2 The Development and Predicament of Smart Cities in the World

1.2.1 Smart City Development in China

China's urbanization is in a period of rapid development, led by dense coastal urban areas and inland central cities, driven by industry and employment, and characterized by large-scale cross-regional population flow. China's urbanization growth rate has been much higher than the global urbanization development average during the same period. Data from the National Bureau of Statistics show that from 1978 to 2013, the urbanization rate of China's permanent residents increased from 17.9 to 53.7%, an average annual increase of about one percentage point. According to the Statistical Bulletin of the People's Republic of China's 2017 National Economic and Social Development released by the National Bureau of Statistics, at the end of 2017, the total population of the country was 1.39 billion, of which 813 million were urban, accounting for 58.52% of the total population, that is, the urbanization rate has reached 58.52%. The trend of urbanization development will continue for another 10–20 years.

The smart city is a new mode of strengthening urban planning, construction and management through comprehensive use of modern science and technology, integration of information resources, and overall planning of business application systems. At the same time, the construction of smart cities is also an important measure to implement the Party Central Committee and the State Council's innovation-driven development, promote new urbanization, and build a moderately prosperous society in all respects.

Since the introduction of smart city pilot management measures in 2012 and the three batches of smart city construction pilot lists announced since then, China has gradually carried out the exploration of building smart cities across the country. In the following years, a series of policies at the national strategic level were successively introduced, and more forward-looking and systematic national urbanization strategic measures were proposed as well as strategic opinions on the promotion of related science and technology fields, while the smart urbanization construction was gradually promoted from pilot to maturity and from shallow level to deep level (see Fig. 1.2) (Table 1.1).

Fig. 1.2 The timeline of smart urbanization construction

Table 1.1 The development of smart cities in China

City practice	Details
Beijing Leading in intelligent transportation, property, and public services	(1) Intelligent transportation Most of China's first-tier cities face the pressure of urban traffic congestion, and Beijing is among them. In order to ease the pressure on the transportation system, Beijing actively promotes the application of new generation information technology in the transportation system as an important part of the construction of smart cities. Through the continuous injection of new technologies and the introduction of new models, traffic congestion is eased and the operation efficiency of the traffic system is improved For example, with the support of Fangshan District's high-end manufacturing base and Zhongguancun Emerging Industry Frontier Technology Research Institute, Doudian Town's smart road infrastructure—enabling autonomous driving and V2X connectivity—was developed. This allowed intelligent vehicles to complete phased testing via synchronized vehicle-infrastructure collaboration, laying a practical foundation for intelligent transportation systems. We actively deploy technical solutions by implementing products in targeted operational scenarios. Through cooperation with Baiyun Airport, driverless shuttles are put into service between the terminal and the parking lot, providing passengers with a technological and futuristic ferry service experience, and improving the convenience and safety of airport commuting. Through cooperation with the Raffles commercial complex project, driverless shuttles are put into the large underground parking lot, and through an automatic identification system, customers are locked into the parking space and are picked up from the elevator entrance of the parking lot to the parking space where their vehicles are located, which effectively solves problems such as difficult-to-find cars in the parking lot and long travel distances In the future, in the context of the coordinated development of Beijing-Tianjin-Hebei, in the process of Beijing's smart city construction, a series of technologies, products, applications, and modes such as driverless driving, vehicle networking, and artificial intelligence (AI) will emerge in an endless stream and gradually light up the capital's transportation arteries (2) Smart property The application of intelligent technology in daily life management has also been fully valued, and smart property management has a positive impact on many aspects of urban people's lives. Some problems faced by the current situation, such as parking difficulties and poor order in old residential areas, uneven management levels in modern residential areas, and energy consumption waste in modern office buildings, will be effectively solved or improved. To build a smart property management system, it is necessary to adhere to the concept of combining administrative fine governance and public participation in joint governance. Through the new generation of information technology such as big data collection, cloud computing, and high-speed Internet of Things (IoT), the integrated management platform is built. Residents can summarize problems to the street through the APP integrated management platform, and the property service company and the administrative department can get involved through the integrated management platform APP to discuss solutions together, and finally the property company will implement it, forming a closed-loop mechanism for problem disposal. Real-time data from office buildings and residential complexes is aggregated through the joint property company. This enables predictive monitoring of fire safety, illegal activities, population trends, and utility risks (water/electricity/heat), while an AI-powered analytics database proactively identifies issues like unauthorized gatherings, high-rise fire hazards, and elderly resident emergencies

(continued)

Table 1.1 (continued)

City practice	Details
	(3) Take the lead in establishing "identity cards" for public facilities In the future, Beijing's public facilities such as bus stops, telephone booths, newsstands and garbage bins on both sides of the road will be equipped with two-dimensional code "ID cards." By 2019, the QR code coverage rate in Beijing's core central business district (CBD) area, Olympic Park and the surrounding areas, Sanlitun, and other areas has reached 100%. Through WeChat, QQ, Weibo, and other software, citizens can scan the two-dimensional code on the facilities not only to understand the basic information relating to these facilities, but also to report the dirty, damaged, and other problems of public facilities online. In the past, public facilities were in a chaotic state of multi-department management, and it was not very clear how many public facilities there were in the city, where they were located, and who should be contacted if they were damaged. Municipal authorities will create standardized digital profiles ('identity cards') for all public facilities to formalize ownership documentation and address the aforementioned operational inefficiencies (4) Big data platforms create a shared society In terms of transportation organization, smart cities will adopt new technologies such as big data, the IoT, and smart connected vehicles. In solving congestion, parking, riding, and other aspects, a series of new forms of information technology has been adopted to make people travel more convenient. A smart city—essentially an urban IoT ecosystem—systematically gathers real-time data from connected devices, mobile sensors, and citizen interactions. This information is consolidated into a centralized urban big data platform for analysis and decision-making. This platform first brings together information from various government departments to achieve sharing. In addition, the information of all social units, institutions, and business sectors should be gathered, exchanged, and shared. Iterative platform enhancements driven by real-world applications create a self-optimizing cycle: aggregated data from organizational and individual activities undergoes systematic mining, analytical refinement, and operational calibration to yield decision-critical patterns. Social organizations and individual activities form a huge database through data aggregation and then, through data mining, analysis, sorting, and optimization, extract some regular things to assist decision-making. At the same time, citizens can also use these data to obtain various convenient life services
Shanghai Its initiatives in smart city and healthcare infrastructure development are at the forefront nationally, with a particular emphasis on leveraging smart technologies to drive industrial upgrading	(1) Smart healthcare Shanghai is committed to building a smart health system. As a key construction project, the Shanghai Health Network has initially built the largest population health big data center in China after two phases of construction, bringing together more than 30 billion clinical diagnosis and treatment data, including one billion outpatient medical records and more than 10 million inpatient medical records, and realizing the interconnection and data sharing of public medical and health institutions in the city. Based on the application and exploration of population health big data, it has played a decisive role in the policy design of medical service price adjustment, community "1 + 1 + 1," and public hospital evaluation, realizing government process management and fine management, and promoting the transformation of government management mode (2) Smart government affairs Shanghai has actively promoted the application of new technologies and models in government administration and services, and has promoted the city-wide connectivity of government information-sharing platforms, the sharing of data across the entire network, comprehensive business coordination, and online service delivery. It has completed the deployment of nearly 200 information subsystems based on the government cloud, realized the sharing and use of enterprise and citizen information in different spatial locations, and carried out cross-departmental collaborative management actions. At present, the coordination and links between the Shanghai municipal government information-sharing platform and the national government information-sharing platform have been realized, laying a solid foundation for solving cross-regional, cross-level, and cross-departmental information sharing

(continued)

Table 1.1 (continued)

City practice	Details
	(3) Intelligent life Shanghai Smart Life Construction started with comprehensive public health services, smart transportation, and weather data services, and built the following platforms: ① The health service integrated management platform. This was designed to create a comprehensive management platform covering the fields of medical care, medical insurance, medicine and public health to realize the links between government policies and resources, establish a comprehensive management platform for health and family planning administrative decision-making, and promote the deep integration and seamless docking of the municipal platform with the district-level platform and business system ② Intelligent transportation travel information release system. This was designed build a comprehensive transportation information service platform to meet the public's travel information needs, and provide interactive and comprehensive information services covering public transport, external transport, and road traffic through a variety of carriers such as mobile terminals ③ Meteorological public data social service cloud platform. Through the open processing of meteorological monitoring data, a meteorological big data platform was built to provide instant meteorological information services to the public and improve convenience in urban life (4) Smart economy Shanghai has introduced a new generation of communication technology for economic development, starting from the development of industrial parks with high efficiency and wisdom (referred to as "two"), and realizing the upgrading of industrial economic development. Among these, the "two" integrated management system implementation promotion project has a greater role in promoting the development of energy economy by carrying out the "two" integration assessment and diagnosis and standard guidance work, enriching the standard implementation pilot enterprises and service institutions, improving and standardizing the standard implementation promotion and evaluation service system, strengthening policy support for the pilot work of standard implementation, and guiding the integrated development of the "two" integrated management system and related standards such as smart parks and industrial Internet
	(5) Smart governance In terms of urban governance, Shanghai focuses on air, energy, and public services, including air governance in cooperation with the Yangtze River Delta region, the construction of the Yangtze River Delta regional air quality forecast and early warning system, the establishment of the Yangtze River Delta regional air quality forecast and prediction center, the establishment of monitoring data opening, data visualization, comprehensive management application, emission inventory, regional air forecast services, and other functions in one system, and improving the level of air quality forecast and prediction in the Yangtze River Delta region (6) New generation of information infrastructure ① User perception improvement project. This will improve the broadband network structure, optimize inter-network connectivity, expand metropolitan area networks, deploy gigabit access to households on a large scale, and further increase network speed ② New service platform construction project. Relying on their own network and facility resources, telecom operators integrate their internet access, business support, cloud computing and big data, user channels and other capabilities, strengthen cooperation with third parties in society, establish an open "Internet+ " comprehensive service platform, and carry out application demonstrations in medical services, transportation, intelligent manufacturing and other fields

(continued)

Table 1.1 (continued)

City practice	Details
	③ Backbone iot private network construction project. Strategic pilot zones—including Lingang, Yangpu, and Disney Resort areas—have initiated phased technical validations and multi-standard network deployments, for different types of users, to provide heterogeneous, ubiquitous, flexible network access, to promote the application in urban management, intelligent manufacturing and other aspects, the initial completion of the material oriented city-wide private network of the IoT and to achieve large-scale application (7) Open utilization of data resources ① Sharing and opening of government data resources, formulating sharing technical specifications and management standards, improving the sharing evaluation and supervision mechanism, building a unified management platform for sharing government data resources in the city, and realizing the centralized storage and unified management of data resource catalogs and the comprehensive sharing of government data resources ② Establishing and improving the city's data trading circulation market. Relying on the Shanghai Data Trading Center, Shanghai will explore and carry out the trading of commercial data derivatives products for application scenarios, improve the relevant legal systems, rules and standards, technical support and certification systems in data trading and privacy protection, standardize the sharing and circulation of data resources, and gradually establish a leading domestic data trading market system, standardization system and regulatory system
Guangzhou Significant achievements have been made in the exploration of smart transportation and smart planning	Guangzhou has accelerated the transformation of government functions, streamlining administration and delegating power, and optimizing services, accelerated the promotion of "Internet+ government services," deeply implemented the information benefit project, and comprehensively promoted the reform of "integrated services" for administrative approval. Guangzhou has achieved a system where all administrative approval and public service matters are handled through a "front desk comprehensive acceptance, back-end classified approval, and unified window issuance" process throughout the city. It has established a four-level linkage mechanism for administrative approval services at the municipal, district, sub-district (town), and community (village) levels, creating a government service environment that features optimized approval processes, high-quality approval services, low approval costs, and high approval efficiency. At the same time, Guangzhou vigorously promote the construction of "social governance government public service platform," build a government service management system of "two-level platform, three-level management, four-level link, and five-level service," realize the resource integration, process re-engineering, data sharing, and business link of the city's government service management work, significantly enhance the ability of social governance, and significantly improve the level of public service. Information integration has been deepened and service management mechanisms have been improved (1) Regional planning and exploration of smart city construction based on smart industry: Tianhe Smart City From 2010 to 2020, the Guangzhou Municipal Government had take "Smart Guangzhou" as an important strategy for urban development, focusing on creating new facilities, new applications, new industries, new technologies, and new life. Through the "planning campaign," the preparation of detailed control plans for key regions have complete the construction of the basic framework of smart city construction in 2015. Among them, Tianhe Smart City, as one of the key areas, is the pilot exploration of smart city construction in Guangzhou

(continued)

Table 1.1 (continued)

City practice	Details
	(2) Integrating modern ecological technology into Lingnan landscape culture to achieve urban and wild symbiosis: smart ecology Tianhe Smart City is an important node in the ecological corridor in the middle of Guangzhou. Surrounded by mountains and hills on three sides, it has the same ecological base as the traditional Lingnan landscape pattern. This project integrates modern technological means such as intelligent collection and analysis with the fundamental base of the Lingnan landscape pattern. It conducts research in three aspects: rain and flood, biology, and recreation, deduces the development patterns, and formulates scientific and reasonable development plans based on these patterns. In terms of stormwater, through the calculation and study of the current water capacity, runoff, and measurement of flood inundation range, a scientific and reasonable spatial layout scheme is established according to the stormwater situation that occurs once every 10 years, once every 50 years, and once every 100 years. In terms of biology, by studying the migration process and environmental adaptability of animals in the region, a safe ecological pattern of protecting organisms and maintaining ecology is arranged. In terms of recreation, through the study of historical monuments, preserved buildings, and ecological parks, the available landscape resources, human resources, and recreation resources are comprehensively analyzed, and different levels of safe recreation flow lines are compiled, interspersed, and superimposed (3) Paying attention to the intelligent restoration ability of ecology and improve ecological infrastructure By emphasizing the regulating and guiding role of the natural environment, the natural environment and urban development are integrated to achieve a symbiosis between the two. The specific measures taken are as follows: (1) through the analysis and calculation of the stormwater experienced in the process of urban development, a number of different flood diversion and flood blocking corridor sections are designed for the future urban development; (2) corridor sections and natural wetlands are used to form a regulation and storage network system, and at the same time use modern technology for water purification to form an ecologically based rain-flood regulation system; (3) the original forms of river channels are restored and repaired, connecting farmland and wetland in series by constructing an ecological green belt, and building a second-level stormwater storage system; (4) an ecological corridor has been built based on the mountain, fully considering the protection of ecological animals and plants, and reserving a limited-level ecological protection space; (5) based on the overall design of recreational routes, ecological corridors, and urban roads, permeable and high-coverage leisure life greenways have been established; (6) the farmland and plant nursery will be retained, constituting an important part of the organic development of the city (4) Building an intelligent and low-carbon transportation system that prioritizes public transportation With the urban subway and ART (Autonomous Rail Rapid Transit) as the core, the traditional bus system as the base, and the public bicycle and public slow lane as the auxiliary, the intelligent and low-carbon transportation system has been built. Guangzhou has increased the density of its new transportation network, strengthened the connection between urban rail transit systems, and enhanced the carrying capacity of the medium and large-capacity public transportation system, aiming to achieve the development vision of reaching the city's core transportation hubs within 15 minutes and the main functional clusters within 30 minutes. It will also improve the transfer convenience and urban service capacity between rail, rail and bus, and bus and self-transport, and creates a slow travel system network combining ecological corridors, traffic nodes, and hubs to achieve 30 min of access to any location within the group

(continued)

Table 1.1 (continued)

City practice	Details
Shenzhen Focus on smart traffic management and smart industry development	In 2016, Shenzhen included "smart street lamps" in the construction of information infrastructure for its smart city. The Dongmen Pedestrian Street in Shenzhen adopted a smart street lamp system as a touchpoint to comprehensively ensure the safety of each street, issued relevant construction standards, and established an industrial alliance. The comprehensive function of the smart point (smart street lamp) is attached to the light pole of the smart street lamp. On the basis of the original public infrastructure of the city, by combining a 4G/5G micro-base station, Wi-Fi equipment, sensors, video surveillance, radio-frequency identification (RFID), public broadcasting, intelligent lighting, information release, charging pile, and other multi-functional modules, to establish intelligent interaction modules and build intelligent perception networks, collect data and provide intelligent services for smart city construction, and help promote the construction of new smart cities Intelligent traffic management In 2017, Shenzhen Traffic Police and Huawei jointly built an industry-leading intelligent traffic lab to build an urban traffic brain. Based on actual combat business scenarios, the two sides have explored a more efficient and intelligent traffic management technology system, and formed a series of innovative results. The urban traffic brain has three kinds of intelligence—computational intelligence, perceptual intelligence, and cognitive intelligence—and focuses on improving the operation efficiency of the traffic system ① Computational intelligence builds an open computing platform for the traffic brain In the field of AI, various intelligent analysis algorithms bloom, but also produce a large number of intelligent fragments. The urban traffic brain provides an open computing platform, effectively solving the dilemma of intelligent debris, and supports the requirements of the sustainable development of intelligent transportation. Atlas, an open computing platform, builds leading AI hardware orchestration capabilities, supports intelligent computing resource pooling such as CPU, GPU, FPGA, NPU, and storage, and can provide hardware resources on demand for unified scheduling and resource utilization. It also provides logical servers at the second level, greatly reducing the service deployment period. The flexible enterprise intelligence (EI) platform can realize real-time scheduling of streaming data and task scheduling of global heterogeneous resources, and can intelligently orchestrate traffic services to adapt to different business scenarios ② Perceptual intelligence, like humans, senses traffic throughout the city Through the deep learning platform and open algorithm warehouse, this accommodates more than 1,000 algorithms such as traffic collection, event collection, violation collection, intelligent analysis, and intelligent rollback to realize the depth perception of traffic flow, events, violations and other behaviors, laying a good foundation for the application of intelligent traffic ecology. Through the algorithm warehouse, application developers do not need to worry about the resource cost, hardware form, and system scale expansion of the deep computing part, but can focus on traffic applications to achieve rapid online and innovative traffic services ③ Cognitive intelligence gives the traffic brain a strong cognitive ability Cognitive intelligence is an advanced ability of the urban traffic brain, which can effectively recognize key vehicle situations and explore intelligence data for special rectification, such as the analysis of "lost driving" vehicles, illegal driving of dangerous chemical vehicles, and the analysis of "late sleeping people's cars." It can recognize traffic travel rules, provide innovative traffic services, and serve as traffic police. The system deciphers mobility patterns to deliver innovative transportation services while providing intelligent decision-support mechanisms for traffic authorities. Through customizable smart scenario configurations, it enhances urban traffic governance efficiency, facilitates the development of comprehensive intelligent traffic management frameworks, and drives optimized urban mobility solutions

(continued)

Table 1.1 (continued)

City practice	Details
	In recent years, the Shenzhen traffic police have focused on building a precise control system supported by big data, adhering to the concept of intelligence-led police work based on big data and information technology, and have built a complete intelligence research and judgment system, while "intelligence-led police" has gradually changed from conceptualization and abstraction to actual combat and concretization. The traffic police department set up a three-level information center to strengthen the leader of intelligence research and judgment, build a big data pool to realize vehicle dynamic and static visibility, use key technologies to realize data comparison collision, establish a new model of data and attack (DA), rely on the big data platform, create big data analysis models such as "lost driving," "drug driving," and repeated violations of the law that have not been processed, and accurately investigate and deal with them through DA special actions.
Hangzhou Focus on the construction and development of urban brains to lay a solid foundation for smart industries	(1) The Alibaba Cloud ET City Brain The Alibaba Cloud ET City Brain is one of the largest AI public systems in the world, which can conduct global real-time analysis of the entire city, automatically deploy public resources, correct loopholes in city operation, and become the infrastructure of the future city. At present, the ET urban brain is operational in Hangzhou, Suzhou, and other places (2) Others In addition to the urban brain, the Ali Cloud ET also builds an open platform in industry, medical treatment, and the environment, and creates a cross-border open ecosystem combining AI and major industries The new generation of AI development planning and major science and technology projects held by the Ministry of Science and Technology of China in 2017 announced the new generation of AI strategy Advisory Committee members, led by the academic Pan Yunhe, The Ali Cloud machine intelligence chief scientist Min Wanli is one of the 27 expert members

1.2.2 Smart City Development in Other Countries

1.2.2.1 Europe

(1) EU—Smart energy construction and smart life application (Fig. 1.3).

The European Commission has been actively promoting the construction of smart cities. It regards smart cities as an important means to promote sustainable development, and hopes to maximize the potential of current infrastructure and capital through the construction of smart cities, and develop new products and services that adapt to social and environmental challenges.

The EU has explored a very innovative model—that is, to technically build a "smart city operating system" model, to build a unified system architecture standard for smart cities, and its relationship with smart cities is like the relationship between Windows and PC terminals. The construction is more typical of the 2013 "EPIC EU Smart city construction platform system," the Barcelona smart city business structure.

(2) The United Kingdom: with the needs of the people as the core, the construction of smart cities pays attention to the application of smart life.

① London. As early as 2002, London began to explore the construction of smart cities. The Beddington Zero Carbon Community (Bed ZED) uses

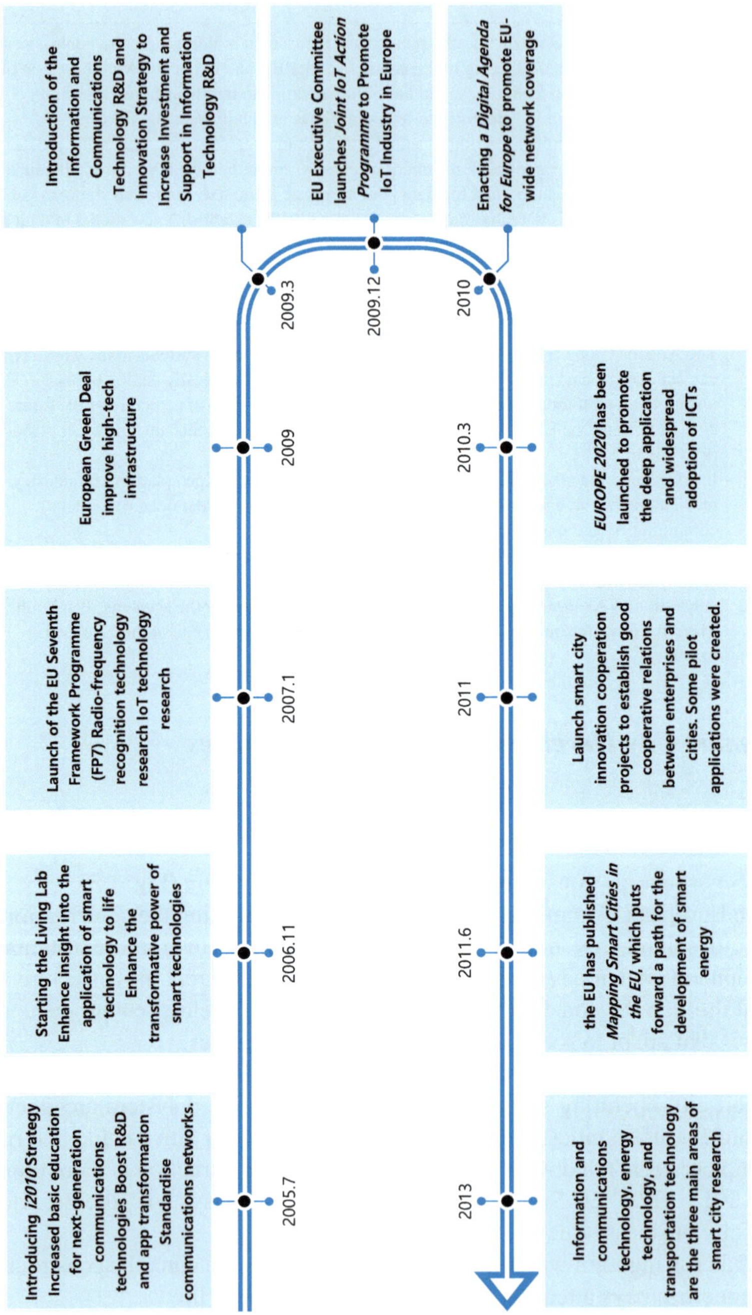

Fig. 1.3 Schematic diagram of the EU smart city development process

environmentally friendly building materials, through intelligent means, the use of building insulation, intelligent heating, natural lighting and other smart design, comprehensive use of solar, wind, biomass and other clean energy, to achieve recycling, zero emissions, and zero energy consumption.

② Gloucester. The Gloucester SmartHouse project was launched in 2007, with a house as a pilot, installing various sensors, through sensors and a central processing system, monitoring the heart rate and blood pressure of residents, and controling the temperature of the room in order to timely alert in the case of danger.

③ Birmingham. The city is tackling climate change by using digital technology. At the same time, the Home Housing Association and Digital Birmingham jointly launched the Home Energy Management project, through the visualization of energy consumption data, to help people understand energy use information and, based on this, provide early warning information for energy facilities and equipment upgrades.

(3) The Netherlands: with the control of greenhouse gas emissions as the core, attention is paid to the construction of smart energy life.

Amsterdam is a model of smart city construction in Europe, and one of the first cities in the world to start smart city construction, with the five "Rs" (reduce, reuse, recycle, repay, and recovery) as the principle of urban improvement. Using sustainable, smart and energy-saving technologies, dozens of smart projects such as sustainable transportation systems, sustainable public spaces, and sustainable living have been established.

(4) Spain: developing smart cities with a focus on green buildings.

Barcelona has the leading experience in the construction of smart cities, and the municipal government has set up a special "urban habitat" department, which is responsible for leading the construction, supervision, and coordination of smart city projects. In 2008, Barcelona launched UrbanLab, a project to experiment with services and technologies in public spaces to obtain information about how these technological practices interact with space. The Media-TIC Building, completed in 2010, is one of the world's most representative smart green buildings and has been awarded the LEED Gold Medal, the world's highest honor for building energy efficiency.

(5) France: focusing on smart transportation and smart tourism.

① Paris. In 2011, the theme of smart street furniture design competition was organized to provide smart improvement schemes for street facilities. Corporate designers and the public participated in the competition, and finally 40 designs were selected and implemented. One example is Concept Shelters, a digital bus stop that lets residents communicate online with city authorities through interactive touchscreen shelters.

② Lyon. Since 2013, Lyon has established a real-time citywide carpooling information service platform on its carpooling portal. Through the site, people can find and further connect with long-term or short-term ride-sharing partners that meet their needs. So far, 9,000 people have signed up on the site and 20% of them are carpooling at least once a week, which works out to 10,000 barrels of gas saved.

1.2.2.2 North and South American Region

(1) The United States: virtual and real interaction—harmonious and unified urban physical world and cyberspace.

The United States is the first country in North America to explore the construction of smart cities,

The United States pioneered two landmark infrastructure initiatives: the National Information Infrastructure (NII) and Global Information Infrastructure (GII), marking the world's first proposals of such frameworks. It focus on the construction of smart city information equipment and facilities, the research and development and application of smart technology, and finally realize the construction of the government-enterprise information interaction platform, the government-community information interaction platform, the digital community, etc., which has brought a good hardware infrastructure for the development of smart cities.

(2) Canada: paying attention to the application of smart energy and smart transportation to reduce urban greenhouse gas emissions.

① Edmonton. Due to limited transportation resources being unable to meet the increasing traffic demand, the urban transportation infrastructure is facing great pressure. Through cooperation with IBM, the city management department uses the internet, cloud computing, geospatial analysis, and other technologies to build urban traffic safety systems, which can instantly understand traffic data, perform overall management of traffic system access, ensure traffic safety, and relieve traffic congestion. At the same time, it also reduces carbon emissions and increased the use of public transport.

② Quebec. Due to the proximity to the polar region, affected by the continental climate, Quebec has a very obvious division of the four seasons—the summer temperature can reach more than 30 °C, while the average winter temperature can be as low as −20 °C, which means urban residents rely on air conditioning, and energy expenditure accounts for a considerable proportion of daily living expenses. In order to reduce citizens' energy costs and energy consumption, the municipal government launched the Green City Project, which uses Delta's *enteli* intelligent energy control system to monitor and manage the energy consumption of households. At the same time, enteli intelligent energy control system integrates the household HVAC control system, the intelligent lighting system, the access control system, etc. to intelligently control the daily public part of the energy consumption, but also to ensure the safety of citizens.

(3) Brazil: paying attention to urban safety and governance, focusing on the construction of the smart city security early warning system.

① Rio de Janeiro. Rio de Janeiro hosted the World Cup in 2014 and the Olympic Games in 2016, which attracted international attention to the city. The 2010 landslide and other natural disasters caused a large number of casualties, and the local government began to attach great importance to the wisdom of natural disaster warnings. Through cooperation with IBM, Oracle, and other information technology industry companies, the Center of Operations has been established to collect and process data information in the city in real time in order to realize early warnings to natural disasters, traffic evacuation, and emergency handling. At the same time, the data information of the urban transportation center is open to the outside world and becomes open data, which can be accessed by the media and the public at any time through the network, ensuring the multi-party participation and supervision of the city's operation.

② Sao Paulo. In the field of smart water use, sensors have been installed on pumps and other water supply infrastructure to avoid water waste and reduce water leaks by 40–50% through 24 h real-time monitoring, immediate maintenance, and regular maintenance.

③ Curitiba. Curitiba has established a smart public transport system to improve the efficiency and reliability of the urban transport system. The government first introduced a three-tier road system, as shown in Fig. 1.4, with intermediate routes divided into two modes: public transport with direct access to the city center and social vehicles with access within the region, with two lanes. The routes on both sides of the north and south are social vehicular roads with direct access to the city center and are one-way lanes. The three-level route system is connected by bus transfer stations. The transfer station is also a service function center, newspaper kiosk, and coffee shop, and provides other service formats.

1.2.2.3 Asia

(1) Japan: paying attention to the application of the smart industry in commerce and tourism, and improving the convenience of shopping.

Japan is one of the early adopters of the construction of smart cities in Asia. Its smart city construction is not only a reflection and exploration on the construction of advanced and comfortable cities in the future, but also a new method to solve the problems of environment and energy under the new situation (see Fig. 1.5). Japan has launched two national strategies: "E-Japan" and "U-Japan." The former has activated the vitality of national information infrastructure and

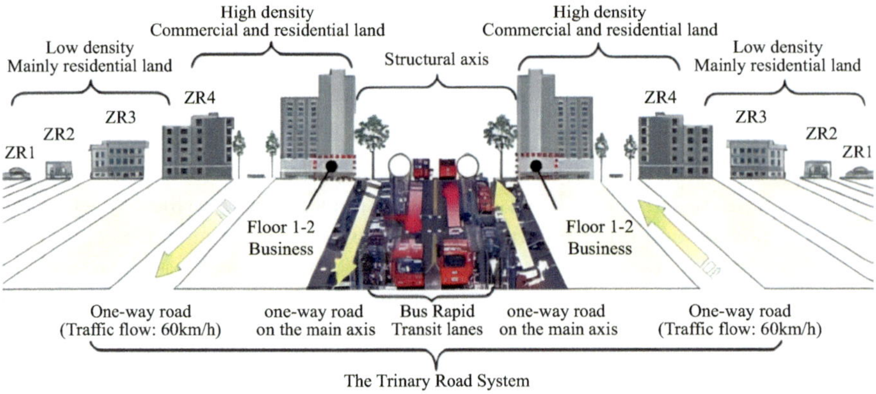

Fig. 1.4 The trinary road system of Curitiba-01

communication technology industry research and development, while the latter focuses on the application of information technology and digital technology to all aspects of life to solve the problems faced by the aging population and enhance national competitiveness.

Based on the "E-Japan" and "UJapan" strategies, the Japanese government developed the "I-Japan" strategy in 2009, focusing on the ease of use and penetration of information technology, aiming to break through various barriers hindering the application of digital technology, focusing on the three major public service areas of electronic government governance, medical and health information services, education and talent cultivation. The goal is to achieve a people-centered, secure, and dynamic digital society.

Fig. 1.5 The Japanese smart city portal

(2) South Korea: paying attention to the application of smart life and medical treatment.

In 2004, South Korea proposed the UKorea Strategic Plan, which aimed to promote South Korea's economic development and social change through digitalization, networking, visualization, and intelligence. In March 2006, the overall policy plan was finalized. According to the plan, the development period of "UKorea" was 2006–2010 and the maturity period was 2011–2015. Through the establishment of a pervasive information awareness network, South Korea can enhance the provision of convenient life services for citizens, thereby improving their quality of life. This initiative will also promote the development of information technology-related industries and bolster the nation's competitiveness. In 2009, South Korea passed the U-City comprehensive plan, which included the construction of U-City into the national budget and strongly supported the localization of core technologies, marking the rise of smart city construction to the national strategic level. U-City is the detailed implementation of U-Korea, through the construction of smart city model city to let the public feel the convenience of smart technology for life, while driving the development of related industries in order to promote the national economy.

(3) Singapore: a pioneer in the construction of smart cities, coordinating the development of smart cities with smart government.

In 2006, the Singapore government announced the "Smart Nation 2015" (IN 2015) plan, hosted by the Infocomm Development Authority of Singapore (IDA), with the participation of the government and enterprises, which aimed to build Singapore into a global leader in information technology within 10 years. In 2011, the Singapore government adopted the "e-Government 2015" master plan and, on the basis of the integration of internal collaborative management and services in 2010, strengthened the government's integration of various functions of external services, improved the management mechanism of government departments, and laid the foundation for the penetrative cooperation between the people and the government. In 2012, the Singapore government established strategic relationships with Dimension Data and IBM to train graduates in big data and cloud computing. At the same time, IT also provides short-term improvement coaching courses on cloud computing technology in the IT industry. Although providing these services is expensive, it will bring about greater benefits.

1.3 Urban Intellectualization Under Emerging Technologies

1.3.1 Social and Economic Conditions Inferred from Aerial Images

Urbanization is one of the challenges of modern society. Even if a city develops in many ways, it will enlarge the social and economic imbalance. Accurately tracking this process as it unfolds has been a challenge for traditional data collection methods, but remote sensing information offers an alternative approach to a more complete picture of these social changes. By providing aerial images in the neural network model, socio-economic information related to the region can be predicted.

For example, in a study of central Paris, France, this approach was used to predict socio-economic conditions (SES) from aerial images and to generate heat maps through the Class Activation Mapping (CAM) method to explain the urban structure. The study shows that trained models can ignore the relationship between urban class and socio-economic status and get predictions directly. This provides a more explanatory model that helps reveal potential correlations between urban structure and high-resolution socio-economic maps to better track and understand urbanization and its consequences.

To improve the accuracy of the study, detailed socio-economic maps and high-resolution aerial image datasets were used to enable CNN to detect local features. The entire research process relied on high-resolution aerial images of the entire French metropolitan territory (20 cm per pixel) taken between 2013 and 2016 and published by the National Institute for Geographic Information (IGN). The orthophoto dataset is distributed as a series of geo-referenced 5 km $\times$ 5 km slices provided at the departmental (administrative demarcation) level. The collection is then supplemented by socio-economic data shared by the French National Institute of Statistics and Economic Research (INSEE) in 2019 (Abitbol and Karsai 2020). This dataset describes the average Winsorized household income per 4 hectares (200 m $\times$ 200 m) of square patches ("census cells") throughout the territory of France. The income comes from France's 2015 tax revenue, which provides a summary of the main features of each dataset. The combination of socio-economic maps and aerial data requires us to identify the aerial images ("aerial tiles") that correspond to each 200 m $\times$ 200 m census cell, and thus be able to obtain detailed information about the census data for each socio-economic block and its spatial match to the aerial images.

1.3.2 *The Spatial Homogeneity of Urban Road Network Quantified by Graph Neural Network*

The homogeneity of urban spatial structure can also be characterized by an AI model. For example, in a study published by the Institute of Artificial Intelligence at Peking University, a machine learning method based on graph neural networks (GNNs) is proposed to quantify the spatial homogeneity of networks. The method was applied to 11,790 urban road networks in 30 cities around the world to measure the spatial homogeneity of road networks within each city and between different cities in an attempt to explore how spatial homogeneity within cities is highly correlated with indicators of socio-economic status such as GDP and population growth (Fig. 1.6). Moreover, the homogeneity across urban areas, obtained by the migration model between different cities, reveals similarities between urban network structures that originated in Europe and were transferred to cities in the United States and Asia (Xue et al. 2022). Using this method to summarize the similarity of different urban structures, it can be used to deepen the understanding of urban spatial characteristics traceability.

A spatial homogeneity metric is a comprehensive metric that captures a variety of existing network statistics, including mean degrees and mean mediations. In this study, it was found that when 30 cities were evenly distributed, cities with lower mean mediations and higher mean degrees (such as New York, Chicago, and San Antonio) had higher spatial homogeneity. They were divided into two groups according to their average range and average degree. Through the information transfer mechanism in the GNN model, the road network nodes receive more domain knowledge, which improves the prediction effect.

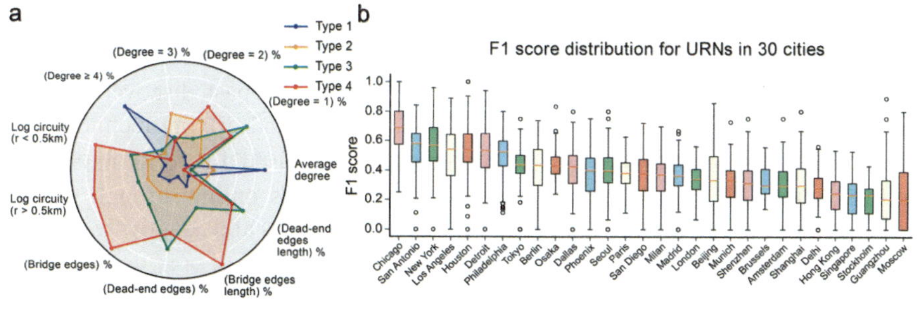

Fig. 1.6 Spatial homogeneity explained by road network type

1.3.3 City Noise Filtered Through Deep Learning Algorithms to Detect Earthquakes

Cities are noisy places. Traffic, trains, and machinery produce a lot of noise. This can become a deadly problem when detecting earthquakes. Researchers at Stanford University have found a way to get a clearer indication of danger. They created an algorithm that improved the detection capabilities of seismic monitoring networks in cities and other built-up areas. By filtering out background seismic noise, the algorithm can improve overall signal quality and restore signals that might previously have been too weak to register.

The Stanford team's deep learning algorithm, called UrbanDenoiser, has been trained on a dataset containing 80,000 samples of urban seismic noise and 33,751 samples that indicate seismic activity. When applied to datasets taken from the Long Beach area, these algorithms detected more earthquakes and made it easier to determine how and where they started. When applying data from the 2014 La Habra earthquake in California, the team observed four times as many seismic detections in the "de-noising" data as the number officially recorded (Yang et al. 2022). The results showed that the AI, named UrbanDenoiser, could process signals from both the array and the LAN (Local Area Network) station. Through its noise reduction processing, people can find some seismic activity that could not be found in the past, thereby improving the understanding of local seismic activity. This will greatly help in monitoring seismic activity in cities, especially in densely populated metropolises such as Los Angeles and Tokyo. The researchers say that although the system was developed for seismic activity, with the right training, it could also be used to monitor other seismic events.

1.3.4 iSDF: Robot Perception Through Real-Time Neural Symbol Distance Field

iSDF is a real-time mapping system developed by Meta AI for robot navigation and operation. iSDF trains neural symbol distance fields online through continuous learning, which is able to fill partially observed regions and adaptively allocate memory capacity to map different levels of detail. It takes a set of pose depth images captured by a moving camera and trains a randomly initialized neural network to map the input three-dimensional coordinates to approximate symbolic distances. In the training process, a self-supervised model is used to limit the predicted symbolic distance by minimizing the loss, and the distance of the nearest sampling point in a batch of actively sampled query points is used. Compared to previous work based on voxel grids, this method is able to provide an adaptive level of detail, reasonably fill in some of the observed regions, and de-noise the observations, while having a more compact representation. When evaluating alternative approaches to real and synthetic datasets for indoor environments, iSDF produced more accurate reconstructions, as

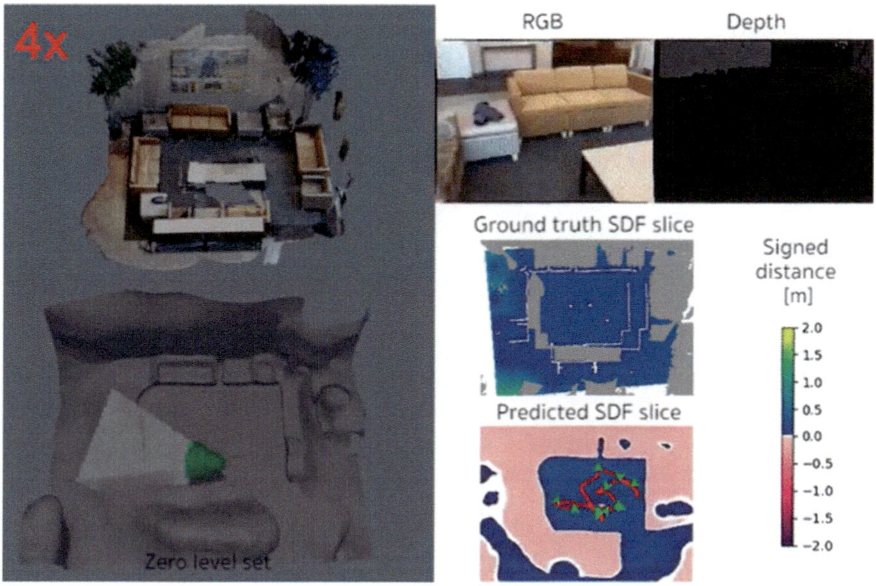

Fig. 1.7 Real-time neural signed distance fields for robot perception

well as a better approximation of collision costs and gradients for different application scenarios in fields ranging from navigation to manipulation, enhancing the robot's perception of urban environments (see Fig. 1.7).

References

Abitbol JL, Karsai M (2020) Interpretable socio-economic status inference from aerial imagery through urban patterns. Nat Mach Intell 2(11):684–692. https://doi.org/10.1038/s42256-020-00243-5

Xue J, Jiang N, Liang S, Pang Q, Yabe T, Ukkusuri SV, Ma J (2022) Quantifying the spatial homogeneity of urban road networks via graph neural networks. Nat Mach Intell 4(3):246–257. https://doi.org/10.1038/s42256-022-00462-y

Yang L, Liu X, Zhu W, Zhao L, Beroza GC (2022) Toward improved urban earthquake monitoring through deep-learning-based noise suppression. Sci Adv 8(15):eabl3564. https://doi.org/10.1126/sciadv.abl3564

Chapter 2
Beyond Smart City: The AI City is Coming

Abstract This chapter delves into the evolution of AI technology, particularly focusing on the transition from traditional AI to AI 2.0. It elucidates advances in seven key areas: machine theorem proving, machine translation, expert systems, gaming, pattern recognition, learning, and robotics. The defining characteristics of AI 2.0 encompass big data intelligence, swarm intelligence, cross-media intelligence, human–machine hybrid augmented intelligence, and autonomous intelligent systems. These features propel innovation and progress in sectors such as smart cities, smart healthcare, and autonomous driving. Big data intelligence facilitates AI learning through vast datasets; swarm intelligence underscores collaborative solutions for complex tasks; cross-media intelligence integrates diverse data types to enhance intelligence; human–machine hybrid augmented intelligence optimizes decision-making processes in industrial and medical fields. Autonomous intelligent systems, including drones, are rapidly approaching human-level capabilities. Additionally, this chapter introduces the emerging concept of the "AI city," highlighting the application of AI technology in urban life, production, and ecosystems. Notably, the AI city pilot project in Maqiao Town, Minhang District, Shanghai, has demonstrated significant potential for practical applications.

Keywords AI 2.0 · AI city · Big data intelligence · Swarm intelligence · Cross-media intelligence · Hybrid Augmented intelligence · Autonomous Intelligence

2.1 The Introduction of New Generation AI Technology

2.1.1 Towards AI 2.0

The concept of AI was initially proposed by Professor John McCarthy from Stanford University in 1956, with the aim of endowing machines with knowledge, reasoning abilities, and learning capabilities akin to those of humans. In other words, it entails harnessing computers to simulate human intelligence—this is what

Z. WU, *The AI City*, The Urban Book Series,
https://doi.org/10.1007/978-981-96-2560-4_2

we refer to as "artificial intelligence." Subsequently, AI has evolved into seven distinct disciplines: machine theorem proving focuses on leveraging computers to emulate human logical and reasoning abilities; machine translation aims at simulating human natural language comprehension; expert systems primarily employ computers for problem solving and knowledge expression; gaming originally relied on tree search algorithms; pattern recognition encompasses voice, image, and text recognition through multimedia cognition techniques; learning involves neural network-based training methods; and robotics represents the seventh discipline within AI development. Throughout this progression, different schools of thought emerged, including symbolic AI research and action-oriented approaches. However, the current landscape surrounding AI has undergone significant transformations compared to previous environments (Fig. 2.1).

First, there has been a notable shift in the information environment. If we reflect upon the past 20 or 30 years, when it was common for several individuals to gather around a single computer system–, today each person may possess multiple computing devices such as laptops carried in bags or smartphones kept in pockets. Additionally, we are surrounded by numerous internet applications along with mobile computing options like supercomputing capabilities offered through cloud computing platforms. Online communities and search engines further contribute to these changes.

Second, social needs have undergone significant changes in conjunction with advances in AI technology. AI endeavors to replicate human intelligence and has given rise to numerous new requirements such as smart cities, intelligent healthcare, autonomous transportation, intelligent gaming, unmanned driving, and intelligent

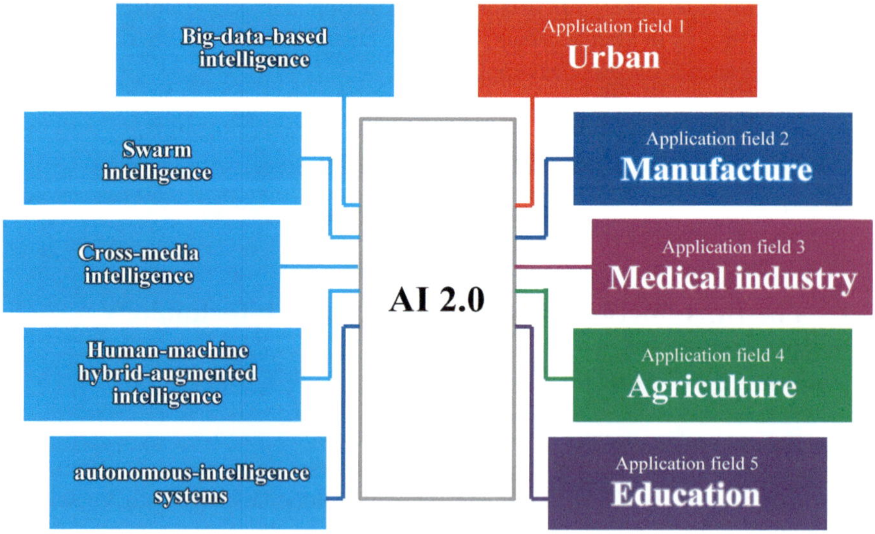

Fig. 2.1 AI 2.0 technologies applied in different aspects

manufacturing. These are not the actions of an individual, but rather those of a system. The challenge lies in how to simulate system intelligence using AI, which will present many novel propositions.

Third, the fundamentals of AI are evolving rapidly. Data-driven approaches form the foundation of AI; however, there is now not only big data but also multimedia and sensor data that humans can only process a fraction of thus far. Additionally, augmented reality and virtual reality technologies will be extensively employed, further complicating matters for traditional AI processing techniques.

Representative experts	Opinions
Pan Yunhe Academic of Chinese Academy of Engineering (Pan 2016)	The first direction is big data intelligence. This will be used for the intelligent development direction of medical treatment and the intelligent development direction of manufacturing, focusing on solving the problems of interpretability and universality from data to knowledge to intelligence. Therefore, it is necessary to combine the data-driven approach and the knowledge-guided approach to form a new and more effective technology of AI, so as to have a wider application in smart healthcare, the smart economy, and social governance The second direction is swarm intelligence. This will examine how swarm intelligence is organized on the internet; how the connection is made; what methods are used to encourage people to participate together; and in the process of participation, how to cooperate with each other, and how to evolve the whole group in a more correct direction and more correct behavior The third direction is cross-media intelligence. This will study all kinds of perceptual learning and reasoning across media and sensors, and connect it with the semantics of language and text. In this way, the language, vision, graphics, hearing, and data conveyed by a variety of sensors can be semantically interlinked, which can make the computer gain a better innovation ability in intelligent security and innovative design The fourth direction is human–machine hybrid enhanced intelligence. Human–machine mixing forms a powerful interactive system and forms enhanced intelligence. Study the environment, interaction, learning, and action control involved in brain-computer collaboration to enable effective cooperation between brain-controlled robots and multiple autonomous agents. The fifth direction is autonomous unmanned systems. The theoretical models and methods of environment perception, self-perception, collaboration between different individuals, behavior planning, behavior decision-making and various behavior execution are studied, which are used in many fields such as unmanned vehicles, drones, service robots, space robots, ocean robots, unmanned workshops, intelligent factories, etc.

2.1.2 D-Intelligence: Big Data Intelligence

Big data take data as the core resource, and the generated data are collected, stored, processed, analyzed, applied, and displayed to finally realize the value of data. AI leverages large volumes of data to transform complex problems requiring machine judgment into manageable data-driven tasks.

Big data intelligence provides rich data accumulation and training resources for AI—for example, the Baidu training face recognition system needs 200 million face portraits. With the rapid application and popularization of AI, the continuous accumulation of big data, and the continuous optimization of algorithms such as deep learning and reinforcement learning, big data technology will be more closely combined with AI technology, and with the ability to understand, analyze, discover, and make decisions on data so as to obtain more accurate and deeper knowledge from the data and discover the value behind the data. New forms and models of business will be created.

Driven by the exponential growth of computing power and high-value data, big data intelligence is constantly extending the breadth of its technology application, expanding the depth of technological breakthroughs and constantly accelerating the speed of technology landing. For example, in the field of new retail, the combination of big data and AI technology can improve the accuracy of face recognition, and merchants can better predict monthly sales. In the field of transportation, the combination of big data and AI technology, based on a large number of traffic data developed through intelligent traffic flow prediction, intelligent traffic dredging, and other AI applications, can achieve intelligent control of the overall traffic network. In the field of health, the combination of big data and AI technology can provide more convenient and intelligent medical services for medical image analysis, assisted diagnosis and treatment, and medical robots. At the same time, at the technical level, big data technology has basically matured and promoted the progress of AI technology at an astonishing speed. At the industry level, intelligent security, autonomous driving, medical imaging, etc. are accelerating.

Representative experts	Opinions
Chen Chun Academic of Chinese Academy of Engineering	With the advent of 5G and the IoT, real-time analytics has developed into a key technology in the field of AI technology. Relying on mathematical statistics and probability theory, the difficulty of time series data analysis lies in two points: large amount of data and high real-time requirements. At the technical level, it includes: how to achieve incremental calculation with complex algorithms, how can we address the issue of data or tasks occurring out of sequence?, how to solve the correlation between time sequence space and feature space, establish a distributed image real-time time sequence data system, and enrich the real-time analysis ecology of big data

2.1.3 S-Intelligence: Swarm Intelligence

The internet-based swarm intelligence theory and method is one of the core research fields of the new generation of AI, which has a basic and supportive role for other research fields of AI. Qian Xuesen, a famous scientist, proposed the integrated Hall of Seminar system in the 1990s, emphasizing the collaborative discussion of expert groups with man–machine integration, and studying challenging problems of complex giant systems together.

Pan Yunhe, academician of the Chinese Academy of Engineering, said: "The global artificial intelligence is moving from 1.0 to 2.0 stage, and the effective combination of computer and human intelligence based on the Internet to form group intelligence is an important direction in the era of artificial intelligence 2.0." China's "New Generation of Artificial Intelligence Development Plan" clearly points out the research direction of swarm intelligence, which is of great significance for promoting the development of a new generation of AI. Currently, with the internet and mobile communication as the connecting medium, human communities, the Internet of Things (IoT), and big data have achieved extensive and deep mutual integration.

Swarm intelligence makes human group intelligence play an increasingly important role in the information environment of the interconnection of everything. At the same time, it has profoundly changed the field of AI, such as open source software based on group development, mass innovation based on crowdfunding and crowdmind, knowledge sharing based on crowdquestion and crowdanswer, Wikipedia based on group editing, and the sharing economy based on crowdsourcing and crowdsharing.

Swarm intelligence also has a wide range of applications in robotics and drones. Researchers at the Georgia Robotics and Intelligent Systems Laboratory (GRITS) have created a swarm of simple robots that can spell words and play the piano. These robots cannot communicate, but based solely on the location of the surrounding robots, they are able to use their own specially created algorithms to determine the best path to complete the task.

In February 2017, Chinese airline Ehang built a fleet of 1,000 drones, which not only performed spectacular high-altitude flying displays, but also demonstrated the ability to react and troubleshoot completely autonomously. On the military front, the US Department of Defense has announced a number of successful tests of microdrones. These tiny drones can perform complex tasks more efficiently and with lower energy consumption. "The micro-UAVs demonstrated advanced group behaviors such as collective decision-making, adaptive formation flying and self-healing," they said.

Representative expert	Opinions
WU Wenjun Professor of Beijing University of Aeronautics and Astronautics	Swarm intelligence refers to the intelligence beyond individual intelligence that emerges when a specific organizational structure and a big data-driven AI system attract, gather, and manage large-scale participants to jointly cope with challenging tasks in a variety of autonomous collaborative ways such as competition and cooperation, especially in complex system decision-making tasks in an open environment In the AI 2.0 stage, swarm intelligence has gradually emerged as a new research direction and a new paradigm. To meet the national strategic needs, we should study the basic theory of swarm intelligence and break through the core technology of swarm intelligence. Finally, relying on the online scientific and technological innovation ecological environment, the group intelligence can be gathered across time and space, can be reorganized efficiently, and can be released more widely and accurately

2.1.4 C-Intelligence: Cross-Media Intelligence

There are two types of data: structured data and unstructured data. Of these, unstructured data, such as images and videos, account for more than 90% of data. These data, although formally heterogeneous, are semantically related to each other. Cross-media intelligence is designed to analyze, identify, retrieve, and reason in heterogeneous big data.

Cross-media intelligence is an important part of the new generation of AI. Through theories and methods such as audio-visual perception, machine learning, and language computing, it constructs a unified semantic expression of the physical world, converts data into intelligence through cross-media analysis and reasoning, and thus becomes an "enabler" for all kinds of information systems to achieve intelligence. Transmedia intelligent engine research can be carried out on existing computing platforms, but its widespread application requires the development of more efficient intelligent chips and hardware, like biological brains and perceptual systems, to efficiently express the complex structure of the external world with very low power consumption.

Traditional AI 1.0 is based on the analysis and application of a single medium. AI 2.0 emphasizes the acquisition, analysis, retrieval, and reasoning of cross-media sources, that is, cross-media intelligence.

A typical integrated application of transmedia intelligence is the smart city. Conduct research on the city's all-dimensional intelligent perception and reasoning engine to address problems related to fragmented perception and information silos encountered during urban development, establish an urban dimensional intelligent perception reasoning engine characterized by "span, perspective, information and service," and realize multi-dimensional, cross-space collaborative perception and comprehensive reasoning of people, vehicles, objects, events, etc.

In addition, cross-media intelligent technology can also promote the transformation of enterprise intelligent manufacturing, inject new vitality into economic growth, and improve the quality of China's economic development. The cross-media intelligent engine will also be applied in important fields such as intelligent medical treatment, which will have an important impact on the national economy, people's livelihoods, and national security.

Representative expert	Opinions
Gao Wen Academic of Chinese Academy of Engineering	The development plan of the new generation of AI is divided into four basic sections, which are technology leadership, system layout, market leadership, and open source In my opinion, the four major advantages of China's development of AI are: (1) the policy advantages of China's development of AI; (2) massive data resources; (3) rich application scenarios; (4) young talents with potential are growing rapidly. At the same time, there are also four shortcomings in the development of AI in China: (1) there is a large gap between the basic theory of AI and the original algorithm, and basic research and algorithms need to be accumulated and precipitated; (2) it is weak in high-end chips, key components, high-precision sensors, etc.; (3) it has not yet formed an open source AI platform with international influence; (4) the lack of high-level talents—China's high-end talents are only 20% of those of the United States, but it also needs to strengthen the cultivation of high-end talents

2.1.5 *H-Intelligence: Hybrid Augmented Intelligence*

Hybrid augmented intelligence refers to the introduction of human roles or human cognitive models into AI systems to create a form of hybrid augmented intelligence (Fig. 2.2). This form is a viable and important growth model for AI. We should realize that people are the service objects of intelligent machines and the arbiters of "value judgment," and human intervention in machines should run through the development of AI. Even if we provide AI systems with ample, or even unlimited, data resources, it is humans who must intervene in intelligent systems.

Zheng Nanning, academician of the Chinese Academy of Engineering and chairman of the Chinese Society of Automation, said: "Introducing the role of human into the computing loop of intelligent systems can closely coupling the advanced cognitive mechanism of human analysis and response to fuzzy and uncertain problems with the machine intelligence system, so that the two can adapt to each other and work together to form two-way information exchange and control. The combination of human perception and cognitive ability with the powerful computing and storage

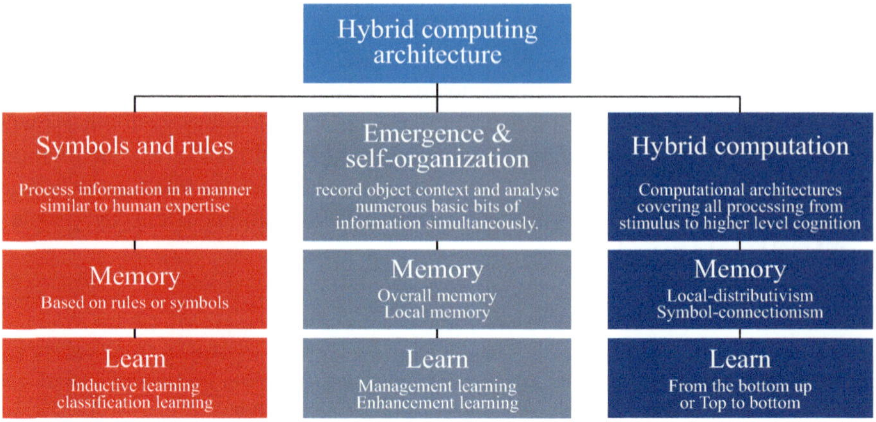

Fig. 2.2 The computing structure of hybrid enhanced intelligence

capabilities of computers constitutes a more powerful intelligence and enhanced intelligence form."

For example, when applying AI systems in the areas of industrial risk management, medical diagnosis, and criminal justice, it is necessary to introduce human supervision, allow people to participate in verification, use human knowledge and wisdom in the best way, and optimally balance human intelligence and computer computing power. To give another example, automatic driving is a highly comprehensive AI system, and it has also been a research hotspot in recent years. With the formation of intelligent transportation systems, as well as the application of 5G communication technology and vehicle networking technology, man–machine co-driving is becoming more and more mature, but in order to achieve complete autonomous driving, it is still facing a difficult challenge: how to coordinate two "drivers" through intelligent man–machine collaboration technology to achieve vehicle safety and comfort. To solve these problems, it is necessary to take "hybrid enhanced intelligence" as the development trend of AI.

In the field, hybrid enhanced intelligence is expected to be widely used in industrial development decision-making, online intelligent learning, medical and healthcare, human–machine co-driving and cloud robots, and may bring about disruptive changes.

Representative expert	Opinions
Zheng Nanning Academic of Chinese Academy of Engineering	In my opinion, in the current "contest" between AI and humans, computers have clearly won in terms of logic, repeatability and normativity. But most of the problems humans face are open, dynamic, and complex, and the imagination and creativity shown by the brain in dealing with such problems, as well as the analysis and description of complex problems, are beyond the reach of current AI methods The human mind makes predictions, pattern classification, and learning on the basis of memory experience and knowledge. In particular, we all have predictive models in our brains, so essentially the brain is a predictive machine. Predictive ability is very important for driving behavior. By contrast, it is very difficult for a computer to make predictions. Computers of the future will need to be able to intuitively understand the physical world, just like people. The process of human cognition has pointed the way to the evolution of computers. The human brain's understanding of non-cognitive factors comes more from intuition and is influenced by experience and long-term knowledge accumulation. These factors play an extremely important role in people's understanding of physical environment, interaction of behavior, and processing of incomplete information Human beings realize learning through interaction with things. The formation of feature concepts in the process of human cognition is often based on semantic interpretation. Human beings rely on the observation of things to build different analytical models in the brain, and use these models to speculate the changes of things. Machine learning takes a completely different path from human cognition. In order for the machine to learn human cognition, it is necessary for the features it learns to conform to the experimental results of neurophysiology to a certain extent, and at the same time to make the features have mathematical and semantic interpretation. In addition, the plasticity of the brain's neural network structure, as well as the interaction between non-cognitive factors and cognitive functions of the human brain, is difficult or even impossible to describe by formal methods

2.1.6 A-Intelligence: Autonomous Intelligence

The level of development of autonomous unmanned systems has become a landmark achievement in the development of AI. The improvement of the intelligent level of autonomous unmanned systems will be more able to reflect human characteristics and closer to the human level, so it can vigorously promote the rapid development of science and technology and economy, and further improve the quality of human life.

Compared with traditional autonomous systems, the research content of unmanned autonomous systems is broader. Various types of intelligent unmanned autonomous systems appear one after another, which will have a significant impact on human life and society. In the present or in the near future, unmanned vehicles, drones, service robots, space robots, marine robots, unmanned workshops, and smart factories may develop into intelligent unmanned autonomous systems.

Representative expert	Opinions
WU Cheng Academic of Chinese Academy of Engineering	I believe that the connotation of the new generation of AI includes three major innovation points: a new environment of information, a new form of intelligence, and a new target that is expected to be upgraded. The intersection of "Made in China 2025" and AI is intelligent manufacturing, which should be both "top to the sky" and "site." Intelligent manufacturing is not only an advanced, cutting-edge technology, but it also plays a critical role across all levels of manufacturing and other industries. It provides technical solutions, generates tangible benefits for enterprises, and promotes sustainable development. Automating knowledge-based work is a key focus within intelligent manufacturing. The improvement of the intelligent level of autonomous unmanned systems will be more able to reflect human characteristics and closer to the human level, so it can vigorously promote the rapid development of science and technology and economy, and further improve the quality of human life. In the next 10–20 years, the autonomous unmanned systems industry will become a new engine of world economic progress, leading the development of intelligent industry and the intelligent economy
CHEN Jie Academic of Chinese Academy of Engineering	Suggestions for the development planning of autonomous intelligent unmanned systems: Focusing on three major scientific issues: autonomous perception and understanding, integration of decision and control, swarm intelligence and collaborative control, the research is focused on intelligent sensors, brain-like controllers, unmanned terminal control systems, network collaboration technology, intelligent chips and systems, security and security of six core technologies, so as to promote intelligent manufacturing, intelligent transportation, intelligent agriculture, intelligent medical, smart city, national security, and other industrial changes The future development of AI needs to focus on enhancing original creativity, take key core technologies as the direction, and consolidate the foundation for the development of AI. The future development of autonomous intelligent unmanned systems urgently requires the integration of various disciplines and the cooperation of experts in various fields

2.2 The Definition of the "AI City"

In April 2016, Pan Yunhe, academician of the Chinese Academy of Engineering, proposed the preliminary concept of AI 2.0, that is, a new generation of AI based on a new information environment with major changes and new development goals. The main features includes big data intelligence, internet group intelligence, cross-media intelligence, human–machine hybrid enhanced intelligence, and autonomous unmanned systems. In July 2017, the Chinese Academy of Engineering established the "China AI 30" top expert community to carry out strategic research on national AI layout planning. On July 8, the State Council issued the "New Generation of Artificial Intelligence Development Plan," which further clarified the basic theory and key common technology system of the new generation of AI, and the new generation of AI officially became the national strategy. The plan proposes to "build an urban big data platform and build an urban operation management system that integrates diverse and heterogeneous data" … Promote the intellectualization of the whole life cycle of urban planning, construction, management, and operation, and to clarify the major strategic direction of applying AI technology to empower cities. In November, the first phase of the Chinese Academy of Engineering Artificial Intelligence 2.0 project was launched, with academician Pan Yunhe as the general manager and academician Wu Zhiqiang presiding over the topic of "Innovative application of Artificial Intelligence 2.0 Technology in Smart Cities." The application of big data intelligence, Internet group intelligence, cross-media intelligence, human–machine hybrid enhanced intelligence and autonomous unmanned systems in urban planning, construction and operation decision-making process is comprehensively studied. In August 2018, academician Wu Zhiqiang released the prototype of the "AI city," which judged that urban development has entered the era of AI. The AI city proposal has brought about changes in ideas, methods and technologies for the planning and construction of future cities, created a large number of scenarios and infinite possibilities for the application of a new generation of AI technology in cities, and opened the way to the innovation experiment of AI cities.

The first generation of AI cities is landing in Maqiao Town, Minhang District, Shanghai, with academician Wu Zhiqiang as the project host. Maqiao is the world's first pilot project of the AI city, providing a large number of test scenarios for the application of AI technology: an AI square, an AI catering street, an AI park, an AI customized bus, an AI town center tower, an AI Master Bay, etc. It will become an AI future town integrating application demonstration, research and development innovation, display training, consumption experience, and product production.

As one of Shanghai's four major platforms for AI integration and innovation, we must adopt a global perspective, dynamically track AI applications in cities worldwide, and host the International AI City Summit quarterly, and gather together the world's top peers to co-innovate.

Representative expert	Opinions
WU Zhiqiang Academic of Chinese Academy of Engineering	The artificial intelligence city, or AI city, is a self-organizing, learnable and iterable highly intelligent urban development form that fully enables urban production, life and ecology with AI technology to solve the needs of urban people under the background of the emergence of AI technology (Wu et al. 2022). Urban development has gone through three stages: digitalization, information technology, and intelligence, and the super-stage of intelligence is the AI city. The difference between an AI city and a smart city mainly lies in four technologies: big data, blockchain, the internet, and cloud computing. If the smart city is mainly based on information processing, AI is the overall coordination of the four major technologies

2.3 The Development and Predicament of Smart Cities in the World

Compared with smart cities, the purpose of AI cities is to solve blocking points, pain points, and difficulties. "AI in the City" is more realistic than "AI of the City." Looking back on the development of urban intelligence, there are two modes: the "green context" and the "gray context." The 'green context' refers to a newly developed city. In the past, smart city projects focused heavily on building technical infrastructure and invested large amounts of money before residents moved into the city, making it difficult to accurately understand and address people's actual needs, in the direction of application deviation, resulting in a large amount of social resources waste. The "gray context" is built on the basis of the existing city; at this time, there are already people in the city, and timely feedback can be generated for any intelligent measures for continuous optimization. In contrast, the "gray context" is more solid and efficient than the "green context," which can directly cut into the needs of the government, society, and the public. Therefore, the city must be people-oriented and demand-oriented construction intelligent rather than equipment-oriented construction intelligent.

The governance of the AI city is aimed at the difficulties and pain points in the current city. The key point of using AI to explore is the grafting point of AI technology and urban governance needs rather than the top-down promotion of AI concepts. This is fundamentally different from the rise and promotion of any "smart city" in the past, which is different from the construction of smart infrastructure and a large and comprehensive technology platform with high investment from the government, and the AI city is reflected in the "peripheral nerve" of urban governance.

There is still an invisible hand behind supply-side reform. Adam Smith argued that the invisible hand that drives markets is capital, while the invisible hand of supply that drives innovation is demand. Generally speaking, the "inconvenience" in the daily life of the people can be used as the traction of technological development. In the AI

Fig. 2.3 Six stakeholders of city construction

technology market, enterprises that see fundamental needs can have a large number of applications for their products. At present, most cities in the world will transform into AI cities; however, this transformation does not start from hardware, but from solving the specific problems that the government, society, and citizens cannot solve, and gradually penetrate into all aspects of urban governance, development and life (see Fig. 2.3).

The AI city has two characteristics. The first is to scientifically empower the judgment of decision makers and the interaction of man–machine decision-making, reduce the burden of machine decision-making, and supplement the artificial, subjective, accidental deviation in pure human intelligence decision-making. The second is that in the process of intervening in a large number of behavioral problems in the city, it can independently distinguish and learn to become more intelligent.

Social needs	Details
AI for the government's needs	At the governmental level, AI can help solve where the city should develop, which industries should be developed, and whether it should be outward development or internal promotion, which are originally very difficult problems in the actual governance of the government. In the past, relying on a chief executive to make decisions on all issues inevitably created great pressure and risk, so AI technology can be grafted onto urban decision-making issues—for example, for the direction of urban development, the use of AI technology for scientific prediction and accurate answers so as to provide a new model of "man–machine intelligence" for government decision-making
AI for society's needs	At the social level, AI technology can effectively assist in solving the production, management, and innovation problems of social organizations such as enterprises, scientific research institutions, and non-governmental organizations—for example, empowering social organizations to find potential partners and explore the need for mutual benefit; enabling enterprises to link factories, industries, and people together, open up the whole chain of production and sales, and save a lot of time, capital, raw materials, and other costs; and enabling service organizations to provide customized, better service experiences and create a new service model
AI for citizens' needs	At the citizen level, AI technology can effectively assist in solving pain points in daily life and personal careers. For example, intelligent matching can be used to help young college graduates find suitable employment opportunities, thereby addressing and removing obstacles that disrupt the career trajectories of college students. In addition, AI technology can also play a role in life's most difficult problems. For example, traffic travel, the choice of residential places, employment, pollution of national concern, and youth safety issues are among the difficulties and pain points of modern cities, but are also the grafting points of AI technology, rather than relying on the top-down layout and implementation of the past "smart city" top-level design

2.4 The Essence of the AI City

AI is an essentially a tool. The development of AI must consider ethical issues. For cities, it is important to deal with the advantages and disadvantages of technology, such as whether AI technology will affect the privacy and security of city people. The ethical issues are heightened by the fact that AI can learn by itself, but we should also clearly recognize that AI is a tool that can be trained to make life better and meet the needs of people in cities. The value of tools lies in how they are trained and how they are used. If AI is not well trained, or if it is trained incorrectly, it can become a major security risk. Therefore, whether AI can benefit humanity depends on the results of human training. By addressing the needs of urban residents as a fundamental goal, AI technology will drive comprehensive improvements across many aspects of urban life, including production, daily living, and ecological sustainability, but also should pay attention to avoiding the situation of technology becoming out of control.

The essence of an AI city is empowerment. In the definition of "AI city," the city obtains strong empowerment in urban organization and civilization development with the help of AI. The past process of urban intelligence emphasized information networking and promoted the comprehensive construction of smart cities. But the AI city is different: the city begins to learn and, after learning, better empowers life, production, and ecology through the learning process in order to continuously improve the energy level. The data of the daily operation of the city has become the different raw materials of AI technology, once data integration is fully achieved—spanning macro-level aspects such as society, economy, environment, and transportation, down to micro-level aspects such as individual and group activities—the overall functioning of the city will significantly improve. It is not the simple general smart city, but the intelligence that can learn. In the AI 2.0 era, with the breakthrough of the five key technologies of big data intelligence, swarm intelligence, autonomous unmanned systems, cross-media intelligence, and hybrid enhanced intelligence, the ability of AI city learning, problem solving, and empowerment has been greatly improved, moreover, numerous patterns and insights can be discovered within massive datasets. Therefore, the city began to iterate, and the urban agglomeration began to interact deeply. After learning, AI can formulate city rules according to a reasonable ideal vision. And when this formulation becomes the goal of deduction, the city can constantly predict, evolve, and revise itself. The 19th National Congress of the Communist Party of China clearly stated that "the principal contradiction in Chinese society has been transformed into the contradiction between unbalanced and inadequate development and the people's ever-growing needs for a better life." In this context, AI cities can empower cities through their strong self-learning, self-regulation, and self-deduction capabilities to help solve the problem of imbalance and insufficiency in the process of urban development in China.

2.5 The Multi-brain Scheme of AI Cities

Compared to smart cities, AI cities require entirely new organizational models. Urban development is not intended to be intelligent; its intelligent development process is in line with its own growth laws. In the early stages of development, the single-center "urban brain" model is the mainstream of smart cities. After the horizontal differentiation of the brain and the cerebellum, as well as the vertical differentiation of the brain and the telencephalon, and the independent development of maturity, the AI city shows a trend of establishing a "multi-brain" structure of multiple intelligent systems, and the city is no longer a singular intelligent entity but rather a community of intelligent entities composed of multiple interconnected life forms. From the perspective of composition, the urban multi brain model includes four aspects—the main brain, the auxiliary brain, the sub-brain, and the telencephalon—which are linked by the communication protocol mechanism. These include the following:

(1) The function of the primary brain is to respond to the decision-making of key urban issues, such as the development strategy of the city, the deployment of major events, and other key issues that need to coordinate the whole system, and only accept the necessary city information.
(2) The function of the assistant brain is to make decisions on sub-systems, such as urban traffic problems, energy problems, environmental problems, and other problems that need to be coordinated within the system.
(3) The function of the branch brain is to complete self-organizing and self-running decisions in local space.
(4) The function of the terminal brain is to make reflective decisions in the terminal perception center, such as an alarm when abnormal data is found.

The protocol mechanism is the information infrastructure to ensure the coordination between various brain systems. The new generation of communication infrastructure based on 5G/6G can support the efficient transmission of cross-region and cross-domain remote information in different intelligent systems. The application of AI technology in cities can build models and conduct community learning and decision responses for residents' lifestyles and behavior patterns from multiple sources.

Representative expert	Opinions
WU Zhiqiang Academic of Chinese Academy of Engineering	Existing smart cities have adopted a centralized system architecture through a centralized operation center to gather and process data. The information flow processing mode corresponding to this architecture is significantly different from the hierarchical and multi-center decision-making in the real society, resulting in the difficulty of information exchange, as well as the long decision-making chain and low efficiency A new generation of smart cities needs to establish a new multi-brain system model, so that the underlying model of smart cities can learn from the collaborative operation of real cities, learn the organization, decision-making, and action ways of social communities, and form a multi-brain community model beyond a single center

References

Pan Y (2016) Heading toward Artificial Intelligence 2.0. Engineering 2(4):409–413. https://doi.org/10.1016/J.ENG.2016.04.018
Wu Z, Gan W, Liu Z, Li S, Zhou M, Zhao G, Zhang X (2022) The AI City: theory and structural model. Urban Plann Forum 5:17–23. https://doi.org/10.16361/j.upf.202205002

Chapter 3
The Prototype of the AI City

Abstract This chapter examines the evolution of urban intelligent structures and their relationship with technological advances. Urban development has progressed through four distinct stages: primitive civilization, agricultural civilization, industrial civilization, and ecological civilization. The characteristics of cities in each stage reflect the societal needs and technological capabilities of that era. Notably, during the ecological civilization phase, cities have gradually developed the capacity to sense, respond, and make judgments, ultimately evolving into smart cities capable of learning and self-improvement. This chapter also analyzes the pivotal technological milestones in urban development, from mechanization to AI, each of which has significantly transformed the form and function of cities. Particularly, AI technologies, including big data and cloud computing applications, have elevated urban intelligence and facilitated the transition from automation to intelligence. Future cities will possess advanced perception, analysis, and decision-making capabilities, enabling them to achieve a higher quality of life and sustainable development through continuous self-optimization. This transformation will profoundly impact urban planning, industrial distribution, and residents' lifestyles.

Keywords Urban intelligent structure · Ecological civilization · Technological wave · Artificial intelligence · Smart city

3.1 The Structural Evolution of Urban Intelligence

The structural evolution of urban intelligence can be categorized into four distinct stages: primitive, agricultural, industrial, and ecological civilization (see Fig. 3.1). The term "civilization" has its roots in the Latin word "civis," which refers to the inhabitants of a city. Originally, it denoted the capacity of people to live in cities and social groups. Additionally, both the Latin words for "city" and "civilization" derive from the same root "cit," suggesting that the city embodies civilization itself, and the urban area serves as the vessel of civilization.

Z. WU, *The AI City*, The Urban Book Series,
https://doi.org/10.1007/978-981-96-2560-4_3

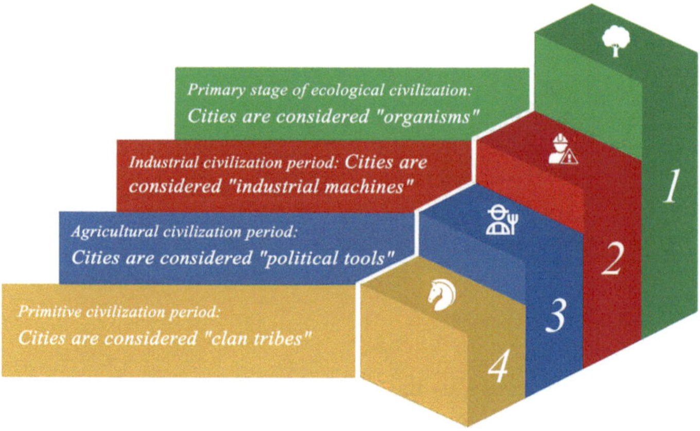

Fig. 3.1 The four stages of structural evolution of urban intelligence

Today, we understand that a city can be likened to a living organism in some respects. However, when examining the four stages of human civilization, we see that a city was successively perceived as a clan tribe, a political tool, an industrial machine, and, finally, an organism, or it exhibited characteristics of these forms. As a result, the diversity in terms of how urban features were depicted and the conceptualization of cities as organic entities across different historical epochs had a profound impact on urban development paths and the quality of life for urban residents during those times.

3.1.1 The First Stage: Primitive Civilization

Many ancient documents record the state of settlements in the primitive era. People "lived in the wild and in the caves, without a room or a house, and living spaces are as same as the birds and beasts" (Lu 2008). They "lived together in groups like beasts and compete with each other by forces" (Guan 2016). "Living in the mountains, they eat birds and beasts … and living near the water, they eat fish, turtles, snails, and clams" (Qiao 1991). From the above records, it can be seen that humans lived in the same domain and coexisted with birds and beasts in the form of tribes.

Labeled as the earliest mode of production, primitive civilization assumes a pivotal role in the evolution of human society. During this epoch, humans grappled with the challenge of food scarcity by organizing themselves into clan tribes, primarily reliant on hunting and gathering practices. Concurrently, humans innovated and crafted diverse tools, refining their methods of labor and adapting their way of life to suit geographic environments through extensive practice. This period witnessed the emergence of production systems, cultural taboos, and social norms, which were transmitted across generations. In this context, the city was conceptualized as being akin to a "clan tribe."

3.1.2 The Second Stage: Agricultural Civilization

The hallmark features of agricultural civilization include its inherent structural rigidity and cultural traditionalism, culminating in a tightly knit, self-contained social framework characterized by gradual change. Although cities during this era were not necessarily diminutive in scale and served as focal points for the consumption of surrounding regions, they often lacked a modern mindset and innovation consciousness. Instead, they tended to prioritize luxury, maintained a self-contained stance, and harbored a sense of historical pride that impeded the embrace of innovation. Consequently, innovation-driven industries were notably absent in these cities, which were primarily characterized by four core functions: governance, commerce, spiritual pursuits, and border defense, thereby being perceived primarily as "political instruments."

As an illustration, Chang'an City during the Tang Dynasty presents a quintessential city of the agricultural civilization. The building layout of Chang'an City generally included three distinct zones: the palace town, the imperial town, and the outer town. The palace town served as the residence of the royal family and the administrative hub for state affairs, while the imperial city housed central government institutions. The outer city encompassed residential areas, commercial districts, and religious sites. Located at the northern center of Chang'an City, the palace city symbolized the locus of imperial power, with the imperial town situated to its south. Surrounding these core zones, the outer town expanded along the eastern, western, and southern perimeters. This urban planning schema not only underscored the emperor's supreme authority but also mirrored the traditional Confucian principle of ruling from the north while facing southward.

In the southern region of the imperial town, two markets, known as the east and west markets, thrived as bustling centers of production and trade. The west market, distinguished by its larger scale, wider array of goods, and broader scope of commerce, stood out as the principal trading hub. Notably, it attracted a multitude of foreign merchants, earning renown as a prominent destination for international trade. Conversely, the east market emerged as the primary locus for handicraft production within Chang'an City. Known as the "gold market," the west market assumed the mantle of Chang'an's primary commercial and industrial zone, surpassing the east market in prosperity following the rise of the Tang Dynasty.

Chang'an City boasted numerous Buddhist temples. To preserve the majestic aura of the palace and other regal structures, city planners intentionally positioned large-scale temples at a considerable distance from the palace precincts. This strategic arrangement, harmonizing the temple layout with that of the principal buildings, solidified the perception of the royal edifices as the paramount landmarks, exerting their dominance over the urban panorama.

Moreover, cities during the agricultural era featured well developed defensing systems, including town gates, fortified walls, corner towers, horse-faced defenses, watchtowers, and moats, among other elements.

Like a living organism, a city has its own inherent laws governing its life processes. These processes can be delineated into seven distinct stages: incubation, infancy, childhood, adolescence, adulthood, old age, and ultimately, regeneration. Understanding the developmental trajectory of a city necessitates a grasp of these fundamental laws. By discerning the specific life stage of a city, one can ascertain its primary requirements for vitality and nutrition, as well as anticipate the prevalent challenges it may encounter.

The disjunction between perceptions of urban life and the actual developmental state of cities across different civilization periods profoundly impacted urban evolution and the quality of life for its inhabitants during those epochs.

Professor Zhiqiang Siegried Wu

Academic of CAE, acatech and IVA

3.1.3 The Third Stage: Industrial Civilization

From the vantage point of industrial civilization, there emerges a demand for a more precise and rigorous social structure. Social production no longer revolves solely around the family unit; instead, it is organized around a meticulously delineated material output process. The whole society is structured in line with the sequence of production that included research and development, production, management, and distribution.

In 1904, Tony Garnier, a young French architect, proposed the prototype of the "industrial city" (Garnier 1917). Grounded in the exigencies of industrial development, Garnier meticulously delineated the functional divisions of various elements within this innovative urban blueprint (see Fig. 3.2). At the heart of the design lies the city center, featuring assembly halls, museums, exhibition spaces, libraries, theaters, and other cultural amenities. Residential zones are elongated and linear, with the sanatorium and medical center strategically positioned on the sunlit northern side. The industrial precinct occupies the southeastern quadrant of the residential area, demarcated by green belts separating each zone. Proximity to transportation infrastructure is ensured, with the train station situated in close proximity to the industrial district. A railway trunk line traverses the urban landscape via an underground route, facilitating efficient connectivity. The urban transportation network includes high-speed thoroughfares and dedicated areas for experimental aircraft fields. Residential

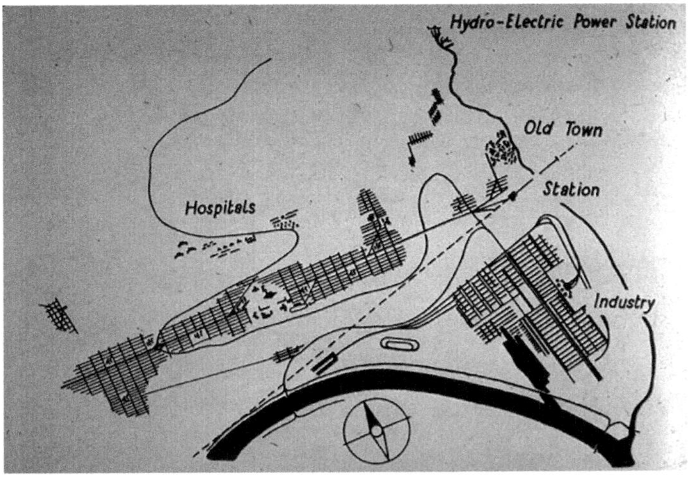

Fig. 3.2 "Industrial city" prototype. *Source* Tony Garnier, *Une Cité Industrielle* (1917)

neighborhoods within the "industrial city" feature 30-m-wide streets adorned with verdant greenery, complemented by neighborhood units housing primary schools and a spectrum of essential service facilities.

The hallmark feature of the industrial city lies in its meticulous and stringent functional zoning, in which industrial areas, transportation hubs, warehouse facilities, and other components wield decisive influence over the spatial layout structure of the city. Exhibiting distinct mechanistic and functionalist attributes, the industrial city prioritizes precision, accuracy, intensity, and efficiency in its design and organization. In essence, the city is conceptualized as a quintessential "industrial machine," emblematic of the era's emphasis on rationalization and optimization in urban planning and development (Wu 2000).

3.1.4 The Fourth Stage: The Initial Stage of Ecological Civilization

Following the Industrial Revolution, cities in Western countries grappled with a myriad of challenges, including congestion, pollution, and epidemics, prompting the public to re-evaluate the traditional urban planning approaches. Howard (1898) articulated the foundational principles of the "garden city" concept in his seminal work *To-Morrow: A Peaceful Path to Real Reform* (see Fig. 3.3).

Howard (1898) made a specific plan for his ideal city and drew a sketch. He suggested that a garden city should occupy 6,000 acres of land. The city is in the center, occupying 1,000 acres; the agricultural land around it occupies 5,000 acres, in addition to arable land, pastures, orchards, forests, etc., and also includes agricultural

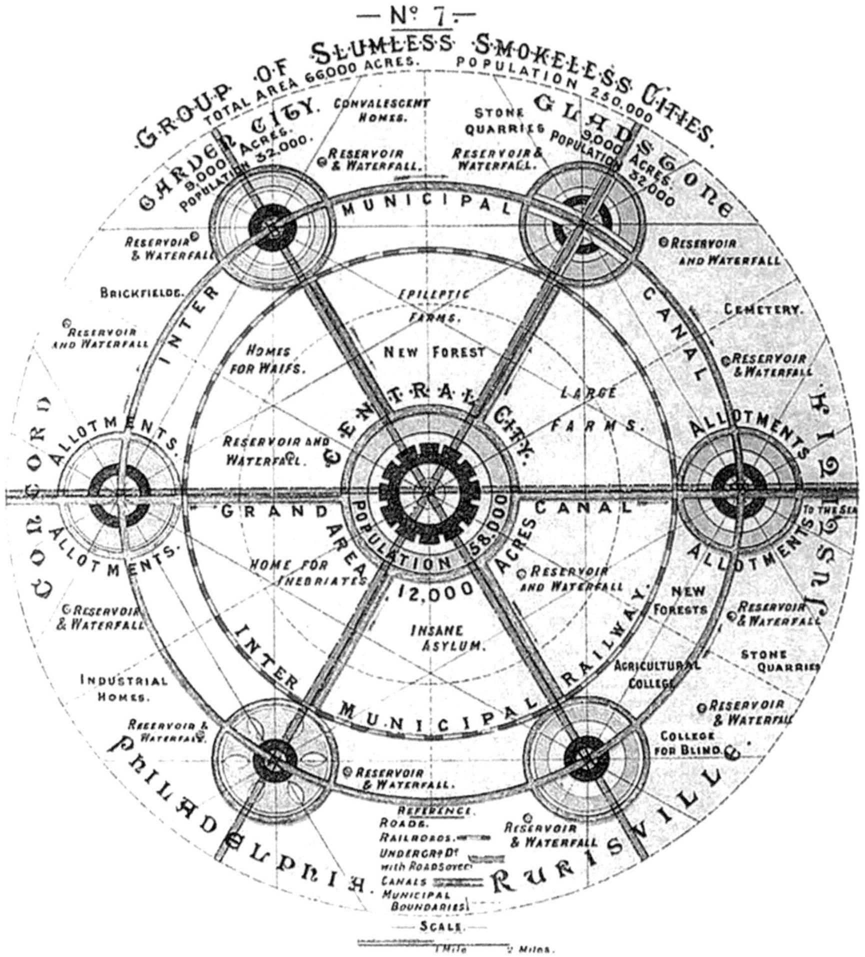

Fig. 3.3 Prototype of a garden city. *Source* Ebenezer Howard, *To-Morrow: A Peaceful Path to Real Reform* (1898)

colleges, sanatoriums, etc. The agricultural land is a reserved green belt, which must never be changed for other purposes. On this 6,000 acres of land, 32,000 people live, of which 30,000 live in the city and 2,000 live in the countryside. If the city's population exceeds the prescribed number, another new city should be built. The garden city has a circular plan, with a radius of about 1,240 yards.

The center is a park with an area of about 145 acres, with six main roads radiating from the center, dividing the city into six districts. The outermost area of the city is built with various factories, warehouses, and markets, with one side facing the outermost ring road, while the other side is a ring-shaped railway branch line, with convenient transportation. Howard proposed that in order to reduce the smoke pollution of the city, electricity must be used as the power source, and the city's garbage should be used for agriculture.

Howard (1898) further envisioned a group combination model for the garden city, in which six individual garden cities encircle a central city, collectively forming a cohesive urban ensemble he termed the "slum-free and smoke-free city group." This arrangement, reminiscent of a planetary system, underscores a distributed spatial organization. The central city, slightly larger in scale, is recommended to accommodate a population of 58,000, with corresponding increases in area. Connectivity between these cities is facilitated by rapid transportation and instant communication networks. Economically self-sufficient, politically aligned, and culturally interconnected, these cities forge a symbiotic relationship. Howard's conception of the garden city group blurs the boundaries between urban and rural realms, creating a permeable region that harnesses the advantages of both while mitigating their respective drawbacks. This multi-centered, integrated urban–rural system embodies Howard's vision for sustainable and harmonious urban development.

Howard's groundbreaking proposals addressed pressing urban challenges arising from modern society, including issues relating to urban scale, layout structure, population density, and the integration of green spaces. His original ideas coalesced into a comprehensive urban planning ideology system, offering innovative solutions to complex urban problems. This garden city theory has profoundly influenced modern urban planning ideas, serving as a beacon of enlightenment for subsequent theories. Notably, Howard's concepts laid the groundwork for theories such as the "satellite city" theory proposed by Graham Romeyn Taylor in 1915, which emphasized the decentralization of urban functions and the creation of self-contained urban satellites. Additionally, Howard's ideas resonated with Eliel Saarinen's "organic dispersion" theory from 1943, which advocated for the organic growth and dispersal of urban centers to achieve harmony with natural landscapes (Taylor 1915; Saarinen 1943). Overall, Howard's pioneering vision continues to exert a significant influence on contemporary urban planning discourse, shaping the trajectory of urban development and design worldwide.

This marks a significant advancement in the evolution of the industrial civilization city, characterized by its design prioritizing human well-being, livelihoods, and productivity. Central to its ethos is the pursuit of harmony between humanity and nature, alongside the synchronization of internal urban systems, fostering sustainable development across urban and rural landscapes. This paradigm shift holds profound implications for mitigating ecological degradation, enhancing environmental quality, minimizing pollution, and enhancing the urban aesthetic. In the nascent phase of ecological civilization, the city assumes the role of an organism, emphasizing the seamless integration of urban and natural environments, as well as the harmonization of internal urban systems.

3.1.5 The Fifth Stage: The Advanced Stage of Ecological Civilization

The prerequisite for a city to evolve into a living organism entails establishing robust material fusion, energy interaction, and information exchange dynamics with its external environment, thereby fostering an interactive ecology. In the advanced stage of ecological civilization, cities will be equipped with sensing, reaction, and judgment systems capable of facilitating material fusion, energy interaction, and information exchange. This represents a pivotal distinction from the earlier stages of ecological civilization.

When a city possesses the capacity to sense, react, and make informed judgments, it attains a heightened level of vitality akin to that of a smart city. Furthermore, in a more advanced stage of civilization, cities will acquire the ability to self-learn, discern patterns, forecast future trends, intelligently self-organize, and self-improve, thus embodying the attributes of an AI city (see Fig. 3.4).

Artificial intelligence city is a highly intelligent urban development form that is self-organizing, learnable, and iterative, which is driven by the needs of urban people and empowers the city's production, life, and ecology under the background of the emergence of new technologies such as big data, AI, the IoT, cloud computing, and mobile communications. In this stage of ecological civilization, a city can be more and more understood as a "living organism."

3.2 The Impact of Seven Waves of Urban Technology

Urban technology lays the foundation for urban production, urban life, and urban ecology. According to the structure, elements, functions, and external environment change of urban technology, it can be divided into the following seven waves (see Fig. 3.5):

- Wave 1: Mechanization technology, predominantly utilizing water power and mechanized production methods.
- Wave 2: Steel and railway technology, centered around steam power, railway systems, and advances in the cotton textile industry.
- Wave 3: Electricity, chemistry, and automobile technology, driven by innovations in electricity, chemical processes, and the proliferation of internal combustion engines.
- Wave 4: Television, aviation, and computer technology, anchored in advances in petroleum-based chemical industries, electronics, and aerospace technologies.
- Wave 5: Biotechnology and information technology, characterized by the digitalization, advances in biotechnology, and the rapid development of information technology.

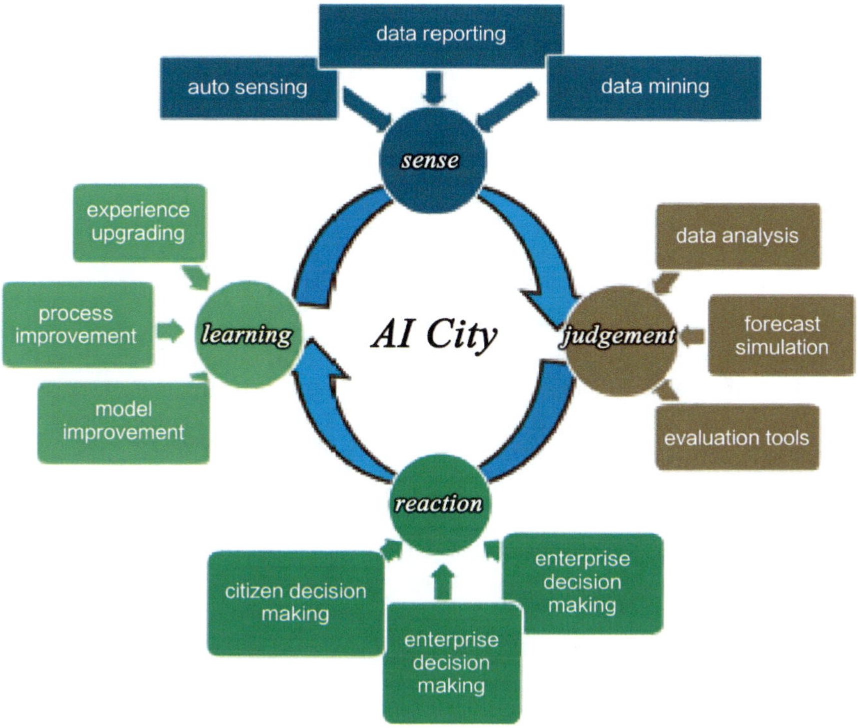

Fig. 3.4 Smart city prototype. **Intensive sense**: making decisions based on sufficient data support. **Accurate judgment**: being able to predict the state and consequences. **Appropriate reaction**: being able to mobilize resources according to situational analysis, and achieve the minimum energy, resource, time, and social psychological consumption. **Continuous learning**: being able to continuously improve the decision model and process, and achieve the continuous progress of the city ontology

- Wave 6: Sustainable development technology, focusing on enhancing material-using efficiency, promoting renewable energy sources, fostering sustainable product design, and advancing green technologies.
- Wave 7: AI technology, leveraging big data analytics, AI algorithms, cloud computing infrastructure, 5G communication, and the internet.

3.2.1 Wave 1: Mechanization Technology

During this period, cities underwent profound transformations as machine-based industries supplanted workshop-based handicrafts. Iron machinery replaced wooden counterparts, while steam power superseded traditional water-based energy sources.

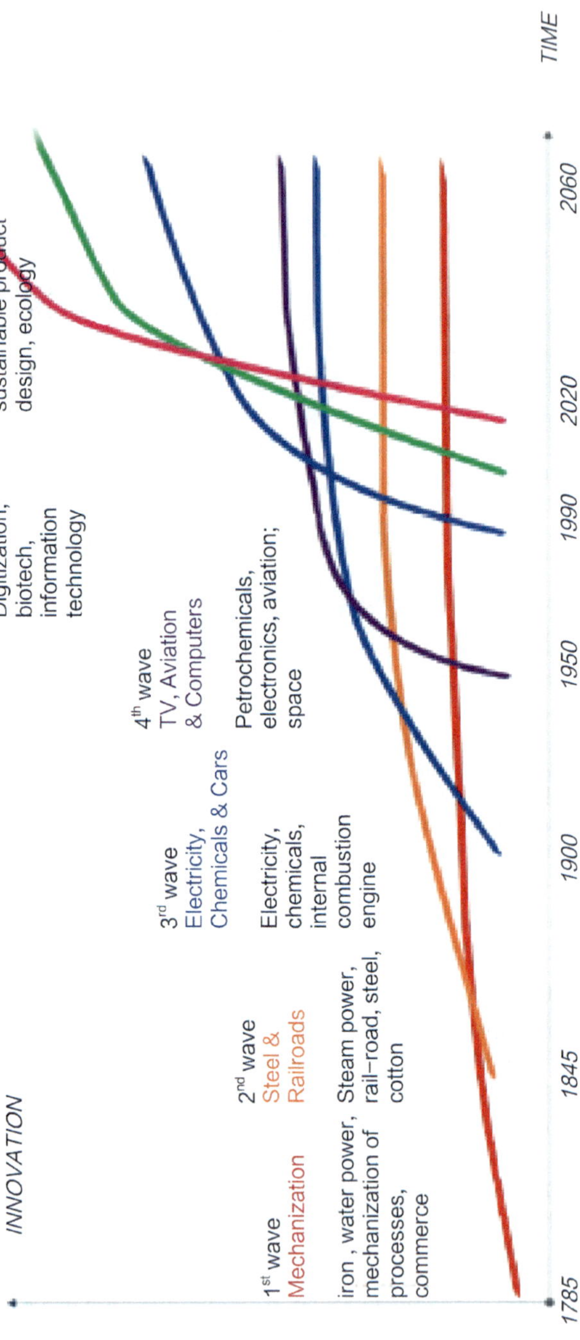

Fig. 3.5 Seven waves of city technology

The advent of new transportation technologies, such as steam locomotives and steamboats, further revolutionized urban landscapes. At the heart of this revolution lay a transformative shift in energy and power dynamics, liberating humanity from the constraints imposed by natural energy sources like wind and water.

As John R. Laverty aptly articulated in his article "Urban Revolution," the Industrial Revolution precipitated a fundamental reconfiguration of human labor dynamics. Formerly, farmers and herdsmen of the agricultural era became beholden to machines fueled by non-biological energy sources. The Industrial Revolution significantly accelerated the urbanization process, leading to a growing concentration of the world's population in urban areas.

A new kind of energy and power played a pivotal role in consolidating production activities in urban centers, fueling the rapid growth of processing industries and invigorating commerce and trade. As a result, urban populations swelled as individuals migrated to cities in search of employment opportunities within the burgeoning industrial sectors.

3.2.2 Wave 2: Steel and Railway Technology

During this period, advances in steelmaking technology led to a significant increase in steel production, consequently driving improvements in steel and railway technologies. Wolfgang Schivelbusch, a German historian and cultural researcher, highlighted in his book *The Railway Journey: The Industrialization of Space and Time in the 19th Century* that the proliferation of large urban railway stations reflects the industrialization of urban space.

The impact of railways on cities is most pronounced in the vicinity of railway tracks and stations. Large urban railway stations necessitate extensive facilities such as garages and public transportation stops to accommodate passengers, occupying substantial space within the city. The influx of railway traffic, particularly in station areas, substantially heightened congestion and noise pollution in the surrounding areas.

To adapt to the railway era, cities like Paris and other European urban centers underwent sweeping transformations in the nineteenth century, fundamentally reshaping the urban landscapes. This marked a significant paradigm shift, with cities increasingly prioritizing circulation needs—such as vehicular, passenger, and cargo flows—over traditional considerations centered on residential requirements during urban planning and development processes.

3.2.3 Wave 3: Electricity, Chemistry, and Automobile Technology

In this period, the widespread adoption of electricity heralded a transformative shift in human production and lifestyle, marking the dawn of the "electrical age." The proliferation of electric lights, trams, telephones, movie projectors, and other innovations proliferated rapidly, vastly enhancing the quality of human existence. This transition marked a pivotal juncture in human history, transitioning from the steam age to the electrical age.

Concurrently, the exponential growth in automobile traffic and the widespread adoption of motorized transportation revolutionized urban accessibility patterns, profoundly impacting urban spatial structures. The automobile emerged as the quintessential symbol of contemporary technological advancement, wielding significant influence over urban morphology. In shaping the urban landscape, the automobile dictates street scales, building connectivity, the necessity for extensive parking infrastructure, and the environmental rhythms crucial for human sustenance.

Furthermore, the widespread adoption of automobile technology precipitated a paradigm shift from the "walking-dominated city"—characterized by high-density land use, mixed development, and narrow streets conducive to pedestrian mobility—to the "automobile-dominated city." This latter model features low-density land use, dispersed development patterns, and a centrifugal layout centered on dominant transportation networks, diverging from the organic, pedestrian-friendly fabric of traditional urban environments.

3.2.4 Wave 4: Television, Aviation, and Computer Technology

During this period, urban technologies such as televisions, aviation, and computers engendered revolutionary transformations in cities. For instance, aviation technology spurred the rapid development of the aviation economy. The aviation economy encompasses a spectrum of economic activities—including transportation, manufacturing, information services, business consulting, and leisure tourism—clustered around airports. These activities leverage the aviation hub as a focal point, bolstered by core industries such as aviation manufacturing and logistics, as well as emerging high-efficiency, high-value-added modern service sectors. This convergence of economic activities gives rise to modern airport metropolitan areas characterized by highly concentrated economic vibrancy (Debbage 1999; Zhang et al. 2010).

In the 1960s, aviation expert M. Conway introduced the concept of the "airport economy," laying the groundwork for subsequent conceptualizations. Scholars such as Huddleston and Pangotra (1990) further refined the concept with their proposition of the "airport city." Weisbrod et al. (1993) delineated the spatial organization surrounding airports into categories such as airport areas and near-airport areas through comprehensive surveys across Europe, Japan, and North America.

Additionally, Kasarda and Green (2005) introduced the concept of the "airport metropolitan area" or "aerotropolis." This innovative urban form emerges from the co-development of various business formats—including aviation, commerce, leisure, entertainment, logistics, and manufacturing—drawn to the airport as a nucleus, fostering synergistic growth and prosperity.

3.2.5 Wave 5: Biotechnology and Information Technology

The fifth wave of urban technology, predominantly driven by biotechnology and information technology, has exerted a profound impact on urban environmental enhancement and the evolution of urban spatial forms.

As urbanization deepens and industrialization accelerates, the proliferation of various urban wastes poses significant challenges. Biotechnology, owing to its comprehensive efficiency and minimal secondary pollution, has emerged as a primary force in urban waste transformation and management.

Information technology has catalyzed a transformation in urban spatial layouts, transitioning from a mere agglomeration to a combination of agglomeration and dispersion. Modern information technology has transcended temporal and spatial constraints in urban dwellers' work, education, lifestyle, shopping, healthcare, and entertainment pursuits. This has reduced dependence on traditional physical spaces such as offices, educational institutions, commercial establishments, medical facilities, and transportation networks. Consequently, industrial production has decentralized, diminishing reliance on resources and fostering a more diversified urban activity space. Urban functions have expanded regionally, diffusing the spatial layout structure of cities.

Moreover, information technology has enhanced the efficiency and scientificity of urban planning, reshaped the industrial composition of cities, offered solutions to urban traffic challenges, facilitated the development of intelligent urban infrastructure, and advanced urban governance and monitoring mechanisms. These advances have permeated various aspects of urban residents' daily lives, fundamentally altering their way of life.

3.2.6 Wave 6: Sustainable Development Technology

In 1987, the United Nations Conference on Environment and Development published *Our Common Future*, which presented a comprehensive framework for sustainable development. This seminal report underscored the imperative of fostering development that fulfills present needs without compromising the ability of future generations to meet their own requirements. In essence, it advocated for judicious use of natural resources, robust ecological stewardship, and the preservation of resource conditions for posterity, all within the context of promoting equitable societal progress.

Subsequently, in 1993, the British Town and Country Planning Association issued *Planning for a Sustainable Environment*, outlining an actionable framework for integrating the tenets and principles of sustainable development into urban planning practice. This initiative aimed to embed environmental management considerations into spatial development planning across various administrative levels.

From a historical perspective of urban planning, the trajectory of urban development has paralleled human civilization's evolution and societal advancement. Urban construction has consistently evolved in tandem with environmental renewal and transformation. During this period, the integration of ecological technology and urban planning emerged as a pivotal ideological and methodological approach. The principles of ecology, such as diversity, independence, and decentralization, were judiciously applied to urban planning endeavors. Additionally, various "ecological devices" or "ecological units," employing ecological methodologies to mitigate anthropogenic pollutants, were incorporated as integral elements of urban design (Shen 1998).

3.2.7 Wave 7: AI Technology

With the advent of new information and communication technologies (ICTs) spearheaded by AI, cities are poised to undergo a paradigm shift. Equipped with smart sensing, analyzing, and decision-making systems, cities are able to autonomously execute tasks such as material, energy, and information exchanges (iResearch and Sensetime 2018). As urban evolution progresses, cities will transcend mere automation to embody true intelligence, capable of self-learning, law recognition, future deduction, intelligent self-organization, and self-improvement—culminating in the emergence of the AI city.

In the mechanical age, cities operated on automatic principles, adhering to preset processes and fixed logic established by humans. In contrast, the AI age empowers cities with autonomy, driven by human-defined objectives and enabled by continuous self-learning and improvement processes.

Moreover, as AI permeates various application scenarios, urban life will undergo transformative shifts. Along with the advancement of technology and industries, the AI-driven cities will transition from top-down policy-driven approaches to bottom-up demand-driven initiatives. Key factors in urban development will be industrial and developmental needs, and economic structural optimization that is unique to each city. The nexus between cities and industries becomes more intertwined, propelling AI penetration from isolated breakthroughs to widespread integration across multiple domains. This evolution fosters forward-thinking and innovative approaches, not merely addressing current needs but also creating new or enhancing existing application scenarios. Consequently, intelligence reshapes urban forms and lifestyles, bringing "urban wisdom" to residents' daily experiences, thus establishing a closer connection between AI and people's lives.

3.3 Future Urban Changes Triggered by AI Technology

3.3.1 The Three-Level System of the AI City

Reflecting on past technological advances and replacements, we observe that disruptive technologies profoundly influence urban life and production methods, presenting challenges to traditional physical space planning and design. The city, as a vessel of civilization, exhibits elasticity and adaptability in its spatial configuration, often trailing behind technological iterations. The juxtaposition of old and new spaces creates a collage-like urban environment that persists throughout history.

AI, big data and cloud computing, mobile internet, sensor networks and the IoT, blockchain, mixed reality, smart construction, robot and automation systems and other emerging technologies in the seventh wave will further act on urban space at different levels (Christidis 2016; Pan 2016). Technological innovation drives the renewal of urban products and services, and stimulates urban space transformation. Traditional land use based on urban function and urban structure is expected to transform toward people-centered pattern.

The emergence of new technologies, particularly AI, is seamlessly integrating into every facet of urban life. This integration significantly enhances the speed and efficiency of urban social operations, catalyzing a cascade of developmental shifts across various urban components, including city-regions and urban agglomerations, community systems, and urban infrastructure networks. Consequently, social relations and organizational structures undergo transformation, leading to the emergence of increasingly complex urban mega-systems.

Using the "backtracking-deducing" approach, we can analyze historical urban transformations driven by technologies progress. By leveraging the characteristics of historical development inertia and making reasonable judgments about the current development trends of emerging technologies, we can speculate on the potential forms and focal points of future AI city subsystems (see Fig. 3.6). This process lays the groundwork for abstracting the theoretical prototype of an AI city.

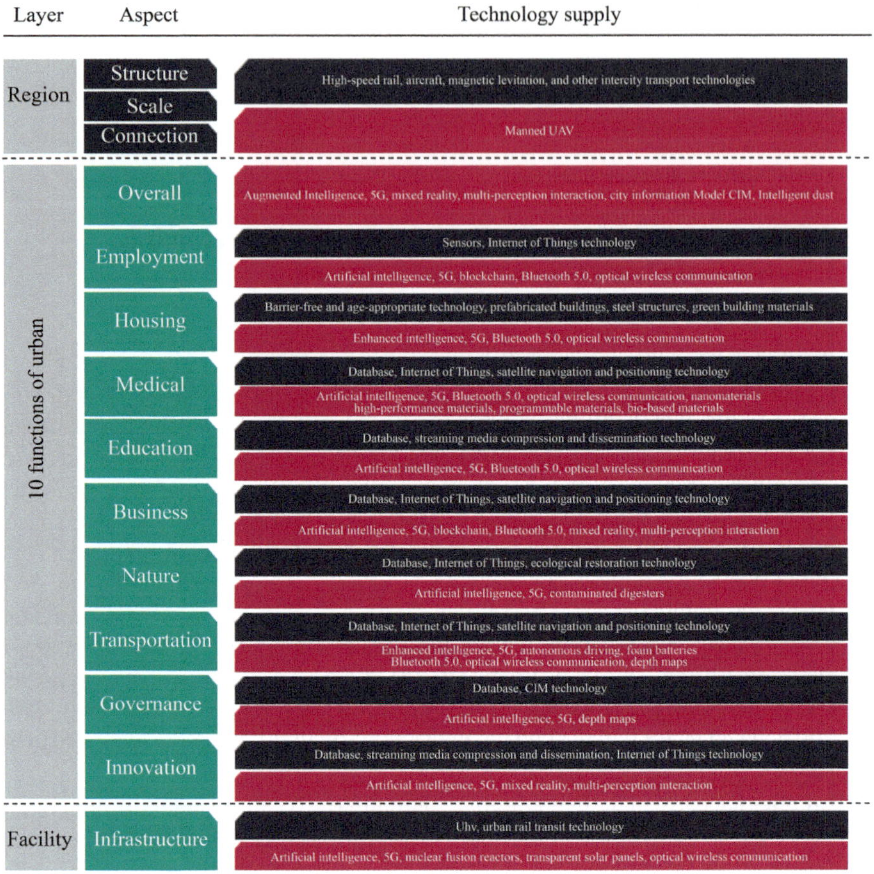

Fig. 3.6 Prediction of possible changes in future cities (space) with the aid of new technologies represented by AI technology

3.4 The AI City Prototype

3.4.1 The Characteristics of the AI City

The AI city embodies five essential abilities: learning from the past, discovering rules, predicting future contexts, intelligent self-organization, and driving technological progress through demand. Figure 3.7 provides an illustration of the prototype of an AI city.

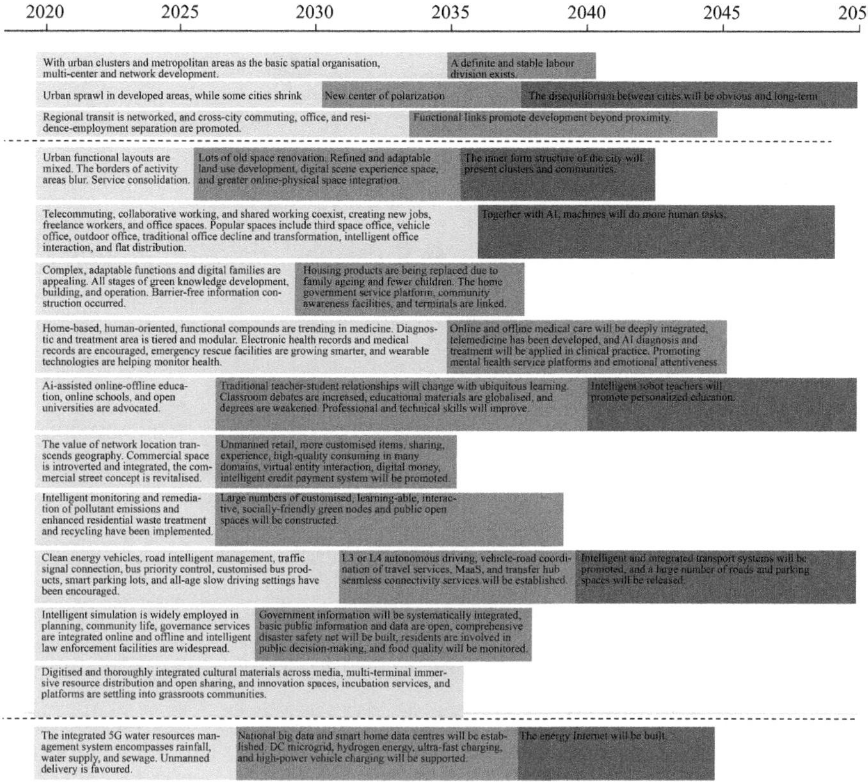

Fig. 3.6 (continued)

3.4.2 *The Innovative Applications of New Generation AI in the City*

Table 3.1 shows the innovative applications of the new generation AI in cities.

3.4.3 *The AI City Prototype*

Wu (2018) introduced the concept of the "AI city," which integrates urban AI hubs and the autonomic nervous system into the framework of smart cities. This concept recognizes that urban development is rapidly entering the era of AI, necessitating the creation of an open ecosystem to facilitate the application of next-generation AI technologies in urban environments. The establishment of the AI city aims to promote innovation experiments with AI technology within urban settings.

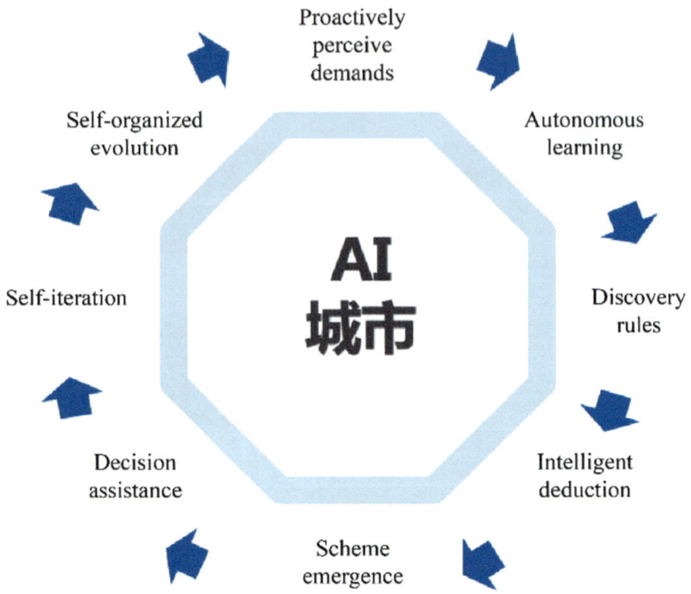

Fig. 3.7 The AI city prototype

AI cities, as previously detailed, address urban needs through adaptive technologies that perceive, analyze, and respond to challenges. This foundation now informs practical prototypes like [example], demonstrating scalable implementation. It fully leverages AI technology to empower urban production, lifestyle, and ecology. It embodies characteristics of self-organization, learnability, and iterative improvement, continually adapting to changing urban dynamics (see Fig. 3.8).

3.4.4 Building the Three-Level System of the AI City

The AI city comprises a three-tiered system, namely: the brain (the strategic decision system); the cerebellum (the urban commanding system); and the nervous system and the autonomic nerve system (see Fig. 3.9).

The autonomic nervous system refers to the network of nerves that branches out in the neck, chest, and abdomen, controlling various organs such as those in the neck, thorax, and most abdominal organs. Unlike brain nerves, the autonomic nervous system does not require processing through the brain; instead, it directly regulates functions like circulation, respiration, and digestion by conducting sensory impulses from the organs and controlling the activities of the cardiac muscle, smooth

Table 3.1 Innovative applications of the new generation AI in cities

Technology type	Frontier problem	Technical capability	Application field
Big data intelligence	Can generalize knowledge computing platform, causal reasoning, visual reasoning	Improving AI's ability to understand, analyze, discover, and make decisions about data. More accurate and deeper knowledge can be obtained from data, and the value behind the data can be mined	In the field of new retail, it can improve the accuracy of face recognition and predict monthly sales. In the field of transportation, intelligent traffic flow prediction and intelligent traffic grooming can be realized Intelligent control of the overall traffic network In the field of health, it provides more convenient and intelligent medical services such as medical image analysis, auxiliary diagnosis and treatment, and medical robots It is accelerating in the application fields such as intelligent security, autonomous driving, and medical imaging
Group intelligence	Emergence and evolution of swarm intelligence, dynamics of swarm intelligence and entropy measurement	Attracting, converging, and managing large-scale participants. A variety of independent and collaborative ways, such as competition and cooperation, to jointly deal with challenging tasks. Intelligence beyond individuals emerges in decision-making tasks in complex and open environments	In the online field, open source software based on crowd development, innovation based on crowdfunding, wisdom and knowledge sharing based on crowd-sourced asking and answering, Wikipedia based on collaborative crowd editing, and the sharing economy based on crowd-sourcing and resource sharing

(continued)

Table 3.1 (continued)

Technology type	Frontier problem	Technical capability	Application field
Transmedia intelligence	Brain-like computing, cloud brain platform, digital retina	Through the theories and methods of audio-visual perception, machine learning, and language computing, a unified semantic representation of the physical world is constructed	In the field of urban decision support, research on the city-wide intelligent perception and inference engine can address issues of fragmented perception and information silos in urban development. It aims to establish a comprehensive intelligent perception and inference engine characterized by a "wide scope", broad perspective, extensive information integration, and enhanced service capabilities. It realizes multi-dimensional, cross-space–time collaborative perception and comprehensive reasoning for people, vehicles, objects, and events
Hybrid augmented intelligence	Machine reasoning and decision-making, robot autonomous learning, safe and trusted human–machine collaboration	The human role or human cognitive model is introduced into the AI system to form the form of hybrid enhanced intelligence	Introducing human supervision into industrial risk management, medical diagnosis, and criminal justice, allowing human participation in verification, using human knowledge and wisdom in the best way, and optimally balancing human intelligence and computer computing power In the field of autonomous driving, intelligent human–machine collaboration technology can coordinate two "drivers" to achieve the safe and comfortable driving of vehicles The fields of industrial development decision-making, online intelligent learning, medical and healthcare, human–machine co-driving, and cloud robots are accelerating

(continued)

Table 3.1 (continued)

Technology type	Frontier problem	Technical capability	Application field
Autonomous intelligence	Autonomous intelligent sensing and decision-making in complex environments, intelligent collaboration of unmanned clusters	Perception, control, decision-making, and system action in complex and variable environments. Machine learning for multi-platform distributed and multi-modal interactive collaborative decision-making	In the field of unmanned vehicles, applied to a new generation of intelligent vehicles, including unmanned vehicles, unmanned aerial vehicles, unmanned ships, and so on Through autonomous intelligent technology, the performance and reliability of vehicles can be enhanced In the field of social production, including intelligent workshop, intelligent factory, service robot, and other applications, it can greatly improve production efficiency and save labor costs In the field of scientific research, space robots and marine robots are being developed through autonomous intelligent systems

muscle, and glands. In the context of urban development, the construction of an urban "autonomic nerve system" facilitates the self-regulation of a vast amount of urban information within the system itself, bypassing the need to go through the urban "brain." This enables more efficient and autonomous management of urban functions and processes.

The urban autonomic nerve system manifests in two forms. First, it involves point-to-point transmission of instructions, where information transmission and feedback occur without the need to pass through the urban brain structure. Second, decisions are made directly at the point of perception. The advancement of computer vision, particularly through the development of convolutional neural networks, facilitates urban end perception. By employing techniques such as end-to-end, pixel-to-pixel training, these networks can achieve rapid and highly accurate image semantic segmentation. This enables efficient processing and decision-making directly at the perception level within the urban environment.

The intricate information flow within the city and the diverse needs of citizens in their daily lives no longer necessitate funneling into the management systems of urban functional departments. Instead, AI technology enables these challenges to be addressed at a low management level. This represents a disruptive breakthrough in the organizational model of cities, facilitated by the capabilities of AI technology to streamline processes, optimize resource allocation, and provide tailored solutions directly at the local level.

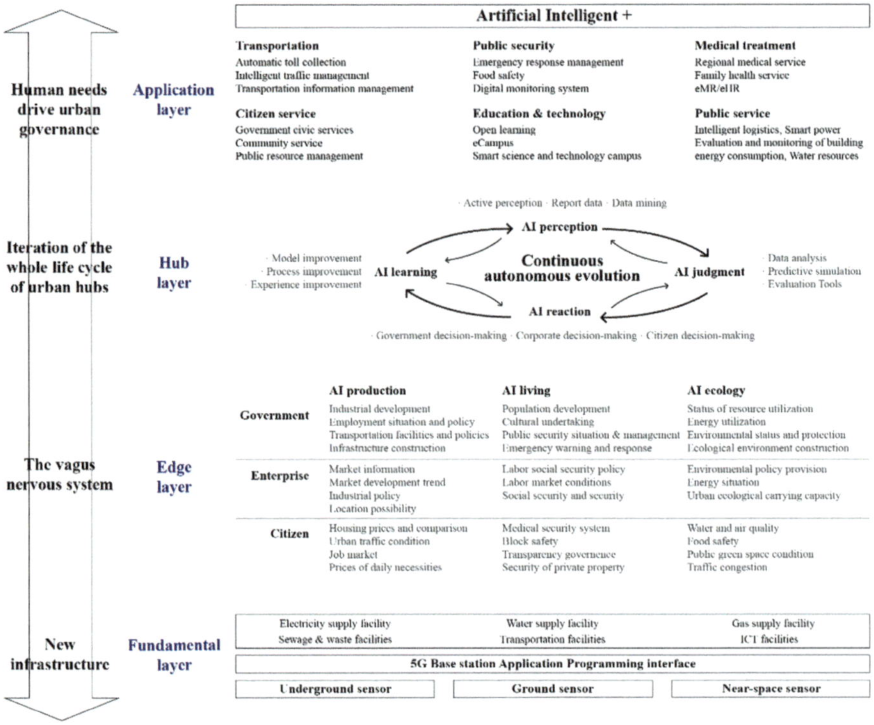

Fig. 3.8 The AI city structure model supported by new technologies

Fig. 3.9 The three-level system of the AI city

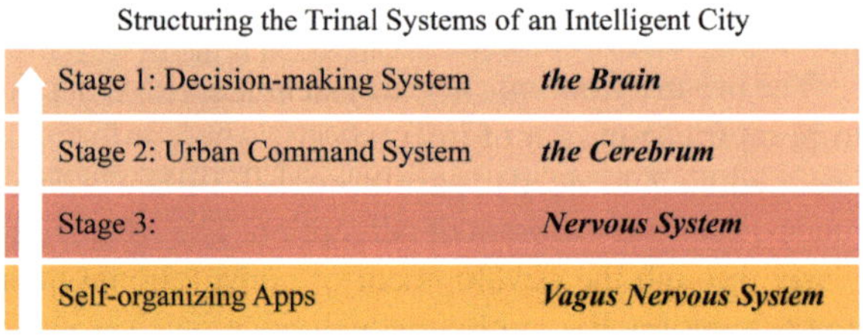

The urban autonomic nerve system disrupts the traditional paradigm where smart city operations and management rely solely on the urban government and functional departments to make decisions. It achieves this by enabling vertical differentiation within the smart city system. In essence, this means that decision-making processes are decentralized and distributed across various levels within the urban environment, allowing for more agile and responsive management of city operations. This shift fosters greater autonomy and efficiency in addressing urban challenges and needs.

3.5 The Planning and Governance of the AI City

3.5.1 The Problems Facing Urban Development

Urban development faces a plethora of complex and diverse challenges. From a temporal perspective, these challenges can be categorized into three main types: "yesterday's problems," "today's problems," and "tomorrow's problems." Although these categories may appear distinct, they are inherently interconnected and mutually influence urban development.

For instance, neglecting to address "yesterday's problems" can exacerbate them, leading to the emergence of "today's problems." Similarly, an exploration of the root causes of "today's problems" often reveals their origins in the past. Failure to accurately identify and address "today's problems" may perpetuate them, potentially resulting in the manifestation of "tomorrow's problems." Moreover, implementing inadequate solutions for "today's problems" may offer short-term relief but could pose long-term risks to future development.

In summary, understanding the interplay between past, present, and future challenges is crucial for effective urban development planning and problem-solving.

From the perspective of the life cycle of problems, urban challenges can be categorized into the following three types:

(1) Self-healing problems: Not all urban issues necessitate planning intervention. Some problems have inherent self-healing capabilities, akin to occasional colds that resolve themselves over time. For such problems, excessive external intervention should be minimized, redundant planning actions should be eliminated, and they should be allowed to naturally resolve themselves.
(2) Continuing problems: Unlike self-healing problems, many urban issues persist and lack the inherent ability to resolve on their own. A significant portion of "today's problems" are actually continuations of "yesterday's problems." Neglecting these issues can pose hidden dangers to urban development. In such cases, planners should promptly assess the situation and propose precise solutions to prevent the continuation of "today's problems" into "tomorrow's problems," or to prevent the emergence of new problems while addressing existing ones.
(3) New problems: With the ongoing development of cities, new challenges inevitably arise. Urban planning should anticipate and mitigate these emerging issues to the best of its ability, fostering the city's sustainable development from its core. By proactively addressing new problems, planners can facilitate the city's positive growth trajectory and prevent the onset of detrimental effects on urban life.

Urban planning is an iterative process aimed at progressively approaching the ideal city by addressing existing urban challenges (see Fig. 3.10). Traditionally, planners continuously identify and rectify issues within the city, akin to treating "urban diseases," and intervene in urban development by adjusting elements such as

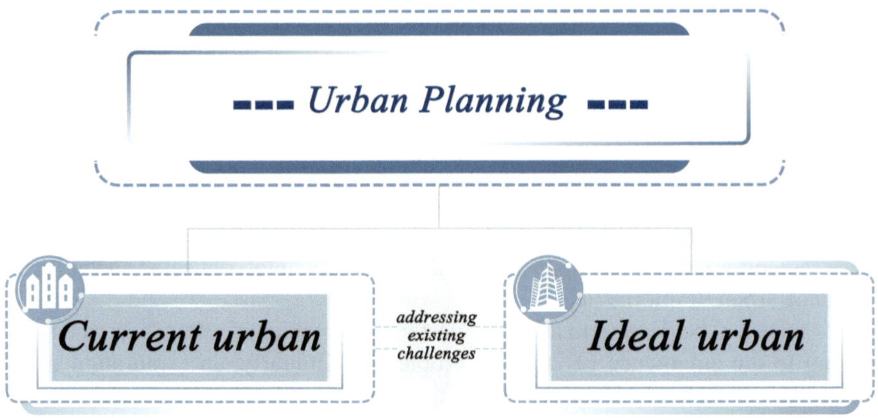

Fig. 3.10 The philosophy of city planning

transportation infrastructure and land use to bring the city closer to its ideal state. However, effectively addressing the complex interplay between self-healing problems, continuing problems, and new problems poses a significant challenge. Urban planning often focuses on present issues or "today's problems." This places urban planners in a defensive position, requiring them to respond to existing challenges rather than proactively shaping the city's future.

To break free from this reactive development paradigm, it is imperative to anticipate and integrate considerations of "tomorrow's problems" into current urban governance practices. This proactive approach involves predicting potential future challenges and evaluating whether today's solutions may inadvertently give rise to new issues. The advent of AI technology offers a promising solution to this urban governance dilemma. AI's diagnostic and predictive capabilities empower planners to identify today's problems accurately and discern their underlying causes. Furthermore, AI technology aids in forecasting the city's future trajectory, enabling planners to preemptively mitigate potential risks and transform urban planning and governance from a model of "treating diseases" to one of "preventing diseases."

3.5.2 The Planning of the AI City

Compared with traditional urban development, AI cities employ different problem-solving methods. AI technology can predict the possible future development status of the city by deducing the current situation, allowing for accurate anticipation of "tomorrow's problems." Additionally, AI cities can identify self-healing problems, prevent new problems, and address continuing issues. This is outlined in Fig. 3.11.

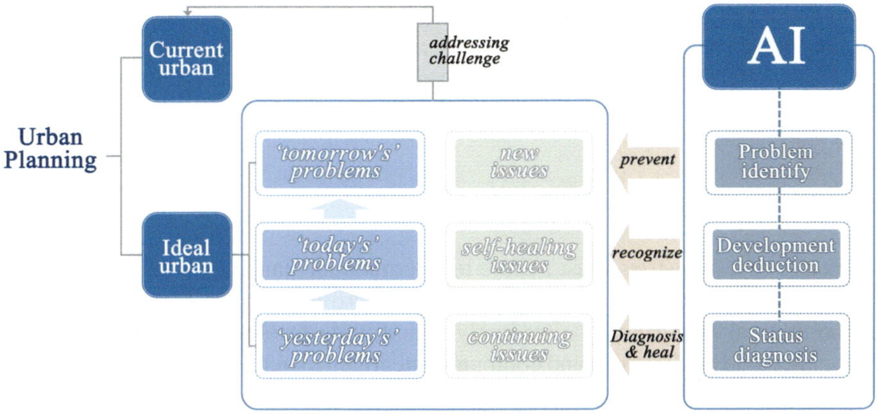

Fig. 3.11 The AI city planning prototype

The core principle of AI city planning is to "prepare today for tomorrow's challenges." The emergence of AI cities introduces new requirements and directions for urban planning and governance. Leveraging technologies such as image recognition and machine learning, planners can accurately identify urban problems and propose effective solutions. With the support of the big data era and computational power, AI can assimilate a vast array of urban cases, allowing for the extraction and synthesis of underlying development patterns within cities. This enables the classification of existing urban issues and the anticipation of future challenges. By distinguishing between "today's problems" and "tomorrow's problems," as well as identifying self-healing aspects and potential future issues, urban planning can offer precise municipal, spatial organization, and construction strategies. In doing so, it promotes the sustainable development of urban life while minimizing unnecessary or detrimental construction and interventions.

Professor Zhiqiang Siegried Wu

Academic of CAE, acatech and IVA

3.5.3 The Governance Paradigm of the AI City

3.5.3.1 Shared Community

In the development of the AI city, it is essential to preserve existing urban elements, uphold the intangible cultural heritage of the city, and maintain the continuity of the historical context. It is also necessary to create a 15 min city which allows for a balanced urban environment for work, residence, education, commerce, healthcare, and leisure. Furthermore, the ultimate objective is to establish a joyful and harmonious living environment, fostering a sense of community and contentment among residents.

3.5.3.2 Intelligent Industry

In the AI city, industries must adhere to international standards to ensure competitiveness and compatibility. The city should possess dynamic intelligent configuration capabilities, allowing it to monitor, analyze, and guide development across all sectors. Utilizing cloud applications and computer-integrated manufacturing frameworks, the city's model can be digitized for efficient management and planning.

3.5.3.3 Vitality

These communities should encourage interaction among residents and promote urban art and innovative culture. Obviously, enhancing vitality is crucial for the AI city, requiring cities to leverage their local advantages and social capital.

3.5.3.4 Smart Ecology

Ecology plays a crucial role in the governance of an AI city. Smart ecology integrates various ecological pathways such as rainwater management, sewage treatment, reclaimed water usage, cold and heat sources, electricity generation, gas supply, waste management, and more in a cohesive manner. This approach aims to develop low-carbon smart energy solutions, carbon–neutral buildings, and establish sustainable green ecological building clusters. Furthermore, guided by end-user demands, the city should establish a comprehensive natural and man-made disaster emergency plan system along with disaster relief spaces to create a resilient security network.

References

Blowers A (1993) Planning for a sustainable environment. A report by the town and country planning association. Earthscan, London

Campbell S, Fainstein SS (1996) Reading in planning theory. Blackwell Publishers, Oxford

Christidis K (2016) Blockchains and smart contracts for the Internet of Things. IEEE Access 2016:2292–2303

Debbage KG (1999) Air transportation and urban-economic restructuring: competitive advantage in the US Carolinas. J Air Transp Manag 1999(4):211–221

Dong J (2004) History of urban construction in China. China Construction Industry Press, Beijing

Ebenezer Howard (1898) Garden cities of tomorrow: a peaceful path to real reform

Faludi A (1973) A reader in planning theory. Pergamon Press, Oxford
Gao W (2021) The open-source ecosystem of the peng cheng cloud brain. Softw Integr Circuit 2021(6):50–51
Gao W, Tian Y, Wang J (2018) Digital retina: revolutionizing camera systems for the smart city. Scientia Sinica (Informationis) 48(8):1076–1082
Garnier T (1917) Une Cité Industrielle
Graham, Romeyn, Taylor (1915) Satellite cities: a study of industrial suburbs. D. Appleton, New York
Guan Z (2016) The monarch and his subjects (Part I), Guanzi. Zhonghua Book Company, Beijing
Howard E (1985) Garden cities of tomorrow. Attic Books, London
Hua X et al (2019) Urban brain: cloud-edge collaborative urban visual computing. AI View, Issue 5:77–91
Huddleston JR, Pangotra PP (1990) Regional and local economic impacts of transportation investments. Transp Q 44:579–594
iResearch and Sensetime (2018) Research Report on the Outlook of Chinese Artificial Intelligence Cities 2017. iResearch Inc., Shanghai
Jang JSR (1993) ANFIS (1993) Adaptive-network-based fuzzy inference system. IEEE Trans Syst Man Cybern 5:665–685
Kasarda JD, Green JD (2005) Air cargo as an economic development engine: a note on opportunities and constraints. J Air Transp Manag 2005(6):459–462
Laverty JR (1978) The urban revolution. University of Queensland Press, Brisbane
Lecun Y, Bottou L, Bengio Y et al (1998) (1998) Gradient-based learning applied to document recognition. Proc IEEE 11:2278–2324
LeCun Y, Bengio Y, Hinton G (2015) Deep learning. Nature 2015(5):436–444
LeGates RT, Stout F (1996) The city reader, 5th edn. Routledge, London
Lu J, Daoji X (2008) Zhonghua Book Company, Beijing
Pan Y (2016) Heading toward Artificial Intelligence 2.0. Engineering 2(4):51–61
Qiao Z (1991) Textual research in to ancient history. Zhonghua Book Company, Beijing
Saarinen E (1943) The city, its growth, its decay. Reinhold Publishing Corp, New York, Its Future
Schivelbusch W (2014) The railway journey: the industrialization of time and space in the nineteenth century, 1st edn. University of California Press, Oakland
Shen Q (1998) Urban ecology and urban environment. Press of Tongji University, Shanghai
Tsen WH (2006) Granger causality tests among openness to international trade, human capital accumulation and economic growth in China: 1952–1999. Int Econ J 2006(3):285–302
Weisbrod G, Reed JS, Neuwirth RM (1993) Airport area economic development model. PTRC International Transport Conference, Manchester
World Commission on Environment and Development (1987) Our common future. Oxford University Press, Oxford
Wu Z (2000) Historical outline of the western urban planning theories in the 20th century. Urban Plann Forum 2000(2):9–18
Wu Z (2018) Artificial intelligence assisted urban planning. Time + Architecture 2018(1):6–11
Zhang L et al (2010) Study on the relationship between airport operation and regional economic growth. Prog Geogr 29(12):1570–1576

Chapter 4
The Determinants of the AI City

Abstract This chapter examines five pivotal factors influencing the development of AI cities: learning capabilities, pattern recognition through learning, predictive analytics, intelligent self-organizing systems, and demand-driven technological advancement. The fundamental strength of AI cities resides in their capacity for continuous self-learning and iterative improvement to model and address intricate urban challenges. Leveraging technologies such as the IoT and big data, AI cities can uncover patterns of urban development through data flow and analysis, forecast future trends, and thereby optimize resource allocation and infrastructure planning. Moreover, AI city management will transition from a traditional top-down approach to a more adaptive and efficient self-organizing and self-decision-making framework. Additionally, the evolution of AI cities is propelled by human needs, with technological innovation addressing issues of environmental and systemic disharmony to foster sustainable urban development. The chapter also cites Wu Zhiqiang, an academician of the Chinese Academy of Engineering, who underscores that the essential elements for AI city development encompass technical feasibility, urban competitiveness, and corporate profitability.

Keywords AI city · Self-learning · Data analysis · Self-organizing management · Technology-driven

4.1 AI City Determinant 1: Learning Ability

In recent years, with the rapid development of high technology in the field of mobile communication and technology, the city has shown a trend of gradually becoming intelligent, so that the internal connection of the city is closer, and the connection of data, information, and resources is more efficient. In the future, with the large-scale popularization of commercial 5G technology, there will be more new products and new services with the characteristics of high speed and low delay, starting from the satisfaction of needs, entering people's lives, better serving urban people,

Z. WU, *The AI City*, The Urban Book Series,
https://doi.org/10.1007/978-981-96-2560-4_4

strengthening the "interconnection and interoperability" within and between cities, and constantly creating and providing efficient and convenient services.

In the urban environment, with the deep integration of the IoT, big data, AI technology and the real economy, digital industries such as industrial Internet and intelligent manufacturing have created new industrial forms, and the era of the Internet of Everything has arrived. However, urban development should not be limited to connectivity alone. The most fundamental distinction between future AI cities and traditional cities lies in their capacity for autonomous learning and adaptive evolution.

On the one hand, the historical data of urban development can be characterized and displayed by the current technology and research means. From the past urban development to the AI city, the city needs to self-learn and update iteratively according to its own development.

On the other hand, AI cities can simulate urban problems while intelligently managing and operating cities, constantly observe, find loopholes, seek solutions, learn from each other between cities, learn from each other at the forefront of urban development and operation, and constantly update and innovate.

Finally, with the development of AI technology, more and more algorithms can iterate and update model parameters based on urban real-time data, so that the model has the ability to constantly evolve with data changes. In the future, algorithms will generally have some self-optimization and learning capabilities, which will promote the AI cities that deploy these algorithms to have learning capabilities.

4.2 AI City Determinant 2: Discovering Laws Through Learning

Alongside convenient and cheap data acquisition, the city uses a series of technology applications, including various sensor systems, IoT monitoring and big data analysis, so that all data within the scope of the city's monitoring and control can fully flow in the management system of various layers of the city, and the operation and development of the city can be restored every day through data deconstruction. Massive city data forms the basis of AI city learning.

The chip with high computing power, integrated with a high-speed, low-delay communication network and interconnected with intelligent platforms and applications at all levels, provides the necessary conditions for city-level data analysis and calculation. Therefore, while collecting and acquiring urban data for self-learning and iteration, AI cities can simulate the urban environment, visually analyze the hidden problems in the city, and help summarize the laws of urban development, operation and management.

At the same time, in the process of providing convenient urban services and promoting the intelligent life of residents, AI cities can build and learn models for the lifestyle and behavior patterns of urban residents, and reveal the laws existing in the data through visualization and related research on model input, output, and explainability. This will help planners deepen their scientific knowledge and understanding of the relevant models, data, and city-related issues. Planners design new technical solutions based on the rules learned from large amounts of data and models to better meet the various needs of the city.

Compared with the technical rationality defect of "not seeing the people, not seeing the flow, not seeing the dynamic, not seeing the rationality, not seeing the relationship, not seeing the context," which can be solved by traditional city data, AI city can realize the big data collection perception of urban development dynamics, cloud computing analysis and diagnosis of urban development status, and AI law identification of urban development process through information technology, provide public participation in the planning and construction decisions of the mobile Internet, so as to quickly achieve the urban research effect of "meeting the people, seeing the flow, seeing the dynamic, seeing the rationality, seeing the relationship, and seeing the context," and support the more reasonable development of the city.

4.3 AI City Determinant 3: Predicting the Future

The decision-making and design of urban planning needs a large amount of data to support it. By learning the spatial and time laws of each subsystem in the city, urban phenomena can be understood more quickly and accurately, urban problems can be diagnosed, and planning schemes can be optimized. At the same time, AI can also obtain a large number of details between the time dimension and the space dimension to perceive the city as a whole and describe the process of urban development and change.

By mining urban laws through AI technology, not only can we see the "problems of today" of the city, but we can also predict the "problems of tomorrow," so that planners can make plans with minimal intervention. On the basis of summarizing the rules, AI technology is used to simulate and deduce the life scenes at different levels of the future city, and scientifically and reasonably predict or intervene in the problems that will be encountered in the process of urban development—for example, using AI to deduce the future of the city, achieve the 15 min living circle of home configuration, achieve the intelligent layout of public facilities location, optimize the urban spatial structure and infrastructure layout, reduce the consumption of urban resources and energy, and improve the level of urban operation efficiency and sustainable development.

Building on this predictive capability, AI-powered urban simulation and evaluation systems tackle development complexities through regional planning collaboration frameworks, multi-stakeholder decision modeling, and adaptive infrastructure optimization. These systems specifically address cross-jurisdictional challenges in transportation network development, water security ecosystems (including coordinated monitoring and disaster preparedness), and sustainable resource allocation across urban-rural continuums.

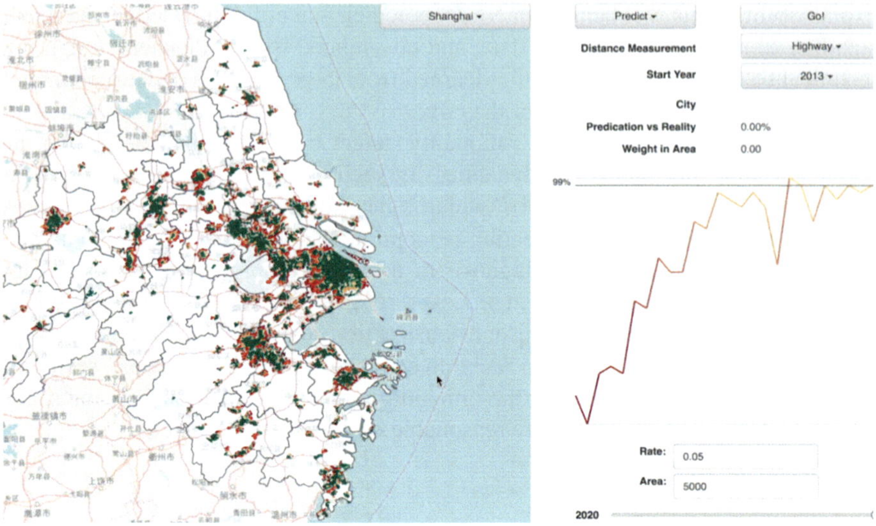

Fig. 4.1 The CityGo urban development platform

For example, the "City-Go" urban development platform of Tongji University (see Fig. 4.1) uses AI technologies such as big data, deep learning, swarm intelligence, and human-machine mixing to simulate the game process in urban planning and decision-making from the perspective of the endogenous laws of urban development, and generate different planning strategies, which can help planners better explore urban laws. It also helps city managers make better planning decisions.

4.4 AI City Determinant 4: Intelligent Self-organization Applications

The management of AI cities will no longer be a single top-down system, but a group of self-organizing, self-decision-making, and self-running systems with the help of AI technology, and then establish a new mechanism of hierarchical decision-making. This mechanism is reflected in social life, such as social networks and virtual communities, a large number of peer-to-peer mobile application smart solutions, and smart services that can accurately push a large number of user data.

Using social networks, mobile phones, bus cards, and other data to study the behavior of urban residents can empower urban space management, traffic governance, social services, and other fields. At the same time, compared with GPS and network log data acquisition methods that require fixed research objects, such methods have the advantages of a large sample size and low cost. With the gradual improvement of the functions of social networks such as Twitter and Weibo and the rapid growth of users, behavioral information obtained from social networks will develop its advantages and reflect the information of residents' activities and trips.

The perception of urban space based on human behavior records is of great significance to urban planning, community service, and allocation of public resources. In recent years, the global urbanization process has developed rapidly, and urban problems such as inefficient management, resource shortage, environmental deterioration, and traffic congestion have become increasingly prominent. People are the main body of a city, and the key to solving urban problems is to understand human behavior, perceive the spatial characteristics of the city according to human behavior, understand the characteristics of public resource consumption, and finally propose the plan to optimize urban management and operation. Using ICTs means to sense and analyze the key information of urban operation, and on this basis to realize the intelligent management and operation of the city.

The complex information flow inside the city and the tedious needs of citizens in their daily life will not all flow into the management system of urban functional departments, but can be solved at the following level of urban management, which is a subversive breakthrough brought about by AI technology for the organizational model of the city. Therefore, the construction of the urban "vagus nervous system" does not have to go through the urban "brain" and self-regulation within the system, which is an element of the AI city.

4.5 AI City Determinant 5: Demand-Driven Technology Development

Human demand is the driving force behind urban development, and the driving force mode of AI city is to use AI technology to solve the problem of human demand in the process of urban development, while the development of technology driven by demand is an important feature. In the city, the generation of human needs includes solving urban problems, satisfying instinctive needs, and realizing human dreams. These reflect the most urgent needs in today's cities, and are the pulling force, thrust, and endogenous power of the development of AI cities, which together constitute the three major driving forces to promote the development of technology.

The first driving force is to solve urban problems. In the final analysis, urban problems can be summarized as follows: (1) the human living environment is not harmonious with the natural ecology, which is summarized as the lack of supply and demand balance; (2) the internal disharmony of the human living environment is summarized as the lack of coordination of the system; (3) the sustainable rupture of the development of human civilization is summarized as the intergenerational sustainability. AI cities need to creatively solve problems such as aging, traffic congestion, energy, and environmental concerns in cities with the help of AI technology, which puts forward urgent requirements for technological development to solve urban problems.

The second driving force is to satisfy instinctual needs. People's instinctive needs have played an important role in promoting the development of AI technology. In the city, people have urgent needs for social interaction, living environment, social safety, and emotional sustenance. Applications such as intelligent social networks, chatbots, intelligent perception and data analytics, smart homes, innovative tools and platforms, intelligent security systems, and emotional computing have emerged in recent years to open up new perspectives on addressing human instinctual needs. The fulfillment of our instinctive needs is the cornerstone of a better future.

The third driving force is to realize the development of new technology of human dream movement in order to realize the transformation of dreams to reality.

Driven by the three driving forces, with the city as the application scenario, the establishment and improvement of the research and development mechanism of new technologies, and the realization of demand-driven technological development will continue to promote the development of AI cities.

Representative expert	Opinions
WU Zhiqiang, Academician of Chinese Academy of Engineering	Digital city, information city, and smart city, when compared to AI city, all represent steps in past explorations. The AI city is a comprehensive utilization and reorganization of the past stage, and in the past more investment in the application of technology, but not in the solution of the problem to achieve a breakthrough across time and space. The system dynamics of AI city development need to cover the following three basic elements (1) Technical possibilities. The above stages did not solve the problem of the essence of the city, and the development of AI technology has brought with it more possibilities (2) Competition between cities. The introduction of emerging technologies by AI in the iterative process will enable some cities to form an intelligent position for other cities, which will enhance their competitiveness and break the competitive pattern of clusters, similar cities, and cities of different sizes. Especially when the perception of the people determines the flow of the people, the AI city has a stronger grasp of the emotions of the group, resulting in a crowd gathering; there will be more young people, while innovative and creative people will promote the city to better development (3) The enterprise is profitable. The demand scenarios of real estate, childcare services, neighborhood committees, and the elderly are borne by the company and ultimately reflected in the contract profits, and the commercial promotion will become an important driving force

Chapter 5
The Main Goal of the AI City

Abstract This chapter delves into the fundamental objectives of AI city construction, with the aim of addressing human needs across multiple dimensions, including instinctual requirements, urban problem-solving, and the realization of future aspirations. AI technology fosters social interaction and innovation by strengthening social connections and propelling economic and social progress. Meanwhile, intelligent systems offer personalized services and efficient solutions to urban challenges such as aging populations, traffic congestion, and environmental concerns. AI cities not only address current realities but also embody futuristic visions, such as underwater, aerial, and space cities. Furthermore, in response to the evolving socio-economic structure in China, diverse human needs have emerged. The application of AI technology in transportation, healthcare, urban management, and other sectors has not only enhanced urban efficiency but has also improved the quality of life for citizens. The development of AI cities is centered on people, striving to create a safe, convenient, and livable environment that meets the personalized needs of citizens—from basic living requirements to cultural innovation activities—thereby promoting the sustainable development of cities.

Keywords AI city · Social demand · Management · Vision · People-oriented

5.1 The Generation of Human Needs

The generation of human needs includes satisfying instinctual needs, addressing urban issues, and fulfilling aspirational needs. These needs embody the most pressing requirements in today's urban environments.

5.1.1 Instinctual Needs

As social beings, humans possess instinctual needs for social interaction with others. Social communication forms a crucial foundation for establishing emotional bonds and building social relationships, and serves as a significant means to promote

Z. WU, *The AI City*, The Urban Book Series,
https://doi.org/10.1007/978-981-96-2560-4_5

creativity, innovation, and enhance socio-economic development. In the construction and development of cities, facilitating communication and interaction among individuals and groups is a paramount consideration. The emergence of AI technology has the potential to bridge the physical and psychological distances between urban residents, expanding social interaction from physical spaces into the digital realm. When constructing AI-driven cities, it is imperative to fully recognize the social nature of humanity and leverage technological advances to optimize relationships between urban residents, residents from other regions, and the broader societal context. The desire to fulfill instinctual needs also propels progress in technological development.

5.1.2 Needs to Address Urban Issues

With the rapid advancement of global urbanization, an increasing number of people are living in cities, giving rise to a variety of urban challenges. The aging population in cities constrains urban development, and intelligent elderly care services can offer personalized, point-to-point assistance to those in need. Urban traffic congestion slows down the pace of cities and increases operational costs, and intelligent transportation systems can redirect and streamline urban traffic, providing efficient solutions for daily commuting needs. Issues related to urban energy and the environment lead to resource waste and environmental degradation. Intelligent energy systems dynamically adjust the city's energy supply structure, reducing energy consumption and improving the ecological environment. AI in cities needs to creatively address challenges such as aging populations, traffic congestion, and environmental concerns, and the urgency to solve urban issues demands rapid technological development.

5.1.3 Needs to Fulfill Dreams

Cities are the crystallization of human civilization and serve as the primary gathering places for humanity, bearing the dreams and hopes of individuals. The developmental process of cities reflects the progress of human civilization, from agricultural to industrial civilization, witnessing significant changes in the appearance, role, and functional attributes of cities. Transforming human dreams into reality within urban landscapes requires continuous technological development to provide robust support. AI cities encompass humanity's optimistic visions for the future urban forms—underwater cities, airborne cities, and even space cities. Achieving human dreams poses unprecedented challenges for technological advancement.

5.2 The Diversity of Human Needs

In addition to the three most pressing categories of needs in today's society, as modernization continues to advance, profound changes in China's economic and social structures have led to the emergence of diverse new demands from the population (see Fig. 5.1).

First, there are new demands arising from the transformation of social structures, such as the needs for elderly care and reproductive services resulting from changes in population structure, as well as the infrastructure, public services, and employment needs brought about by rapid urbanization.

Second, new demands have emerged due to technological progress, including the promotion of technology sharing, increased convenience in utilizing technology, strengthening information technology infrastructure, and improving the quality of network services.

Third, new demands have arisen to mitigate various unexpected risks, such as the construction of social security systems, improvement of social governance and service systems, and the establishment of a comprehensive public safety system. The generation of these diverse needs indicates that in the era of AI, people are increasingly focused on quality of life, social identity, and the realization of personal values on nonmaterial levels.

The application of AI technology in areas such as transportation, healthcare, municipal management, urban and rural environments, disaster reduction and relief, social assistance, elderly care services, labor and employment, cultural education, quality and safety, consumer rights protection, and community services enables the realization of intelligence in various fields of smart cities, contributing to the construction of a well-rounded intelligent city.

In these scenarios, AI, with its enhanced sensing capabilities and optimal algorithmic prioritization and resource allocation, brings about a series of groundbreaking changes. These applications are closely linked to the urban development process,

Fig. 5.1 Diverse citizen needs

altering the organization and operation modes of cities, further enhancing urban operational efficiency and quality of life, and exerting significant influences on the physical and social forms of cities.

Representative expert	Opinions
PAN Yunhe, Academician of Chinese Academy of Engineering	First, societal demands have evolved. In the past, AI research focused on simulating individual intelligent behavior using computers. This was the approach for the first 60 years of AI research. However, contemporary society presents new demands, requiring solutions for issues such as smart cities, intelligent healthcare, smart transportation, smart games, intelligent manufacturing, and more. Many of these problems do not involve simulating the intelligence of an individual, but rather simulating the intelligence of a group of people. The emphasis is now on researching the intelligent operation of complex systems. While individual intelligence is essential, system intelligence holds greater significance. For instance, in the case of the transportation system, the solution was initially thought to be autonomous vehicles, but recent findings suggest the need for a collaborative vehicle-road system Second, there has been a tremendous shift in the information environment. Sixty years ago, AI targeted the intelligent simulation of a single computer, but today we are faced with an information environment consisting of the internet, mobile computing, supercomputing, wearable devices, the IoT, cloud computing, online communities, the World Wide Web, and search engines. These tools constitute a complex information mega-system. If AI does not fully utilize such a new information environment, it will inevitably be a weaker form of AI. Therefore, it is crucial to research and establish AI within a mega-system composed of computers, interconnected networks, and large datasets generated by computers, and various wearable and mobile devices Third, the foundation and goals of AI have undergone significant changes. Sixty years ago, the hope was for computers to become as intelligent as humans. However, in the subsequent decades, it became clear that computers can be more intelligent than humans in certain aspects—they can remember more, compute faster, and excel even in activities like playing chess. This indicates that computers will undoubtedly outperform humans in certain domains, much like how cars can travel faster than humans on roads. However, certain aspects of human intelligence are challenging to describe with precision, and if they cannot be described, they cannot be programmed. If they cannot be programmed, they cannot be implemented using computers. Now, an increasing number of AI scientists recognize that machine intelligence and human intelligence are two distinct forms of intelligence—one is the intelligence of silicon chips and the other is the intelligence of the human brain. These two have their respective strengths, and the best approach is to integrate them seamlessly to create an intelligence entity smarter than both humans and machines. This should be the new goal for the development of AI Based on these understandings, I believe that AI is undoubtedly moving toward a new generation

5.3 Meeting Human Needs is the Essence of Urban Intelligence

Human needs serve as the driving force for urban development, and the power model of AI cities is to use AI technology to address the needs of people in the urban development process. The crucial characteristic is the development of the city being driven by these needs.

Researching the technical support services required for intelligent city construction should start with citizens' needs, guided by overall design, aiming for efficiency improvement, and conducting end-to-end, closed-loop service design around various aspects of intelligent city construction.

In the planning and design of AI cities, it is essential to strengthen planning guidance based on the increasingly diverse and enriched needs of the people for a better life. Tailored planning should be considered, enhancing the quality of the living environment. This involves a comprehensive consideration of citizens' demands for urban spaces, including occupational, residential, educational, medical, commercial, recreational, road network, river network, green space, and cultural heritage spaces.

In the construction of AI cities, the basic life needs of citizens should be thoroughly considered. Activities such as commuting, dining, recreation, shopping, and entertainment should be seen as reflections of urban vitality, while the spontaneous cultural and social activities of young people should be viewed as symbols of urban innovation capability.

In the operation and management of AI cities, a people-centric approach should be adopted, providing corresponding services tailored to the needs of different demographic groups. Moving from single management to diverse intelligent management, a combination of "top-down" and "bottom-up" approaches should be employed. This involves offering intelligent and personalized services to citizens, establishing a standardized platform that can gather together a consensus from all parties, and achieving unified, standardized, and proceduralized urban management. Urban management should in particular highlight its role in safeguarding and improving people's livelihoods, ensuring that every resident (especially newcomers) feels the warmth of the city, enhancing their sense of identity and belonging.

Adhering to a people-centric approach in AI cities, while addressing urban issues, should be rooted in the notion of "putting people first." Understanding the common needs of different demographics, planning for production, life, ecology, and shared spaces based on people's needs, feelings, and holistic development are is crucial for innovating the development methods of AI cities. This includes promoting balanced and efficient allocation of resources such as industrial development, infrastructure, and public services at a macro-level, while actively responding to the education, healthcare, housing, elderly care, green open spaces, community life circles, and urban safety concerns at a micro = level. Implementing the concept of "people-centered" through AI 2.0 technology in various corners of the city can maximize the safety and convenience of spatial layout, allowing people to enjoy high-quality intelligent services and personalized living experiences, ultimately enhancing the livability of the city (see Fig. 5.2).

Representative expert	Opinions
YAN Shuicheng Associate Professor at the National University of Singapore, Vice President at 360 Group, Director of the Artificial Intelligence Research Institute, participant in the thirteenth batch of the National "Thousand Talents Program," Chief Technology Officer at SenseTime, and Fellow of IEEE (Institute of Electrical and Electronics Engineers) and IAPR (International Association for Pattern Recognition)	The core mission of an AI startup and a major AI laboratory is to achieve the practical implementation of AI, requiring solutions to two key aspects First, in terms of algorithms, it is essential to ensure that algorithms are "usable," meaning they have sufficiently high accuracy to truly unlock a scenario. Additionally, algorithms must be "applicable" as many scenarios nowadays cannot be adequately addressed by single-modal algorithms alone Second, regarding computing power, it is crucial to make it "affordable" for users. For example, AI chips supporting computation need to have sufficiently high concurrency performance Simultaneously, the power consumption of this computing power must be low enough to make it "affordable" for users, as high energy costs may hinder its utilization even if users can afford to purchase it As AI becomes increasingly integrated into various scenarios, the technology has reached a stage where it is practically deployable. Now, the emphasis is not only on the growing demands for computing power and algorithms but also from an "affordable" perspective To ensure the successful implementation of AI in a given scenario, the two crucial engines are (1) Efficient AI models: This falls under the algorithmic dimension. Achieving an efficient AI model can be approached through two methods: one based on different motivation patterns and the other based on Neural Architecture Search (NAS). The primary goal is to address the "affordable" issue in both research and application (2) Efficient AI chips: This pertains to the computational dimension. Chip manufacturers must adhere to algorithm and chip principles to ensure the chip achieves high efficiency in a sufficiently large range of scenarios. Additionally, they need to anticipate the main trends in algorithm development in the field to ensure the chip remains effective in the coming years. Finally, the construction cost for users must be sufficiently low for them to afford and utilize the chip As AI is applied in an increasing number of scenarios with higher precision and goals, the demands on algorithms and computing power continue to rise. At this juncture, the "affordable" issue becomes increasingly critical. Turning AI into "Affordable Intelligence" requires high-performance AI models and high-performance AI chips, which serve as the dual engines propelling this transformation. Only by doing so can end-users afford to purchase and utilize these technologies effectively Based on these understandings, I believe that AI is undoubtedly moving toward a new generation

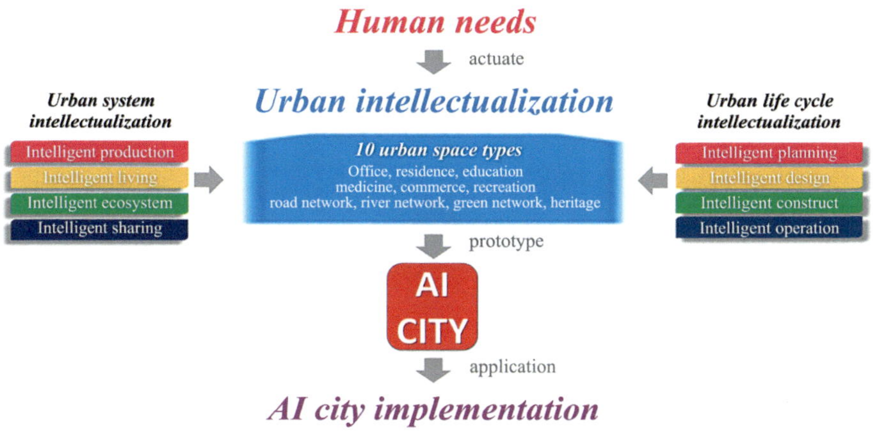

Fig. 5.2 Meeting people's needs is the essence of urban intelligence

Chapter 6
Matching Between New Generation AI Technologies and Urban Demands

Abstract This chapter examines the alignment between next-generation AI (AI 2.0) technology and the requirements of urban environments, with a focus on the application of AI 2.0 across ten key urban functions: nature, governance, housing, mobility, commerce, healthcare, education, industry, infrastructure, and innovation. By developing a matrix model that maps technological capabilities to urban needs, this chapter proposes a suite of AI-driven urban solutions designed to establish a robust feedback loop between technology and demand. The distinguishing characteristics of AI 2.0—such as big data-driven learning, swarm intelligence, cross-media intelligence, hybrid augmented intelligence, and intelligent unmanned systems—have significant potential in terms of enhancing various aspects of smart cities. Specific applications encompass optimizing energy consumption through advanced data analytics, optimizing resource allocation via swarm intelligence, assessing urban conditions using cross-media intelligence, improving human–machine collaboration efficiency through hybrid intelligence, and advancing urban automation and convenience through intelligent unmanned systems, all of which contribute to fostering sustainable urban development.

Keywords Urban functional demand · Big data intelligence · Swarm intelligence · Intelligent unmanned system

6.1 The Matrix of AI Technologies and City Needs

Interpreting and responding to the various needs of people in the city is an important goal of the AI city, and the realization of this goal relies on the continued development and practical application of AI technology, especially the new generation of AI technology: AI 2.0. This involves disassembling and matching the main technical directions and key technologies of AI 2.0 with the ten major functions of the city, including nature, governance, residence, travel, commerce, medical care, education, industry, facilities, and innovation, to build a matrix model of new-generation AI technologies and city needs (see Fig. 6.1), and thus researching and developing a series of

Z. WU, *The AI City*, The Urban Book Series,
https://doi.org/10.1007/978-981-96-2560-4_6

individual AI city products based on the matrix is an important working framework for realizing the mutual feedback mechanism of AI city technologies and demands.

Compared with the concept of AI 30 years ago, AI at this stage has entered a new stage of development, namely AI 2.0. The main technical changes from AI 1.0 to AI 2.0 include: from only knowledge engineering to big data-driven learning combined with knowledge engineering, from researching individual intelligence to establishing swarm intelligence services based on the internet, from using single structured data to integrating a variety of unstructured data, from being machine-centric to emphasizing the interaction between humans and machines, and from optimizing individual robots to building an overall autonomous unmanned intelligent system.

Currently, the five major technical directions of AI 2.0 are big data intelligence, swarm intelligence, cross-media intelligence, hybrid augmented intelligence, and intelligent unmanned systems.

6.2 The City Applications of Big Data Intelligence

Big data intelligence technology, or B-intelligence, focuses on the in-depth analysis and mining of big data to achieve knowledge learning with comprehensive reasoning capabilities. Its key technologies include knowledge computing engines, visual interaction engines, innovative design knowledge service technology, digital creative knowledge service technology, business intelligence knowledge service technology with visual media as the core, and general AI development technology based on holographic data, etc. The latest advances in digital intelligence technology include Google and DeepMind training neural networks based on weather forecasts and massive historical data from turbines to achieve power generation predictions within 36 h, thus increasing the utilization value of the 700 MW capacity wind power plant in the central United States.

The urban products of B-intelligence technology involve all aspects of the ten major functions of the city, including smart perception, smart security, smart life, smart transportation, smart retail, smart medical care, smart creation, smart construction, smart catering, smart entertainment, smart sports, and smart weddings, smart dating, smart exhibition, and other fields, which have broad application prospects (see Fig. 6.2).

Examples of the integration of B-intelligence technology and urban needs include the scientific allocation and rational utilization of urban energy and water resources with the help of AI 2.0 big data intelligence. For example, in the design of the Qingdao Sino-German Ecological Park, by collecting and accumulating power generation and consumption data of urban power plants and residential groups, the total power consumption of residential groups at different times of the day is predicted, thereby predicting the power supply of power plants to different urban groups. The total power supply is adjusted, and the potential energy generated by the height difference of the reservoir is used to generate electricity as an effective supplement in order to fully allocate and use urban electric energy and water resources.

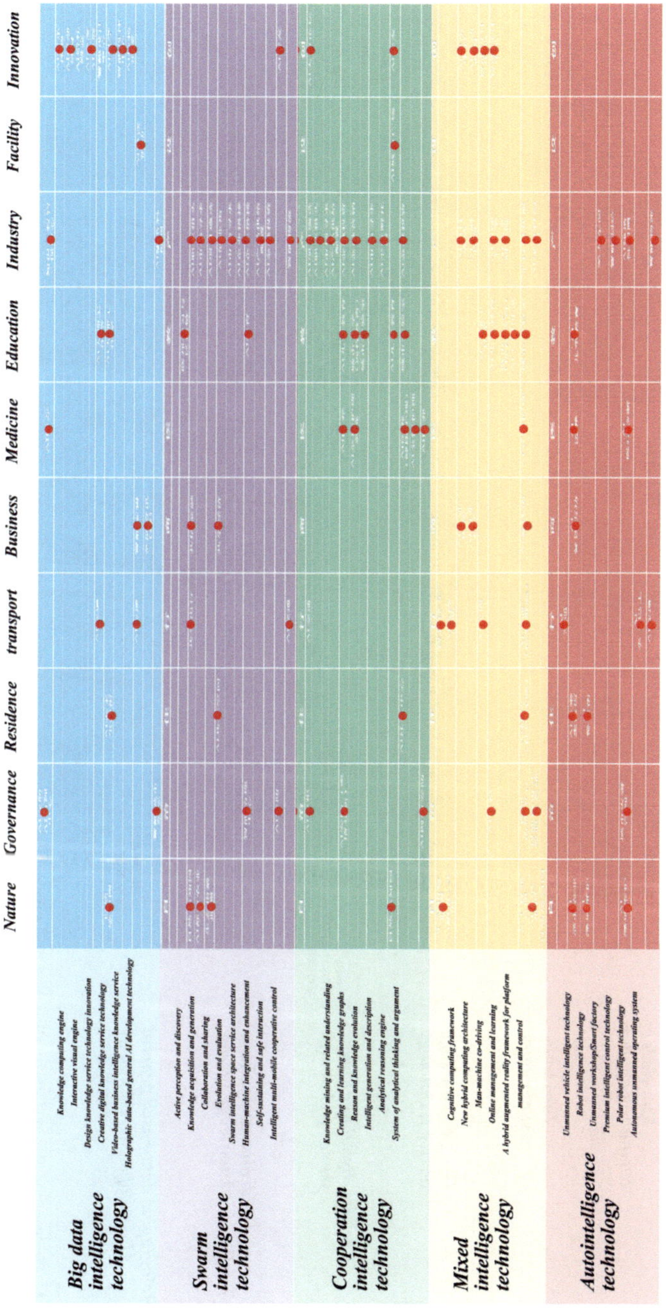

Fig. 6.1 The matrix of AI technologies and city needs

	Nature	*Governance*	*Residence*	*Transport*	*Business*	*Medicine*	*Education*	*Industry*	*Facility*	*Innovation*
Knowledge computing engine		AI security system Intelligent governance center				medicine system		Intellectual property intellectual protection center		
Interactive visual engine										Entertainment Sports gym Exhibition
Design knowledge service technology				AI transporta-tion			Master studio			Design center
Creative digital knowledge service technology	Natural perception garden		AI Future Life Street				Master studio			AI Pavilion Design center AI Principals Forum
Video-based business intelligence knowledge service				AI transporta-tion	AI retail Intelligent financial information				Catering street	
Holographic data-based general AI development technology		Smart city system						Science & Innovation Park		

Fig. 6.2 The matrix of big data intelligence and city applications

6.3 The City Applications of Swarm Intelligence

Swarm intelligence technology, or S-intelligence, emphasizes the intelligence beyond individual intelligence formed by large-scale autonomous participants under internet conditions. Its key technologies include swarm intelligence active perception and discovery, swarm intelligence knowledge acquisition and generation, swarm intelligence collaboration and sharing, swarm intelligence evaluation and evolution, the service architecture of swarm intelligence space, human–machine integration and enhancement of swarm intelligence, self-sustainment and safe interaction of swarm intelligence, and multi-mobile group intelligent collaborative control. The latest developments in S-intelligence technology include OpenAI Five's use of the Rapid system to simulate train an agent with basic human abilities using 2,000 data represented game states and won two games in a row in Dota2 5v5, the first time in an e-sports game that the human world champion was defeated (OpenAI 2019).

The urban products of S-intelligence technology involve the city's nature, governance, residence, travel, commerce, education, industry, and innovation functions. They span fields such as smart agriculture, smart monitoring, smart security, smart sharing, smart travel, smart finance, smart education, smart recruitment, smart investment, smart logistics, and smart socializing, each demonstrating promising application potentials (see Fig. 6.3).

Examples of the combination of S-intelligence technology and urban needs include the use of AI swarm intelligence to achieve the coordinated development and element allocation of urban clusters at the region scale. For example, the regional planning of the urban agglomeration in central Zhejiang proposes a total of ten allocation functions: green, governance, housing, transportation, commerce, medicine, education, industry, infrastructure, and innovation. Under the "15 min pedestrian neighborhood planning" rules of the 15 min walkable living circle, through the four-party game of the government, citizens, capital, and planners established and improved the decision-making model of various game subjects, and allocated each function in the urban agglomeration under swarm intelligence (see Fig. 6.4).

6.4 The City Applications of Cross-Media Intelligence

Cross-media intelligence technology, or C-intelligence, pursues comprehensive cognition, learning, and reasoning of various perceptions such as vision and hearing. Its key technologies include cross-media association understanding and knowledge mining, cross-media knowledge graph construction and learning, and cross-media knowledge evolution and reasoning, cross-media intelligent description and generation, cross-media analysis and reasoning engines, and cross-media analysis and reasoning verification systems. The latest progress in C-intelligence technology is that researchers at Carnegie Mellon University have established a multi-task learning framework, used a multi-layer LSTM model to achieve label prediction and paragraph writing, and annotated abnormal areas of the image to automatically generate medical images reports to assist doctors in diagnosis and treatment.

	Nature	*Governance*	*Residence*	*Transport*	*Business*	*Medicine*	*Education*	*Industry*	*Facility*	*Innovation*
Active perception and discovery										
Knowledge acquisition and generation						Federated Learning and blockchain				
Collaboration and sharing	Natural perception garden Smart urban agriculture			AI transporta-tion	Intelligent financial information			Professional headhunter Market search Project select		
Evolution and evaluation	Ecological index monitoring							Business incubation Market search Enterprise bond		
Swarm intelligence space service architecture			Sharing space		Sharing economy					
Human-machine integration and enhancement		Intelligent governance center					AI Education	Enterprise bond Product supply allocation Financial investment		
Self-sustaining and safe interaction		AI security system								Making friends
Intelligent multi-mobile cooperative control				AI transporta-tion				Intelligent logistics		

Fig. 6.3 The matrix of swarm intelligence and city applications

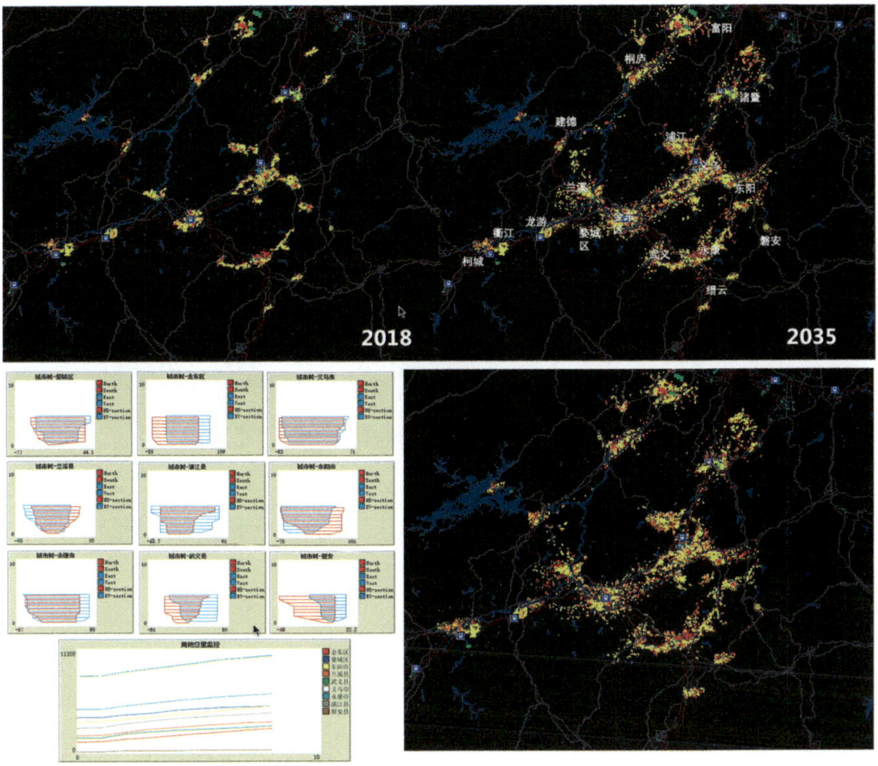

Fig. 6.4 Application of Swarm Intelligence: Scenario Simulation of Zhejiang Central Agglomeration

C-intelligence technology's urban products involve the city's nature, governance, residence, travel, medical care, education, industry, facilities and innovative functions. In the areas of smart network security, smart communities, smart transportation, smart care, smart education, smart marketing, smart recruitment, smart manufacturing, smart squares, and smart forums, C-intelligence technology has great application potentials (see Fig. 6.5).

An example of combining C-intelligence technology with urban needs is the use of AI cross-media intelligence to achieve global urban intelligence evaluation based on massive data from multiple sources. The Urban IQ diagnostic service of the Smart city Knowledge Service System from the UNESCO International Engineering Science and Technology Knowledge Center automatically collects more than 100,000 pieces of text, picture, and video information from major cities around the world every week and extracts and integrates the data from each source into city's five dimensions, like economic and industry, management services, environmental construction, hardware facilities, and residents' literacy, to measure and evaluate the urban intelligence levels of global cities in real-time (see Figs. 6.6 and 6.7).

	Nature	*Governance*	*Residence*	*Transport*	*Business*	*Medicine*	*Education*	*Industry*	*Facility*	*Innovation*
Knowledge mining and related understanding		AI hub		AI transporta-tion				Professional headhunter Market search Project select Product supply allocation		Master studio
Creating and learning knowledge graphs		Public opinion analysis				Medical care system	AI Education Distance education City lab	Investment and marketing		
Reason and knowledge evolution										
Intelligent generation and description	Natural perception garden						AI Education	Market search Business incubation	AI city center	
Analytical reasoning engine			Community center			Medical care system	AI Education	Financial investment		Making friends
System of analytical thinking and argument		Public opinion analysis				Medical care system				

Fig. 6.5 The matrix of cross-media intelligence and city applications

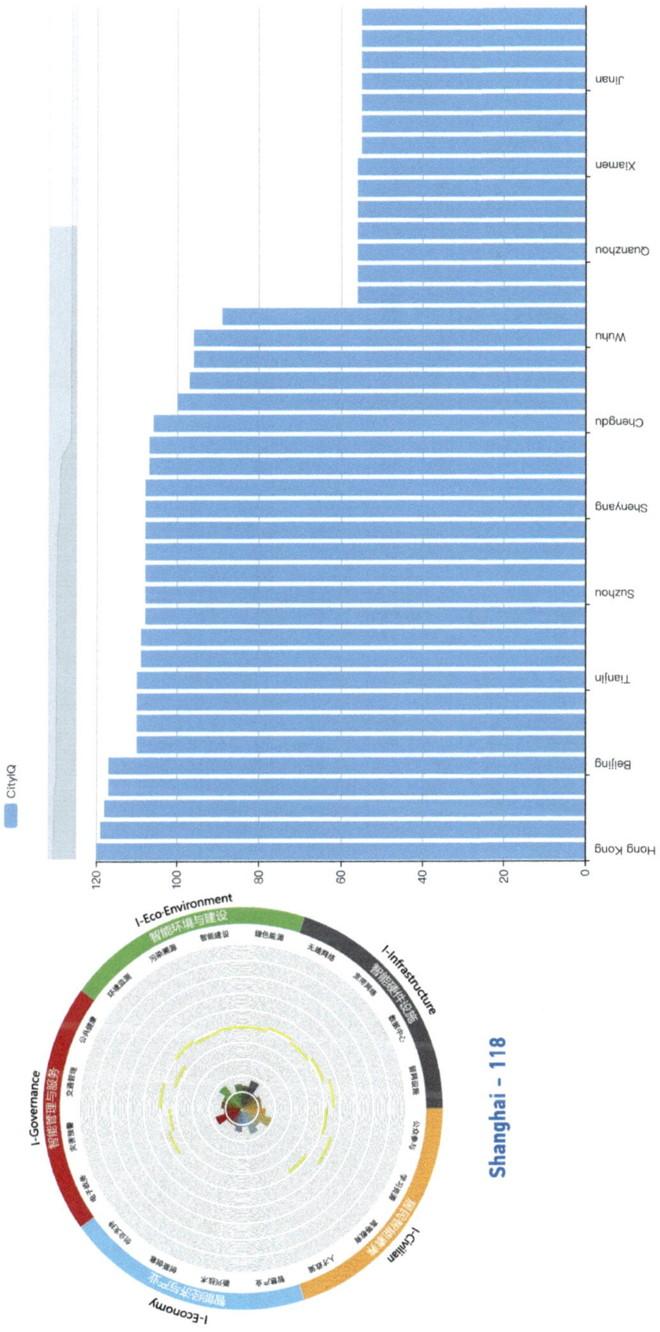

Fig. 6.6 Cross-media intelligence application in CITY IQ of Shanghai in 2019

Profile indicators	Value	Unit	Year	Value	Unit	Year
Total city population	24,183,300	Person	2017	21,707,000	Person	2017
Population ages 65 and above		undefined			undefined	
City area	6,340	km2	2017	16,411	km2	2017
Population Density	3,814	Person/km2	2017	1,324	Person/km2	2017
Urban Population	2,120,875	Person	2017	1,879,600	Person	2016
Gross Domestic Product (GDP)	3,013,386	Million CNY	2017	2,566,913	Million CNY	2017
GDP per capita	124,600.0	CNY	2017	118,198.0	CNY	2017
Economy	Value	Unit	Year	Value	Unit	Year

Fig. 6.7 Cross-media intelligence application in CITY IQ comparison between cities

6.5 The City Applications of Hybrid Enhanced Intelligence

Hybrid enhanced intelligence technology, or H-intelligence, focuses on playing a human role in AI systems or drawing on human cognitive models. Its key technologies include cognitive computing framework, new hybrid computing architecture, human–machine co-driving, and online intelligent learning and hybrid augmented intelligence frameworks for parallel management and control. The latest progress in hybrid intelligence technology includes, for example, Neuralink announced at a press conference at the California Academy of Sciences that it has found a way to achieve an efficient brain-computer interface and is seeking FDA approval for human trials. The trials involve connecting micron-scale wires to the brain, using a specialized surgical machine capable of implanting six wires per minute, and employing custom chips to read, process, and amplify neural signals.

The urban products of H-intelligent technology involve the management of nature, governance, residence, travel, commerce, medical care, education, industry, and innovation functions of the city, including living, traveling, commerce, and medical education. There are broad application prospects in the fields of smart runways, smart parks, smart green spaces, smart services, smart parking, smart entrepreneurship, smart nursing, smart education, smart construction, and smart design (see Fig. 6.8).

Examples of the combination of H-intelligence technology and urban needs include the use of AI hybrid enhanced intelligence to achieve human–machine collaborative decision-making to address various urban problems. For example, in Qingdao Sino-German Future City Smart city Hub, real-time city data streams such as traffic, electricity, water supply, and rainfall are directly integrated into the system and are visually displayed through data panels and three-dimensional models. A control panel is provided for human interaction to view and adjust various facilities and resources in real time. Human–machine cooperation and decision-making under hybrid augmented intelligence are performed when dealing with urban problems (see Fig. 6.9).

6.6 The City Applications of Intelligent Unmanned Systems

Intelligent unmanned system technology, or U-intelligence, focuses on realizing autonomous operation and management integrating intelligence and action without intervention. Its key technologies include unmanned vehicle intelligent technology (drones, unmanned vehicles, rail transit, etc.), robot intelligent technology (service robots, space robots, ocean/polar robots, etc.), unmanned workshop or smart factory intelligent technology (discrete manufacturing and process industries, etc.), high-end intelligent control technology, and autonomous unmanned operating systems. The latest advances in U-intelligence technology, such as DeepMind, can collect data center cooling system data every five minutes, calculate a series of operations that

	Nature	*Governance*	*Residence*	*Transport*	*Business*	*Medicine*	*Education*	*Industry*	*Facility*	*Innovation*
Cognitive computing framework	Ecological index detection AI runway and garden			Intelligent parking Fault diagnosis						
New hybrid computing architecture					Enterprise bond Financial investment			Project selection Financial investment		
Man-machine co-driving				AI transportation						
Online management and learning		AI hub					AI Education Distance education Master studio	Master studio Sharing lab		Design center
A hybrid augmented reality framework for platform management and control	Green space maintenance Natural perception garden	Intelligent governance center Smart city open services	AI Community	AI transportation	AI Catering street	Medical care system	City lab	Business incubation builds science & Innovation Park		

Fig. 6.8 The matrix of hybrid enhanced intelligence and city applications

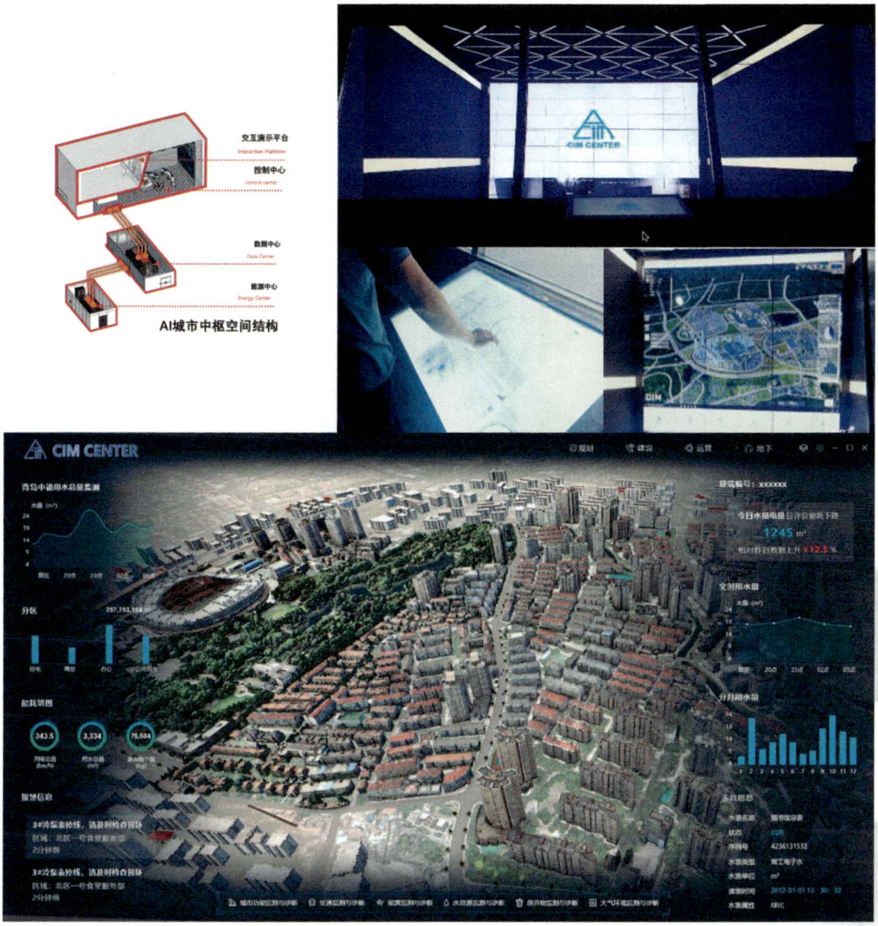

Fig. 6.9 Hybrid enhanced intelligence application in the CIM system of QINGDAO Sino-German Future Park

minimize energy consumption under safe settings, and realize safe and automatic data center cooling and industrial control through the control system.

The urban products of U-intelligence technology involve the city's nature, governance, residence, travel, commerce, medical care, education, and industrial functions. There are broad application prospects in fields such as smart agriculture, smart disaster prevention, smart catering, smart medical care, smart education, smart manufacturing, smart education, and smart logistics (see Fig. 6.10).

An example of combining U-intelligence technology with urban needs is the use of AI autonomous unmanned intelligence to realize unmanned public transportation systems in urban transportation. For example, the planning and design of Maqiao Artificial Intelligence Town in Shanghai focused on recording and analyzing travel times and transportation modes among different resident groups,

	Nature	*Governance*	*Residence*	*Transport*	*Business*	*Medicine*	*Education*	*Industry*	*Facility*	*Innovation*
Unmanned vehicle intelligent technology				AI transporta-tion						
Robot intelligence technology	Green space maintenance Urban agriculture		AI Future Life Street Catering street		Catering street	medicine system	Kids education			
Unmanned workshop/Smart factory								Unmanned workshop Intelligent manufacturing		
Premium intelligent control technology	Green space maintenance	Disaster management				Disease diagnosis		Science & Innovation Park		
Polar robot intelligent technology				AI Under-water bus						
Autonomous unmanned operating system				AI transporta-tion				Intelligent logistics		

Fig. 6.10 The matrix of intelligent unmanned systems and city applications

Fig. 6.11 Intelligent unmanned systems application in the unmanned city transportation system design in Maqiao, Shanghai

integrated this data with real-time urban traffic operations, and utilized autonomous rail transit technology to implement daytime fixed-route/flexible-station scheduling while promoting nighttime free-moving station-based unmanned rail buses, gradually establishing an intelligent driverless transportation system for urban public mobility (see Fig. 6.11).

Reference

OpenAI (2019) OpenAI five defeats Dota 2 world champions. https://www.openai.com

Chapter 7
Frontier Application of New Generation AI Technology

Abstract This chapter examines the evolution of intelligent manufacturing, intelligent agriculture, intelligent healthcare, and intelligent education in contemporary society, along with their influence on urbanization. In the context of Industry 4.0, intelligent manufacturing is transitioning from traditional mass production models to more customized and intelligent systems, thereby enhancing resource utilization efficiency and transforming production paradigms. China has fostered the advancement of smart manufacturing through its Made in China 2025 initiative, promoting high-quality development in this sector. In agriculture, particularly urban smart agriculture, fragmented spaces and cutting-edge technologies are utilized to boost productivity, streamline supply chains, and ensure product freshness. Smart healthcare leverages big data analysis, image recognition, and other advanced technologies to improve diagnostic accuracy, especially in elderly care, where smart home and IoT technologies provide enhanced security and health management for seniors. Intelligent education employs digital technology to refine teaching methodologies, addressing the challenge of balancing standardization with individualization, and offering new prospects for educational reform. The intelligent development across these sectors not only enhances production efficiency but also optimizes resource allocation, contributing to the sustainable development of society.

Keywords Intelligent manufacturing · Industry 4.0 · Intelligent agriculture · Intelligent medical treatment · Intelligent education

7.1 Intelligent Fabrication

Manufacturing is the cornerstone of the national economy. From the first Industrial Revolution to the present, the mode of industrial production has evolved from centralized mechanized production to assembly line production, and then to systematic production. In the Industry 4.0 era, the production mode is once again evolving toward customization, intelligence, and miniaturization (see Fig. 7.1). For a long time, the country has attached great importance to the development of manufacturing. Since

Z. WU, *The AI City*, The Urban Book Series,
https://doi.org/10.1007/978-981-96-2560-4_7

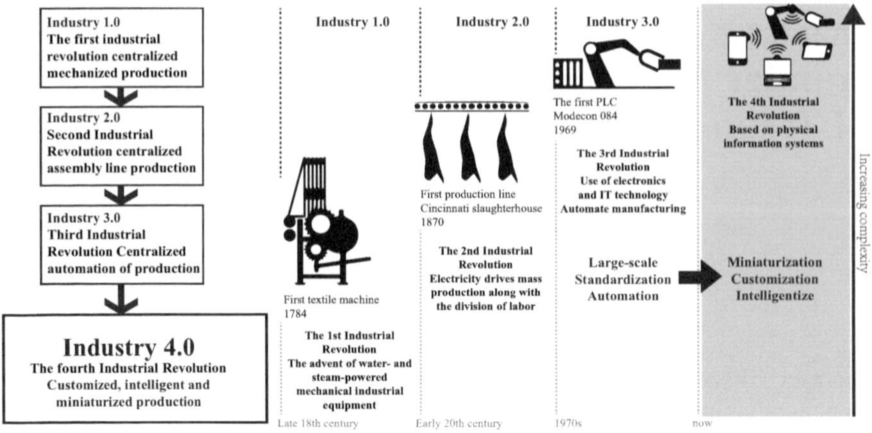

Fig. 7.1 The history of industrial revolutions

the release of "Made in China 2025" in 2015, numerous documents have been issued to promote the high-quality development of manufacturing, focusing on the development of advanced manufacturing, intelligent manufacturing, shared manufacturing, and other areas (see Fig. 7.2).

7.1.1 Conceptual Framework of Smart Manufacturing and Industry 4.0 Cities

The core of smart manufacturing lies in digital production innovation oriented toward user demand. The concept of Industry 4.0 cities is based on the Industry 4.0 concept, extending from production to digital innovation through supporting all industries of the city. The concept of Industry 4.0 is divided into three levels—production, industry, and city (see Fig. 7.3):

- The first level is Industry 4.0 production, which achieves digital innovation in production, focusing on smart products, smart production, and smart logistics.
- The second level is Industry 4.0 industry, which achieves digital innovation in the industry, focusing on collaborative production and shaping industrial ecosystems.
- The third level is Industry 4.0 city, which achieves digital innovation in the city, focusing on urban innovation driving, smart spaces, sustainable development, and modern governance, supporting the future of industry and production through urban innovation.

Fig. 7.2 Intelligent fabrication policies in China

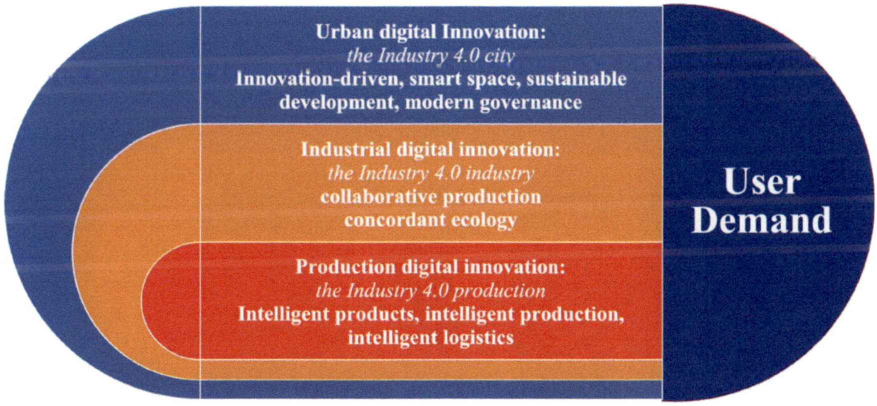

Fig. 7.3 The Industry 4.0 framework

7.1.2 Five Characteristics of Intelligent Manufacturing

The first major characteristic of urban smart manufacturing is utilizing AI to establish regional spatial connections for urban production, surpassing the production mode of individual factories and achieving breakthroughs from single-factory production arrangements to cross-factory production organizations (Fig. 7.4).

Within the city, enterprises are no longer confined to producing a single product; the production of a single item may involve collaboration among multiple different businesses. Through algorithmic allocation, precise access to the most suitable processing capabilities and equipment from a series of related enterprises within the city is obtained, resulting in products that surpass the quality of those produced by a single enterprise.

The second major characteristic of urban smart manufacturing is demand orientation. Smart manufacturing in the Industry 4.0 era has reconstructed the origin of production (se Fig. 7.5). In the past, the origin of production was the product, and all production organizations adhered to manufacturing standardized products. In the Industry 4.0 era, the origin of production is the user's demand, and all production organizations revolve around users' order demands in terms of product appearance, functionality, production time, and overall delivery location. Furthermore, future production will originate from users' most basic needs and instinctive desires. Designers and companies will provide flexible solutions that meet user demands by analyzing users' essential desires.

Existing industrial production is mainly based on mass production. A series of judgments from manufacturing to production and market entry are based on guesses about future customer needs by investors and producers. The production is based on past experience and the individual understanding of potential users. However, there is still great uncertainty over whether the product is what consumers truly need, leading to significant waste of energy and resources. In contrast, smart manufacturing in future cities is based on human needs, adopting an order-based production model,

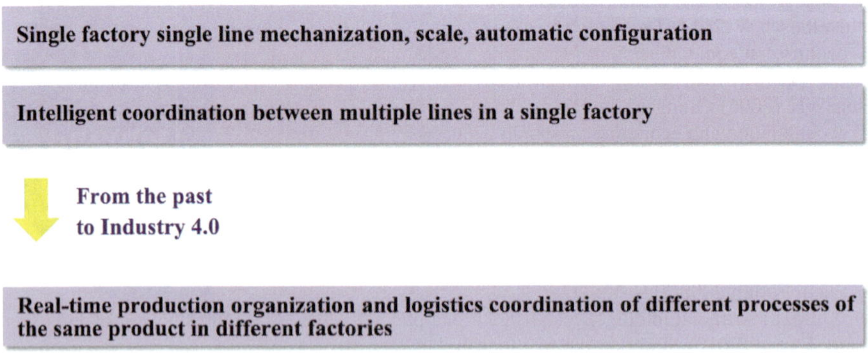

Fig. 7.4 The breakthrough from the single factory production arrangement to cross-factory production organization

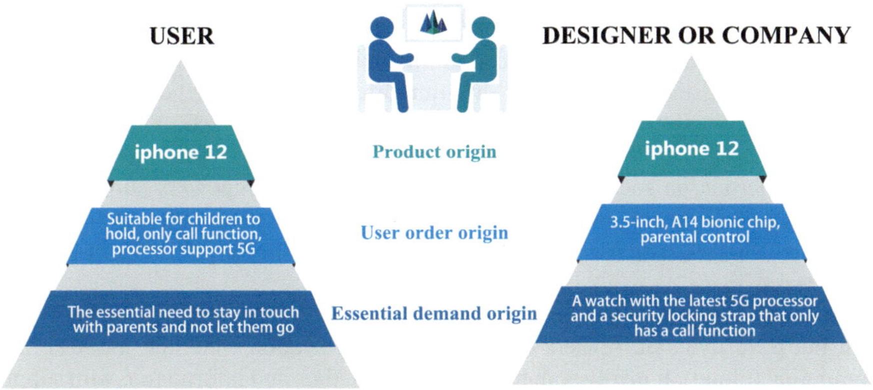

Fig. 7.5 Industry 4.0 production origin reconstruction

greatly reducing blind investment and waste of resources. This is the trend of urban customized production.

The third major characteristic of smart manufacturing is the transition from large-scale mass production to flexible production time, known as the "just-in-time" model (see Fig. 7.6). In the past, every pause in the production process, from raw material entry to production and storage, required significant warehouse space. In the future, with clearer product timing requirements, inventory time will be greatly reduced. Production will be scheduled based on target times, eliminating the need for extensive storage space. After the product is processed, it goes directly to the customer, significantly reducing waiting times. This trend is referred to as "smart logistics."

The fourth major characteristic of smart manufacturing is low energy consumption. The scattered distribution of production and consumption areas increases carbon emissions. Through intelligent learning and configuration, product manufacturing is no longer heavily globalized, leading to a significant reduction in carbon emissions. This trend is known as "localized raw material production."

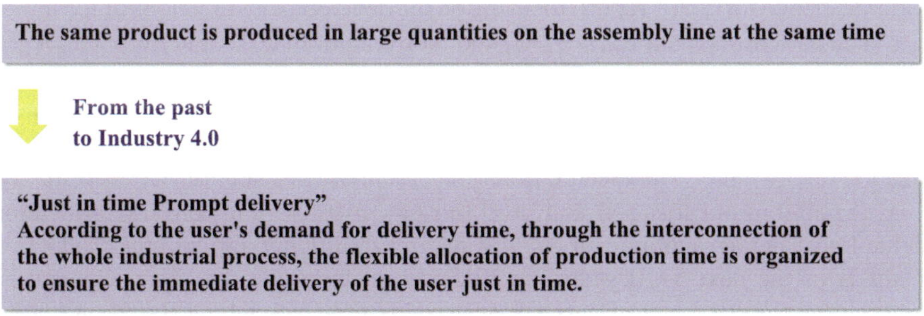

Fig. 7.6 The breakthrough from mass production to "just in time"

The fifth major feature of intelligent manufacturing is full life-cycle learning and intelligence. The most significant trend in smart city industrial production is the digitized monitoring and supervision of the entire life cycle of product demand, production, and sales terminals. This involves identifying issues such as time wastage, material wastage, and labor wastage throughout the entire flow process, which impose a burden on society and natural resources. This empowers humanity with powerful tools for more efficient use of limited energy resources in future production processes. This learning process marks a groundbreaking milestone in city production empowered by AI.

Industry 4.0 precision smart logistics is a set of collaborative technologies that integrate dynamic sensors (the IoT), communication (internet, mobile), and computing (cloud). It involves sharing data, knowledge, and information with supply chain partners to transform critical logistics processes into user-centric decisions enabled by real-time event synchronization.

7.2 Intelligent Agriculture

7.2.1 The Development Situation

Since the 13th Five-Year Plan, during the wave of the new round of technological revolution, developed countries such as the United States, the United Kingdom, Canada, and Japan have been deploying development strategies and technology research and development plans in areas such as the IoT in agriculture, agricultural big data, agricultural AI, agricultural robotics, and blockchain. Smart agriculture, represented by the in-depth application of agricultural big data, agricultural AI, and agricultural robotics, is becoming a new direction and trend in the world's agricultural science and technology development. In 2018, the National Academy of Sciences, the National Academy of Engineering, and the National Academy of Medicine of the United States jointly released the "Breakthroughs in Food and Agriculture Science for 2030" report, focusing on the development directions of technologies such as sensors, data science, AI, and blockchain. In 2017, the European Agricultural Machinery Association proposed the "Agriculture 4.0 (Farming4.0)" plan, emphasizing that smart agriculture is the direction of future agricultural development in Europe. In 2015, the Canadian federal government's Prediction and Strategy Organization released the "MetaScan3: Emerging Technologies and Related Information Chart," pointing out that soil and crop sensors, livestock biometric identification technology, and agricultural robots will disrupt traditional agricultural production methods in the next 5–10 years. In 2015, Japan launched the "Next-Generation Agriculture, Forestry, and Fisheries Industry Creation Technology Based on Intelligent Machinery + Intelligent IT" project. According to the international consulting firm "Research and Market," the global smart agriculture market value is expected to reach $68.389 billion by 2025, with the Asia–Pacific region, especially China and India, experiencing the fastest growth, with a compound annual growth rate (CAGR) reaching 14.12%.

On September 25, 2018, during his inspection of the Jian Sanjiang National Agricultural Science and Technology Park, Xi Jinping pointed out that "China's modernization cannot be separated from agricultural modernization, and the key to agricultural modernization lies in science and technology and talent. We must prioritize the development of agricultural science and technology, vigorously promote agricultural mechanization and intelligence, and give agriculture modernization the wings of technology." Documents such as the "Rural Revitalization Strategy Plan (2018–2022)," the "Outline of Digital Rural Development Strategy," and the "Development Plan for the New Generation of Artificial Intelligence" have all made important deployments for the development of smart agricultural technology. China's urbanization rate has reached 58.5%, the area of land transfer has exceeded one-third of the total area of family-contracted farmland, and the average age of rural primary labor force is now over 60. Implementing the rural revitalization strategy and comprehensively achieving agricultural and rural modernization have put forward more urgent demands for smart agricultural technology.

7.2.2 Smart Urban Agriculture

In the context of AI cities, agriculture refers specifically to smart urban agriculture rather than the general concept of smart agriculture. The fundamental difference lies in the fact that smart urban agriculture focuses on consumer-oriented agricultural production, whereas traditional smart agriculture emphasizes production-oriented agricultural production.

Urban agriculture refers to agriculture located in urban and peri-urban areas, closely linked to and serving urban areas. It relies on the technological, human talent, financial, and market advantages of cities to conduct intensive agricultural production, providing urban residents with better ecological environments and agricultural products, and serving multiple functions such as leisure, tourism, education, and innovation.

One major characteristic of smart urban agriculture is spatial fragmentation. Agricultural cultivation utilizes fragmented urban land, such as balconies, rooftops, and vertical green spaces. Smart urban agriculture is more closely aligned with individualized human needs. Instead of producing goods solely based on production capacity, it focuses on people's preferences, such as preferences for certain types of food or interest in the agricultural production process. Another feature of smart urban agriculture is its short sales channels, directly from balconies to kitchens, ensuring the freshness, organic nature, and lack of toxicity of urban agricultural products. Self-production and self-sales, as well as sharing with neighbors, are the main destinations for urban agricultural products. With the introduction of AI and the establishment of credit systems, urban agricultural products are poised for a longer-term, wider-reaching future, providing important intelligent support for the sustainable development of urban agriculture itself.

The smartification of urban agriculture in China focuses on two main key areas:

(1) The cultivation of urban agriculture requires a collective mindset shift from city governments and street offices to residents' committees and property committees. Like ancient feudal cities in China, modern Chinese cities are characterized by high-density urban forms where urban agriculture lacks a foundation, and many people equate urban agriculture with "idle pursuits" within the city. This perception has gradually evolved with the advent of industrialization and post-industrialization. Urban managers and developers are increasingly paying attention to fragmented areas such as urban balconies and rooftops, and policies encouraging urban agriculture are emerging, promoting a top-down change in mindset. In this process, big data precision perception can support the identification of urban spaces with potential for agricultural production. Many familiar urban spaces have the potential to become sites for urban agriculture, transforming into the battleground for future urban agriculture.
(2) The smartification of urban agricultural products involves the establishment of a knowledge graph and configuration. By creating knowledge graphs and intelligent question-and-answer systems, households interested in urban agriculture can receive more scientific and intelligent configuration schemes for their rooftops, balconies, and other spaces around their homes. This enables citizens to quickly understand the local climate and suitable planting seasons for crops, as well as dynamically obtain information on plant health and maintenance.

Leveraging agricultural knowledge graphs, each household can identify and upload information about the nutrition and quality of the agricultural products they cultivate, receiving scientific feedback and guidance. This will serve as a guarantee for the quality and refinement of future urban agriculture.

Urban agriculture in China is a virtually untapped frontier. The introduction of AI will lead to a historic development of urban agriculture in China. In particular, the measures taken by major cities to control large-scale epidemics have promoted public awareness of the importance and safety of food, preparing society for the future development of urban agriculture and its smartification. This could be a significant opportunity for industrial development and social change.

7.2.3 Application Scenarios: Urban Meta Farms Empowered by the Metaverse

As China's urbanization continues to advance, most urban children have not had the opportunity to experience rural life or agricultural production. Through the "Meta Farms" virtual reality experience interaction system, urban children can expand their understanding and perception of agriculture from both a temporal and a spatial perspective.

Using virtual reality/augmented reality technology, we aim to promote the integration of the real world with the virtual world, enabling realistic perception and virtual feedback in the experience. By incorporating features such as inputting information from growers, generating the imagery of "Meta Farms", sharing perception data, providing personified outputs, facilitating educational interactions, and enabling emotional experiences throughout the entire interaction process, we establish an interactive mechanism between "Meta Farms" and the real world (see Fig. 7.7). This initiative aims to create an enjoyable educational experience for children in relation to agriculture, fostering a sustainable visiting mechanism, increasing user engagement, and encouraging children to willingly engage with agricultural production.

7.3 Intelligent Healthcare

7.3.1 Development Forms

The application of AI technology in healthcare has long been recognized as a crucial direction and field for the development of AI. People hope that AI can provide convenient medical services, reduce medical costs, and enhance the precision of diagnosis and treatment.

Currently, most countries have issued strategies for the development of AI, with a particular focus on the application of AI in healthcare in countries such as the United States, the United Kingdom, Japan, and India, which are advancing overall promotion at the national strategic level. China has scientifically laid out the basic research, key technologies, and key applications relating to intelligent healthcare and has initially established a technological innovation system for the healthcare industry.

With the improvement in processing performance and optimization of machine learning algorithms, AI is expected to reach a critical point of technological breakthrough, becoming a new driving force for the transformation and development of healthcare. Major global enterprises have deployed technologies such as cloud computing, big data, 3D printing, robotics, cloud engineering, and cloud services in the medical field. They have achieved outstanding results in research areas such as visual recognition, speech recognition, deep learning based on big data, innovation design driven by big data intelligence, brain-machine interfaces and interactions, virtual reality/augmented reality, providing strong support for the development of intelligent healthcare. Currently, the main applications of intelligent healthcare include clinical examination and diagnosis assistance, treatment decision support, health risk assessment, patient monitoring, safe medication monitoring, and assessment of infectious disease transmission in populations.

At the industry level, since 2009, there have been 1,153 new AI medical enterprises worldwide, with business scopes mainly concentrated in areas such as drug research and development, medical imaging and applications, virtual assistants, and health management.

Fig. 7.7 Metaverse-empowered urban intelligent agriculture

7.3.2 Trends in Intelligent Healthcare

(1) Integration of intelligent diagnosis with modern medicine

By employing collective intelligence and cognitive computing capabilities, AI automatically extracts disease features and logical relationships from various structured and unstructured information. It integrates evidence-based medicine discrimination criteria and prior knowledge from multi-disciplinary medical experts to automatically construct knowledge graphs and inference engines for diseases. These are combined with high-performance computing frameworks to rapidly learn knowledge from vast medical literature and electronic medical records, and to complete disease diagnosis inference. Utilizing the latest advances in AI, there is deep integration of computer vision technology and medical image pattern recognition technology to accurately identify and assess radiological lesions, thereby improving diagnostic accuracy. By developing AI technologies that effectively analyze daily mobile health monitoring data, it assists in achieving early disease diagnosis. This approach fully utilizes omics data such as genomics, proteomics, and metabolomics, in conjunction with traditional data, to achieve an "all-in-one" intelligent disease diagnosis system from phenotype to genotype.

(2) Integration of intelligent treatment with patient medical behavior throughout the process

On the one hand, based on clinical big data and guided by clinical disease diagnosis and treatment guidelines, research is conducted on intelligent treatment scheme decision support and intelligent treatment methods. This is supported by perception and cross-media intelligence, hybrid intelligence, etc. It achieves flexible human–machine interaction surgical robotic systems for surgical treatment and physiological compensation of human motion. Utilizing medical imaging and augmented reality technology, preoperative simulation and intraoperative navigation are employed to precisely guide the surgical process and provide real-time feedback, achieving high-precision and minimally invasive surgery. Surgical positioning and surgical approaches are suggested based on patient information, and surgical operating steps are formulated according to intraoperative visual conditions, achieving real-time human–machine interaction and intelligent communication during surgery. On the other hand, based on drug databases and massive patient electronic medical records, unsupervised clustering algorithms, supervised classification methods, and association rules are used to analyze interactions between drugs, drug-food interactions, personalized prediction of adverse drug reactions, prediction of low-frequency adverse drug reactions, and analysis of the correlation between single-drug adverse reactions. This facilitates effective monitoring and prediction of adverse drug reactions, reducing the incidence and mortality of related diseases caused by adverse drug reactions, as well as economic losses.

7.3.3 Application Case: Intelligent Healthcare Empowering Home Elderly Care

According to the Seventh National Population Census (2020), the population aged 60 and above in China is 264.02 million, accounting for 18.70% of the total population. Among them, the population aged 65 and above is 190.64 million, accounting for 13.5% of the total population. It is estimated that by 2030, the elderly population will reach nearly 300 million, with the proportion of "empty nest" elderly people possibly reaching 90%. In this context, the issue of elderly care has attracted more attention and emphasis.

For the elderly, as they age and their physical functions decline, familiar living environments gradually pose safety hazards. Situations such as forgetting to turn off water, electricity, and gas at home, accidental falls without anyone noticing, and accidental ingestion of various medications often occur among empty-nest or solitary elderly people. Intelligent home systems based on the IoT and sensors can effectively eliminate hidden dangers in daily life and provide safe home support for the elderly.

By establishing medical records for the elderly based on wearable devices and the perception data of smart homes, integrating the medical history and health status of the elderly, and leveraging big data, cloud computing, and AI technologies to analyze and predict elderly diseases, potentially malignant diseases can be detected in a timely manner, and early health interventions can be provided. With the help of intelligent home response systems, suggestions and support for home rehabilitation and health maintenance can be provided to the elderly (see Fig. 7.8).

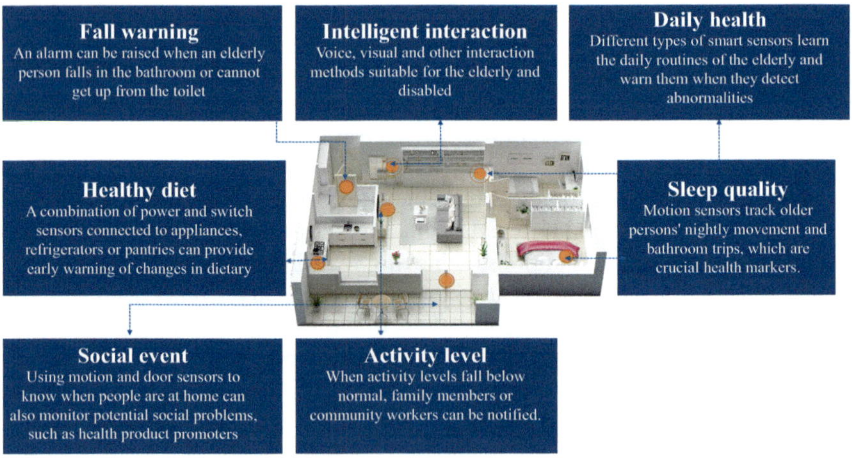

Fig. 7.8 Intelligent healthcare-empowered "aging in place"

7.4 Intelligent Education

7.4.1 New Opportunities for Smart Education

(1) AI resolves the contradiction between standardized teaching for multiple individuals and personalized tutoring for individual students

Adaptive classroom scenarios, after analysis through cloud computing, will automatically match corresponding scenario variables and change teaching activities to better assist teachers. For example, if students in the classroom are chatting, voice technology can capture this variable, and the classroom background will automatically dim or brighten, or the teacher's icon will automatically enlarge to the center of the screen, prompting students to pay attention.

If a teacher forgets to ask a question to a particular student during the entire class, that student's icon will glow to remind the teacher to ask them.

If a student frequently mentions a particular interest point when answering questions, the system can capture that interest point and match corresponding-level, interest-based picture books or short texts for practice through a database.

If students in language classes frequently mispronounce certain words when answering questions, the system can diagnose which aspect of natural phonics or vocabulary exercises they lack through big data analysis. At the end of the class, personalized recommended reading lists and assignments are automatically generated for each student.

(2) AI helps teachers optimize teaching methods

Highly intelligent classrooms can collect data on learning outcomes through speech recognition, motion capture, exercises, etc. They can also gather data on the teacher's language output through keyword extraction, thus providing better insights into which teachers and teaching methods are more effective. The captured teaching scenario variables include: (i) the frequency of teacher questioning in a class; (ii) the proportion of different types of teacher questions, such as open-ended questions versus judgmental or prompting questions, questions focusing on a specific knowledge point versus those addressing context before and after; and (iii) the proportion of different types of feedback given by teachers to students, such as inductive feedback versus merely informing the final answer (see Fig. 7.9).

Fig. 7.9 Student-centered education

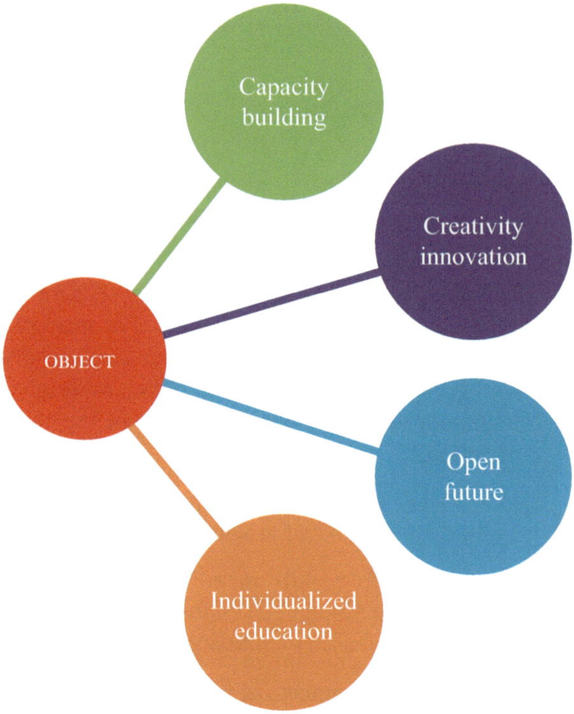

7.4.2 *Common Directions in Education Reform Reflected by International Cases*

(1) Putting learners at the center

Learners need to transition from acquiring knowledge to shaping abilities in order to adapt to the rapid creation and iteration of knowledge in contemporary society and the changing environment of human-AI interaction. In particular, in the face of the fundamental challenge posed by machine labor to various professions, abilities such as interpersonal communication, perception and operation, and the creative application of knowledge to address unknown challenges will become the core of future education.

Creativity and innovation are essential human capabilities that distinguish us from machines. Therefore, all educational models must change and accommodate the cultivation of creativity and innovation. While specific knowledge points may have fixed definitions, the network of connections between knowledge lacks a fixed pattern, and the reasons for forming connections have no fixed rules.

Society is not static, and the long-term development of individuals should not be rigidly determined by early education. Individual development inevitably changes with the times, various opportunities, and challenges. Education should provide every individual with continually evolving capabilities and create an adaptable and open future. Education should not mass-produce talents with a standardized mold or evaluate talents with a single yardstick, but should instead tailor unique capacity-building plans based on each person's interests, strengths, and background.

(2) Removing barriers from the educational process

In 1877, Johns Hopkins University first used the term "major" to express a specialization. The division of knowledge that emerged in the nineteenth century should not become a shackle in the twenty-first century, but in fact, it has led to a state of tribalism in knowledge, and people often have to expend multiple times the effort to extract valuable content from multiple knowledge tribes to support specific goals. Today, more and more innovations arise from collisions between different disciplines, and future education should comprehensively reorganize the knowledge system of education, making connections rather than nodes the dominant factor.

Knowledge becomes meaningful only when applied in context, and skills can only be truly mastered through experiential learning. So-called Project-Based Learning (PBL) education, mission-based education, and connection with the real world all involve integrating education into specific contexts.

Whether exploring the unknown or innovating, future society increasingly relies on the collaboration of different roles and partners. The old individual-based education model should largely give way to supporting collaborative learning among multiple learners, while also facilitating everyone in terms of finding the best collaborative partners more conveniently.

Digital technology is an important component of education, yet currently, education itself makes limited use of digital tools. With the integration of various sensing devices, digitalization of the educational process, widespread adoption of big data analytics, and the proliferation of AI technology in education, unimaginable potential will be unearthed to support the transformation of education (see Fig. 7.10).

7.4.3 *Facing the Accelerating Changes in Intelligent Education*

The world is undergoing unprecedented changes. In 2013, analysis suggested that 47% of jobs in the U.S. job market were at risk of being replaced by computers (see Fig. 7.11). More and more factories are employing robots, and various unmanned concepts are continuously permeating our lives.

The challenges that human education urgently needs to address include:

(1) The accelerating iteration of knowledge makes it difficult for textbooks to keep up with the pace of change.

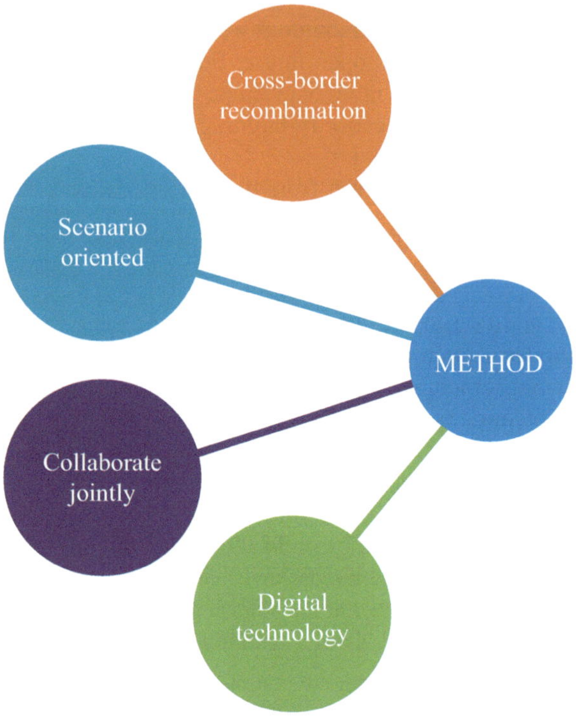

Fig. 7.10 Four aspects of intelligent education

(2) Standardized education systems cannot accommodate the knowledge backgrounds, individual characteristics, and developmental needs of every student.
(3) A single evaluation system emphasizes learning knowledge rather than developing skills, leading to the burial of many potentially talented individuals.
(4) Competitive non-collaborative structures treat winning in competition as the direct goal of education, neglecting the fact that collaborative cooperation is the cornerstone of future society.
(5) Education and careers are separated and are unable to provide continuous support for human development.
(6) The center of abilities has shifted: creativity, interpersonal skills, perception, and hands-on abilities are far more important than knowledge, as these are the abilities that AI cannot replace.

In the face of the new era, the cultivation of three dimensions is crucial for individual development: social intelligence, creativity, and perception and manipulation (see Fig. 7.12).

Students should not only learn rapidly updating textbook knowledge but should also spend more time engaging in personal or team innovation projects, such as poetry creation, coding, filmmaking, robotics, painting, or experiments related to physics or mathematics—remembering that initially, mathematics, science, and engineering are essentially no different from art, only the names differ.

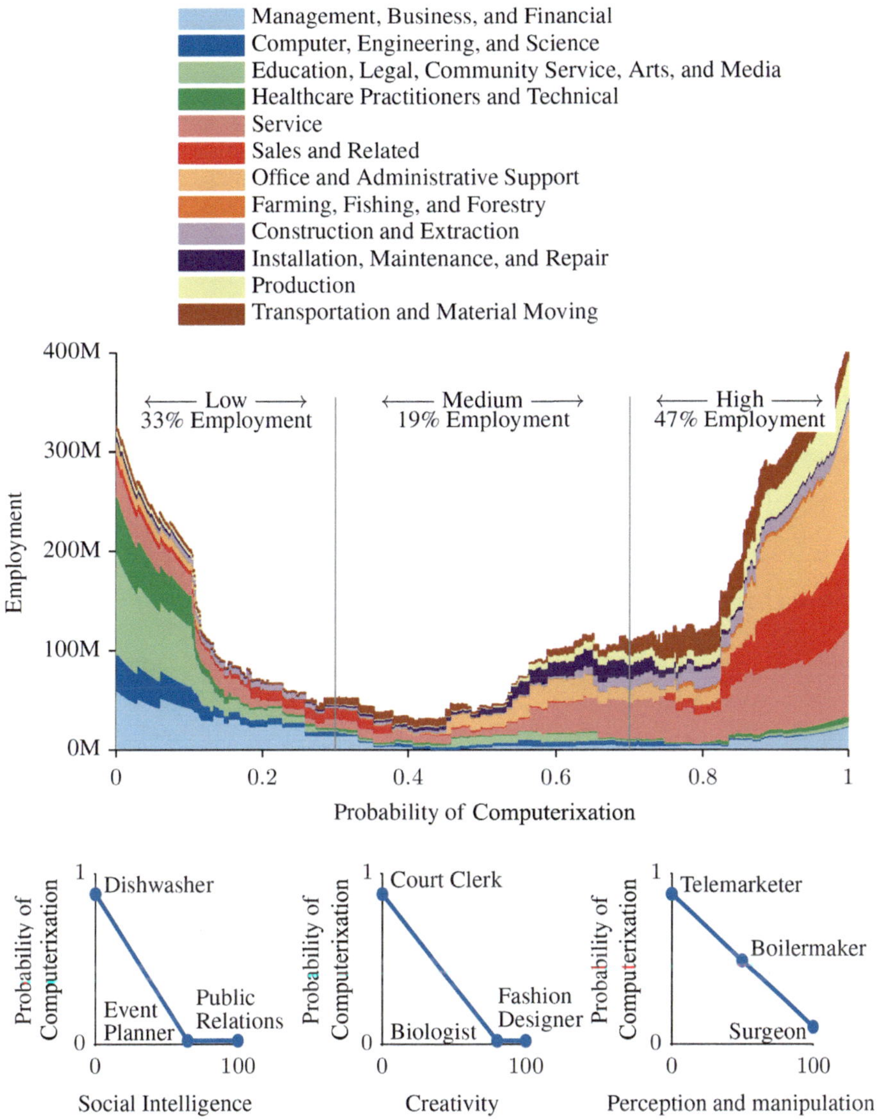

Fig. 7.11 Probability of computerization

Fig. 7.12 Three key dimensions for individual development

Social Intelligence

Creativity

Perception and manipulation

Chapter 8
The Technical Framework of AI Cities

Abstract This chapter delineates the technical framework of an AI-driven city and its pivotal components, with a particular emphasis on data perception and database management, intelligent feedback mechanisms, decision-making technologies, and their application scenarios. It provides an in-depth examination of the establishment of CiMA (Urban Intelligent Mapping Alliance) and the evolution of its database architecture, which facilitates large-scale urban data storage and processing nationwide, thereby fostering the collaborative construction and sharing of foundational digital city data. Regarding intelligent feedback and decision-making technologies, the AI city achieves precise configuration of urban functional facilities through multi-agent simulations and collective intelligence algorithms, achieving spatial accuracy within 5 m × 5 m × 3 m, surpassing traditional urban simulation systems. Moreover, cloud-based decision chains and intelligent configuration decision technologies emulate biological neural transmission mechanisms to enhance the city's responsiveness and governance capabilities. Additionally, the chapter explores the specific implementation of AI in various application scenarios, such as the urban happiness index, carbon–neutral intelligent design, and the integration of virtual reality and real-world construction, promoting the development of cities toward smarter and greener futures.

Keywords Intelligent feedback mechanism · Urban data platform · Swarm intelligence · Urban application scenario

8.1 Data Sensing Platform and Database

8.1.1 The CiMA Database and Platform

The City Intelligent Mapping Alliance (CiMA) was officially established in May 2021. Its goal is to promote the co-construction and sharing of basic digital city data among urban scientists.

Z. WU, *The AI City*, The Urban Book Series,
https://doi.org/10.1007/978-981-96-2560-4_8

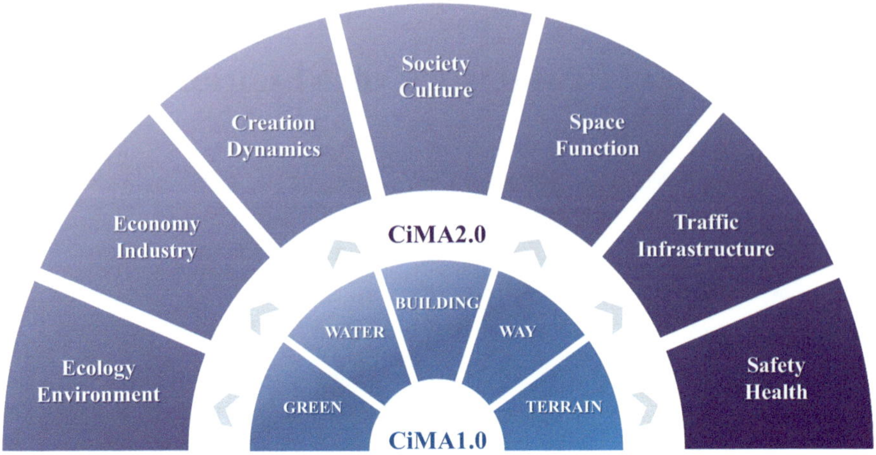

Fig. 8.1 The CiMA 1.0 and 2.0 framework

(1) CiMA database architecture

CiMA is divided into different versions according to data content (see Fig. 8.1). CiMA 1.0 mainly involves the five basic elements of urban form: buildings, roads, water systems, green spaces, and terrain. Based on these five types of elements, basic urban morphological models can be quickly constructed and guide urban design work. CiMA 2.0 is based on CiMA 1.0 and involves seven major urban planning areas: ecological environment, economy and industry, innovation dynamics, social culture, spatial function, transportation and facilities, and health and safety.

(B) CiMA database

CiMA data covers all regions across the country, and the amount of data is extremely large, with 12 million pieces of building data alone. All data is stored in the Postgres database, and efficient database query technologies are employed to extract target region data from this vast dataset. This technical breakthrough enables rapid establishment of local databases based on the national database, providing a solid foundation for subsequent construction of local data platforms. (see Fig. 8.2).

(C) CiMA platform display

Use Python to call the database and build a background program to realize the data flow process of "postgres database-Python backend-HTML frontend." The HTML interface integrates all spatial data in various fields of CiMA 2.0 on one platform. Taking Jinan as an example (see Fig. 8.3), various types of data from different sources of the city (such as statistical data, remote sensing images, three-dimensional models, and real-time monitoring data) are displayed on one platform, and data interaction functions can be realized. Users can gain an overall overview of urban development from a macro-level, including industry, transportation, space, and ecology, or they

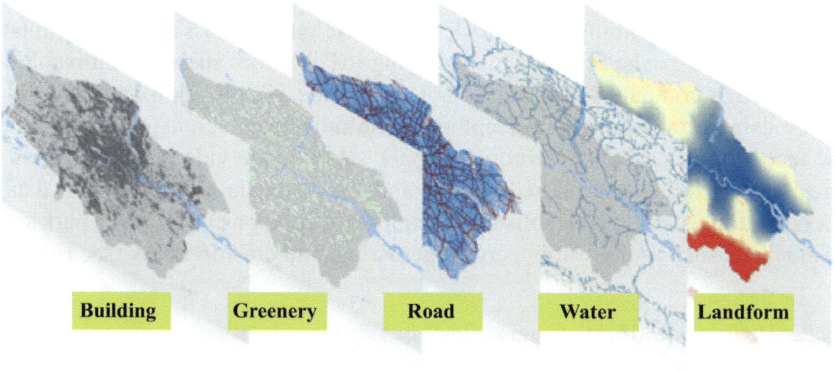

Fig. 8.2 The five elements of CiMA

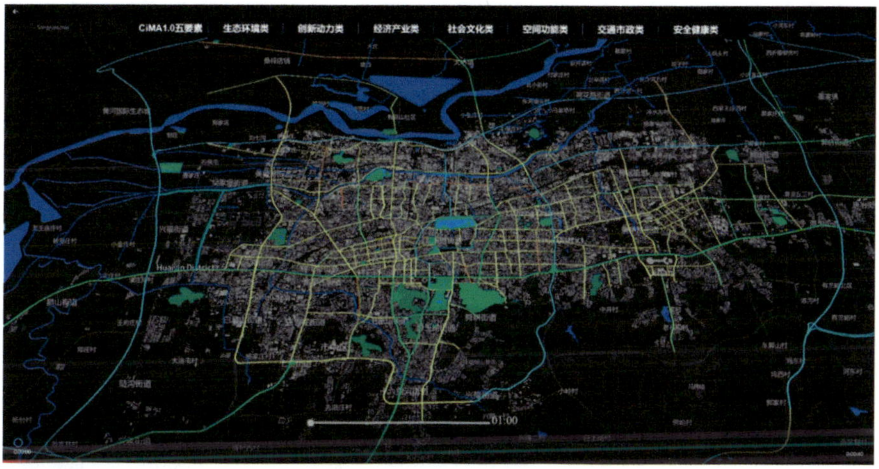

Fig. 8.3 The CiMA 2.0 platform for Jinan

can carefully examine the current situation of a certain land parcel at a micro-level, such as land performance, functional layout, and the traffic situation. Based on this platform, urban planners can grasp the dynamics of urban operations and calculate various related indicators to guide planning and design work.

8.1.2 Industrial Park Sensing

Industrial parks are important urban spaces. By studying the relationship between the flow of people in the park (the flow of people and the relationship between people), the spaces of different scales in the park, and the activities in the park, we can establish an objective understanding of the park space. The purpose of sensing park-related human flow data can be achieved by deploying IoT facilities such as high-resolution cameras, edge computers, and sensors. Through the visualization and analysis of sensory data, the mining and perception of multiple data such as real-time people flow recognition ‘and data recording of park surveillance videos, visualization of corresponding three-dimensional spaces, and social media public opinion data, a park operation database is established to explore the relationship between park space and elements such as innovation, crowd gathering, and crowd vitality (see Fig. 8.4).

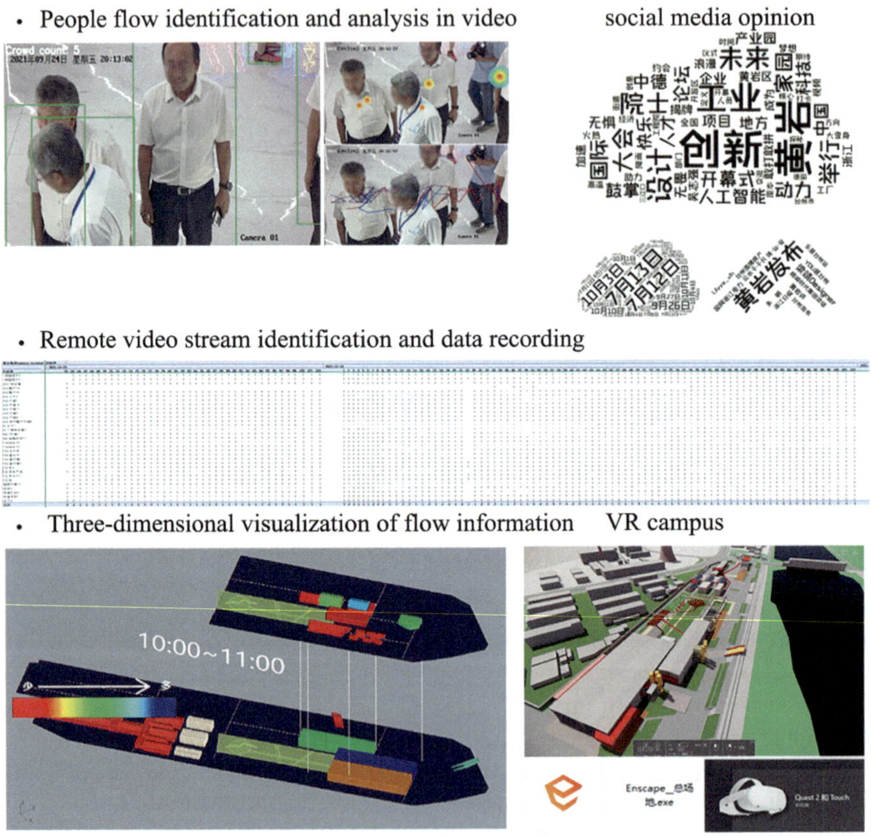

Fig. 8.4 Data sensing at Taizhou innovation park

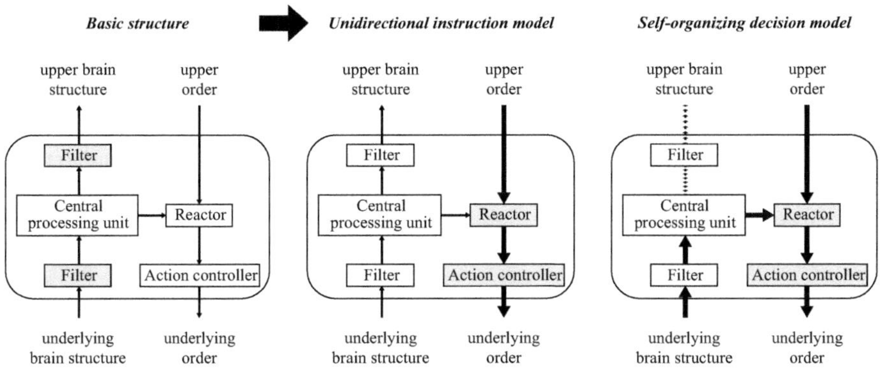

Fig. 8.5 The intelligent feedback unit of the AI city

8.2 Intelligent Feedback

8.2.1 The Unit Module of AI City Intelligent Feedback

Cities in the mechanical age have frequently used automatic control systems. However, in the AI era, such control systems no longer operate according to fixed logic, but are autonomous; they can continuously learn and improve on common goals. Each brain structure in the city is a micro-unit of information processing, with the function of filtering input data for the lower layer and feedback information for the upper layer (see Fig. 8.5). In the self-organizing mode, the information transfer process can send instructions directly downward through the reactor, thereby avoiding the one-way flow of information and forming a loop. This micro-circuit builds a sophisticated network for the city to respond to many individuals' cumbersome daily needs. As a traction force for AI technology research and development, it has gradually expanded to all aspects of urban governance, production, and life.

8.2.2 Design Feedback: Intelligent Dynamic Configuration of Urban Complex Functions

Using multi-agent game and swarm intelligence collaboration algorithms, based on deep learning of the evolution rules of urban block business formats at a scale of 1 km^2, we independently calculate the five relationships between urban functions, like integration, dependence, avoidance, repulsion, and separation, and deduce the precise combination of ten urban functions in space, intelligently configure urban functional facilities, and integrate intelligent technology intor urban functional decision-making. The configuration accuracy reaches 5 m $\times$ 5 m $\times$ 3 m spatial units, greatly improving urban scientific decision-making efficiency. The scenario application of this technology surpasses the urban simulation system UrbanSim developed by the University of California, Berkeley, in terms of learning intensity, model elements, three-dimensional space configuration capabilities, and configuration accuracy, showing excellent performance. It can achieve a more refined urban functional configuration close to the scale of functional units in real cities and dynamically simulate the spatiotemporal evolution process of ten types of urban functional elements (see Figs. 8.6 and 8.7).

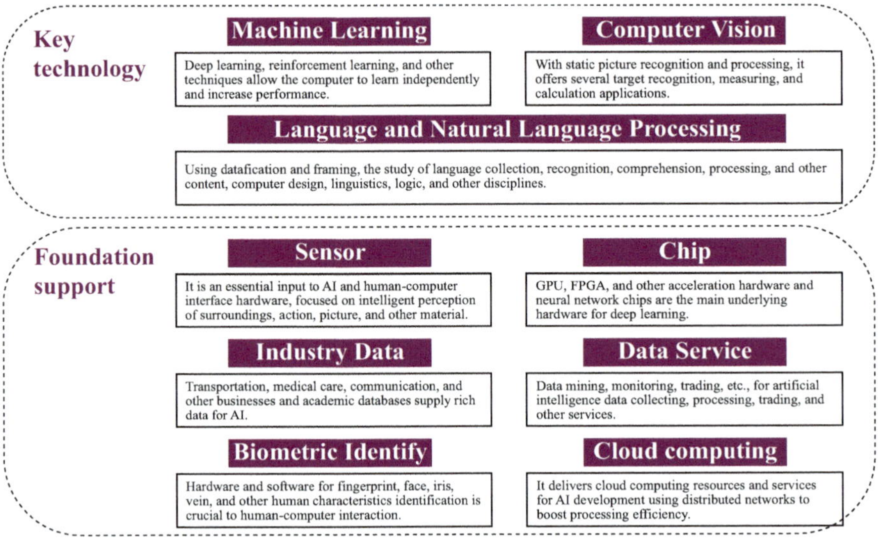

Fig. 8.6 AI-empowered infrastructure

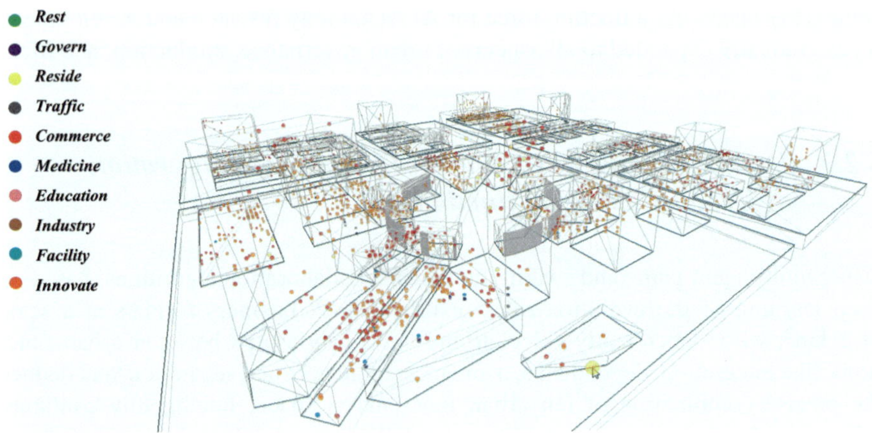

Fig. 8.7 The intelligent allocation of urban points of interest (POI)

8.2.3 *Scene Feedback: The Virtually Empowered Metaverse Community*

AR-augmented reality technology realizes the ingenious integration of virtual information and the real world, superimposes virtual information content in the real world, meets the different needs of people in different scenarios, and enables scenarios to be empowered. Through the community meta-farm established by AR technology, users can experience the fun of nature and planting in urban scenes (see Fig. 8.8). Ubiquitous education is a new entertaining learning method that combines boring knowledge with real scenes through virtual reality to enhance the sense of situation and fun of learning. The meta-museum uses AR technology to realize spatio-temporal dialogue, which can present the history and culture of the neighborhood and enhance the interaction between people and space.

Fig. 8.8 The reality and augmented reality (RAR) urban scene

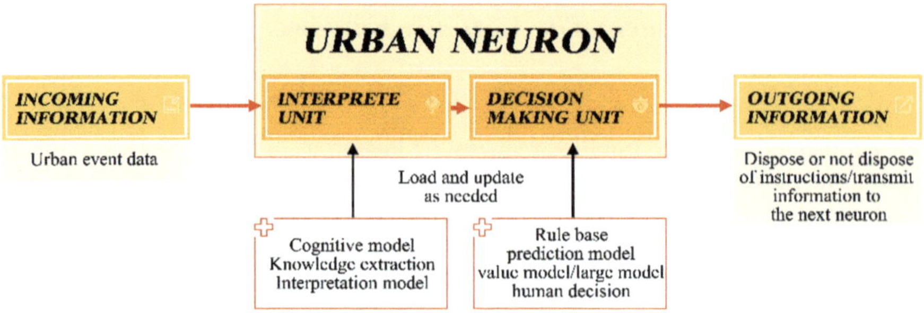

Fig. 8.9 The cloud decision-making chain

8.3 Decision-Making Technology

8.3.1 The Cloud Decision-Making Chain

The decision-making chain of the urban cloud reflection arc is one of the core technologies of the AI urban crowd-brain model (see Fig. 8.9). By imitating biological neural conduction mechanisms, we establish interconnected information transmission and decision-distribution mechanisms among urban neurons (intelligent agents). This system enables event-complexity-adaptive decision responses through optimal pathways, ultimately forming an urban cloud reflex arc that connects urban events to decision-making processes. The reflex arc should be open, inclusive, and robust, supporting network collaborative decision-making with complex information chains and simple decision-making in independent scenarios.

8.3.2 Intelligent Configuration Decisions for Urban Composite Functions

This system utilizes multi-agent gaming and swarm intelligence collaboration algorithms, combined with deep learning to analyze the evolution patterns of urban block formats within a 1 km^2 area. It autonomously identifies five types of relationships between urban functions—integration, dependence, avoidance, repulsion, and separation—and dynamically simulates refined spatial combinations of ten urban functional categories. Operating at a high-precision spatial resolution of $5m \times 5m \times 3m$, the system intelligently generates urban facility configuration plans, integrating decision-making technologies to significantly enhance urban planning efficiency. Compared to UC Berkeley's UrbanSim, this solution demonstrates superior performance in learning intensity, model element coupling, 3D spatial adaptability, and configuration precision. It supports urban sample learning at a 1 km^2 grid scale and enables

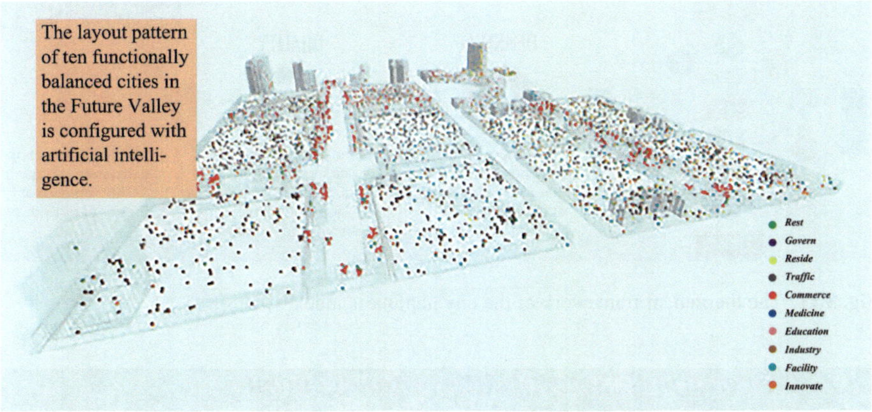

Fig. 8.10 Deduction of Ten-Yuan POI at Urban Block Scale in Fengxian Future Valley

real-time dynamic configuration of 10 functional categories, achieving precision that closely aligns with real-world urban functional unit scales (see Fig. 8.10).

8.4 The System of Application Scenarios

8.4.1 The City Happiness Quotient

Based on the "Have·Happiness·Blessing" theoretical model (see Fig. 8.11), we employ multimedia intelligence and big data algorithms to analyze multi-source heterogeneous data from non-governmental sources, independent and reliable interventions. We identifie key factors affecting neighborhood happiness at 1 km^2 scale urban communities across economic development, social support, life expectancy, personal autonomy, emotional well-being, and other dimensions. We also determine precise quantitative thresholds, discover the laws of happiness, realize the integration of intelligent governance technologies to enhance public welfare and proposes scientific improvements for urban management capabilities.

Taking Shenzhen as an example (see Fig. 8.12), the City Happiness Quotient (City HQ) was developed, with the following four characteristics:

(1) Accurately identify the key influencing factors of urban happiness. By building a machine learning model, the study calculated the influence of different indicators on City HQ and obtained the eight indicators that have the greatest impact

Fig. 8.11 The theoretical framework of the city happiness index

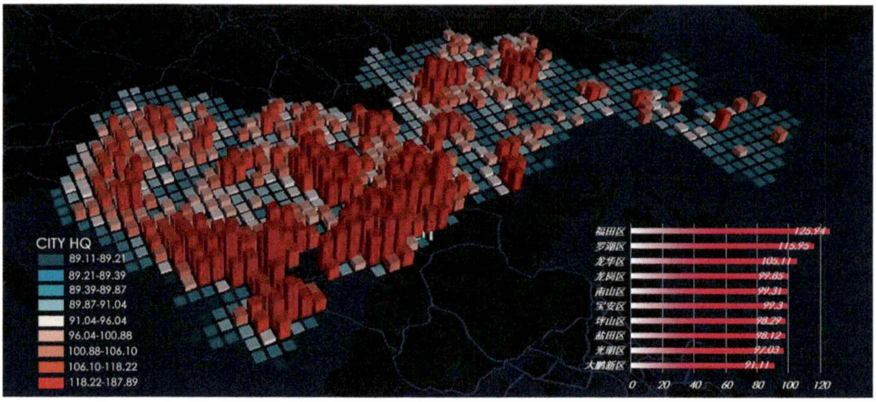

Fig. 8.12 The City HQ of Shenzhen

on Shenzhen City HQ: GDP per capita, rental-price-to-income ratio, travel-POI density, facility-POI density, and housing-POI density, employment rate, housing quality and high-tech enterprise density (Fig. 8.13).

(2) Accurately identify the threshold range of key elements and enable spatial intervention. For example, build a machine learning model to obtain the impact of park green space quality on the urban happiness index. The threshold of positive and negative effects was found, and it was found that when the quality of park green space is higher than 4.06, it will positively contribute to the happiness index. The park green space POI rating data provided by Baidu Maps (the evaluation is based on the real evaluation feedback of a large number of users after actual experience of POI points) is used to rasterize the green space and calculate the quality of the park green space. The current value of park green space quality in Longgang District is 2.29, which is lower than the current value of park green space quality in Shenzhen (4.33) and far below the threshold range of the impact on the happiness index. This shows that Longgang District can significantly improve the urban happiness index by improving the quality of park green space (see Fig. 8.14).

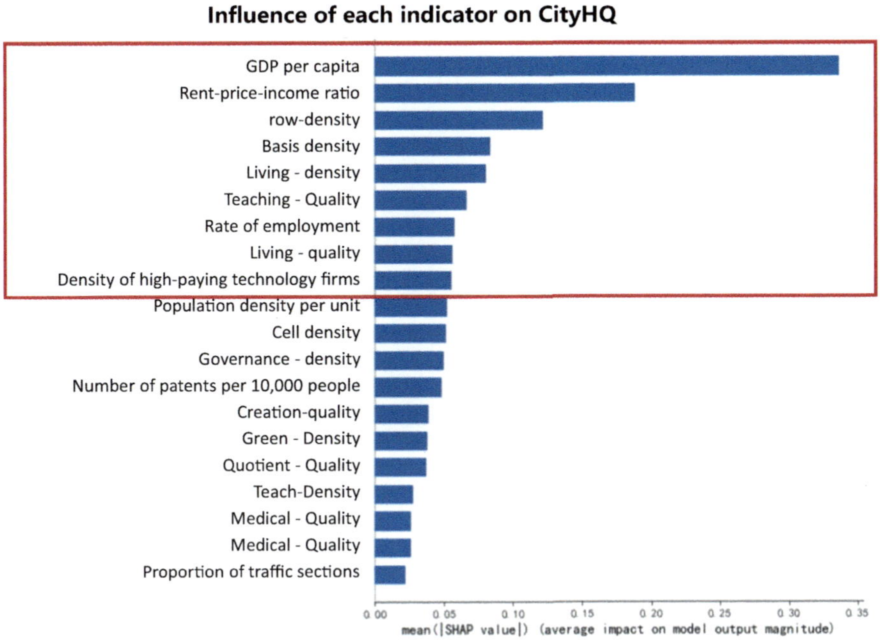

Fig. 8.13 The key factors affecting Shenzhen's City HQ

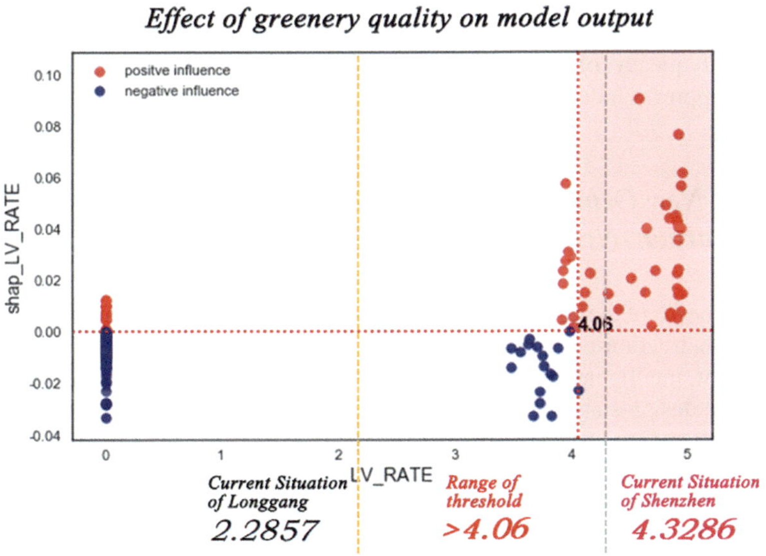

Fig. 8.14 The threshold range of key elements and spatial intervention

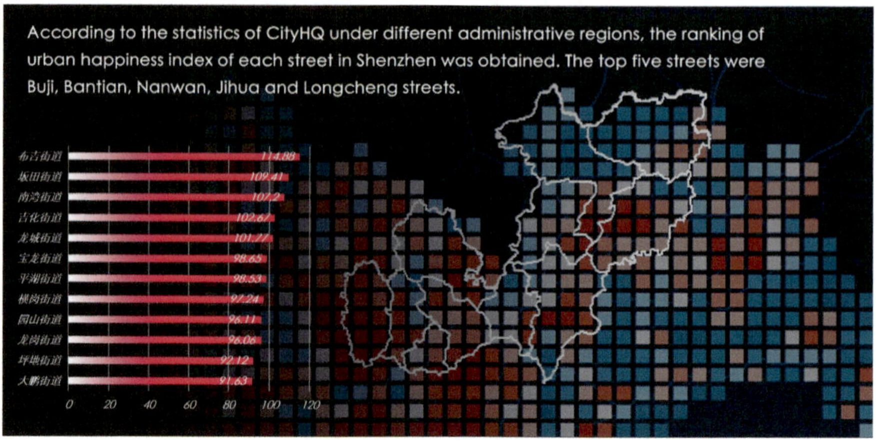

Fig. 8.15 Shenzhen City HQ evaluation at different administrative levels

(3) It can be implemented at different levels of administrative responsibility entities. Since the research is based on Shenzhen's gridded urban happiness index evaluation, City HQ can be implemented in administrative entities at different city levels, like districts, streets, and neighborhoods. The comprehensive innovation point (2) can provide accurate information to administrative entities at different levels for policy recommendations (see Fig. 8.15). Real-time monitoring of City HQ can be completed at any spatial scale; since the evaluation data sources are high-frequency, of high granularity, and open source, real-time monitoring of the happiness index at any spatial scale can be achieved.

8.4.2 A New Generation of AI-Assisted Urban Carbon–Neutral Intelligent Design

Facing the needs of the national dual-carbon strategy, the next-generation AI-assisted "design-construction-operation" full life cycle is the architectural goal to achieve independent, intelligent prediction and evaluation of carbon sinks and carbon emissions in the design stage. Machine learning is used to sample carbon emission data from similar regions, linking the three-dimensional model with key indicators of green development. Carbon neutrality results are dynamically calculated during the design process based on intervention methods such as morphological layout, policy guidance, and technology selection. Then, the optimal allocation of urban resources toward green development through human–machine hybrid enhancement is achieved (see Fig. 8.16). A focus on solving the problem of three-dimensional space platform

Fig. 8.16 The AI carbon balance design platform

aggregation of AI technology gives full play to the core advantages of urban intelligent application scenarios, and integrates energy, water resources, and carbon emission calculation tools into a unified spatial carrier. The reinforcement learning algorithm is used to extract the influencing parameters of similar regions automatically and correct the regional differences of the model. The calculation results are intuitively presented to assist in predicting carbon emissions and carbon sinks in different city areas. The calculation accuracy reaches a 30 m × 30 m grid, which can directly serve the carbon–neutral dynamic prediction of a single construction project. The performance in the above aspects surpasses the European carbon emissions dynamic monitoring and analysis platform CarbonSpace.

8.4.3 Urban Scene Construction Where Virtuality and Reality Coexist

Through technologies such as vehicle–road collaboration, driverless lanes, and smart urban transportation centers, we will create a more optimized urban travel environment and connect all aspects of transportation, building an integrated and all-round smart transportation system to achieve the organic integration of infrastructure, traffic management, vehicles, pedestrians, and roads (see Fig. 8.17).

Through intelligent element configuration, built-in sensors to explore and perceive innovative behaviors, and office spaces with built-in smart furniture, office spaces will provide a suitable working space for innovative people to the greatest extent (see Fig. 8.18).

Fig. 8.17 AI transportation

Fig. 8.18 The AI innovation district

Emerging interactive technologies such as the Metaverse and virtual reality, as well as AI algorithms such as big data and personalized recommendations, will provide citizens with a new audio-visual feast, and visitors can immerse themselves in a holographic and full-sense personalized journey (see Fig. 8.19).

AI-enabled services such as fall alarms, telemedicine, interest recommendations, and early diagnosis and prevention of malignant diseases can improve the quality of life of the elderly, making them content and happy in old age (Fig. 8.20).

By accurately sensing the needs of local residents and intelligently configuring corresponding land and service facilities, it will be possible to build a carbon–neutral green home platform to help optimize urban design layout, balance urban energy consumption, and empower urban vitality (see Fig. 8.21).

Fig. 8.19 AI recreation

Fig. 8.20 AI elderly care

Diversified education models such as VR classrooms, online education, and study abroad break the limitations of educational resources and educational space. The emergence of technologies such as the Metaverse and virtual reality provides students with an immersive learning experience (see Fig. 8.22).

Automatic inspection and production line technologies such as energy consumption optimization and industrial knowledge graph accelerate the realization of Industry 4.0, compress production time, reduce logistics and warehousing costs, and make products closer to user needs (see Fig. 8.23).

Fig. 8.21 AI Jiayuan Scenario

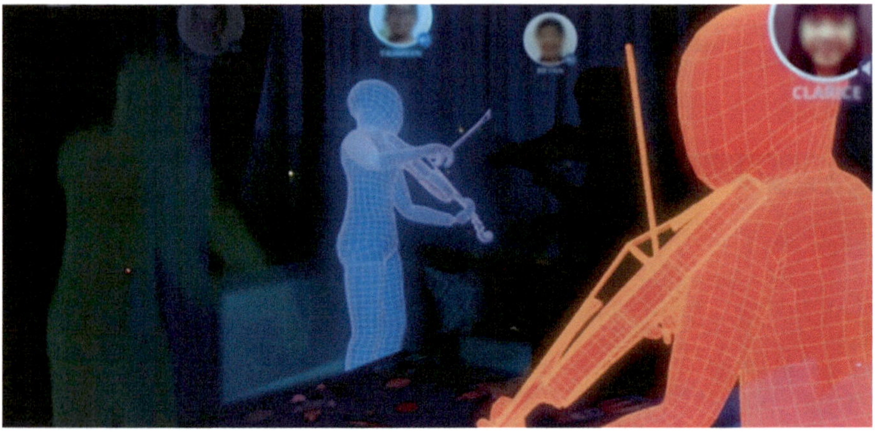

Fig. 8.22 AI education

Technologies such as intelligent habitat identification and detection, plant pest health detection, automatic irrigation, and agricultural knowledge graphs make urban agriculture possible, allowing residents to fully explore the corners of their daily spaces that can become rooftop gardens, integrating farms into the city (see Fig. 8.24).

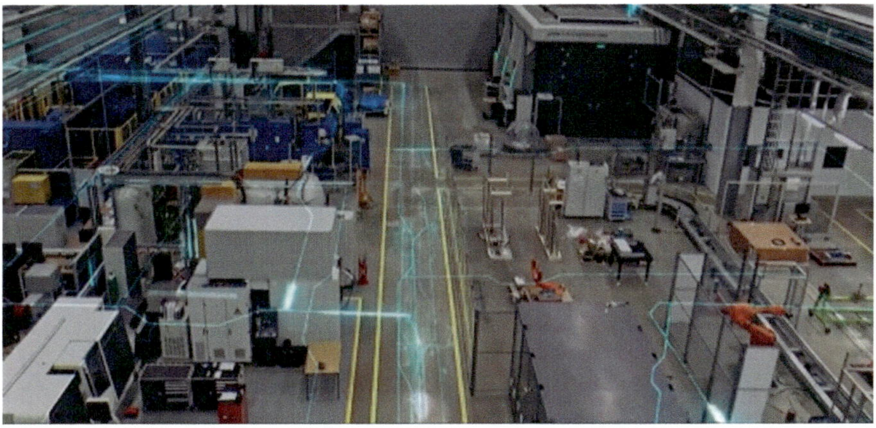

Fig. 8.23 The AI factory

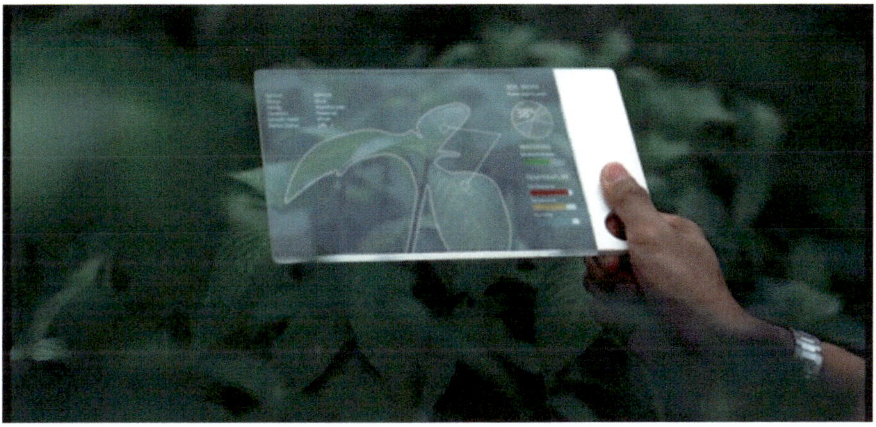

Fig. 8.24 AI agriculture

Chapter 9
Case Study: Qingdao Sino-German Future-Park

Abstract This chapter presents the development of the AI City Hub within the Qingdao Sino-German Future City, situated in the West Coast New District. This project represents the inaugural sustainable development initiative resulting from collaboration between the Chinese and German governments, focusing on the establishment of an intelligent ecosystem and fostering industrial transformation. The centerpiece of this development is the AI City Hub, which leverages the City Information Modeling (CIM) platform to integrate Building Information Modeling (BIM), Geographic Information System (GIS) technologies, and IoT devices, thereby enabling intelligent urban planning, construction, and management. The CIM platform harnesses big data, AI, and 3D simulation technologies to facilitate informed decision-making and optimal resource allocation, particularly concerning energy, water resources, and urban planning. The platform's architecture comprises three tiers—"data," "computation," and "application"—incorporating advanced functionalities such as intelligent perception, decision-making, response, and learning capabilities. These features allow for real-time monitoring and optimization of urban operations, enhancing urban management efficiency and sustainability.

Keywords Qingdao Sino-German future-park · AI city · CIM platform · Intelligent ecosystem · Urban construction information modeling

9.1 Construction of the AI City Pivot in the Qingdao Sino-German Future City

The Qingdao Sino-German Eco-Park, covering an area of 2.68 km^2, is situated in the core region of the Sino-German Ecological Park in the West Coast New Area. It represents the first collaborative endeavor between the governments of China and Germany dedicated to sustainable development and the establishment of an intelligent ecosystem. This remarkable park serves as an exemplar of bilateral cooperation, fostering research and development innovation, driving industrial transformation, and advocating for environmentally conscious living. Furthermore, it stands as a

Z. WU, *The AI City*, The Urban Book Series,
https://doi.org/10.1007/978-981-96-2560-4_9

Fig. 9.1 Masterplan of the Qingdao Sino-German future city

pioneering demonstration zone for smart construction and the practical application of AI technologies (see Fig. 9.1).

The planning of the Sino-German Future City is a pioneering step and serves as the cornerstone of its construction. From the outset, the planning and design phase has integrated a Construction Information Modeling (CIM) platform, underpinned by AI and grounded in rational methodologies. This platform is a critical infrastructure within the AI-driven urban core, evolving from Building Information Modeling (BIM) to a city-wide scale (Wu et al. 2021). It integrates Geographic Information System (GIS) technology and connects with IoT devices to create a digital platform that offers a comprehensive view of real urban information. By harnessing big data, AI, and high-precision urban 3D simulation technologies, the platform supports intelligent urban planning, construction, and governance. It safeguards the approval and management of construction projects, reduces the challenges of project implementation, and enhances the efficiency of government services.

9.2 Rational Allocation of Energy and Water Resources

Leveraging big data intelligence facilitates the scientific allocation and rational utilization of energy and water resources.

Big data intelligence focuses on the in-depth analysis and exploration of large datasets to develop a knowledge learning system endowed with comprehensive inferential capabilities. Utilizing digital intelligence technologies, the Qingdao Sino-German Future City collects and accumulates data on electricity generation and consumption from urban power plants and residential clusters. It predicts the total electricity consumption of different residential groups at various times of the day. This enables the adjustment of the total power supply from power plants to different urban clusters. Additionally, by harnessing the potential energy generated from the elevation differences in reservoirs for power generation, it serves as an effective supplement. This approach ensures the full allocation and utilization of the city's electrical and water resources (see Fig. 9.2).

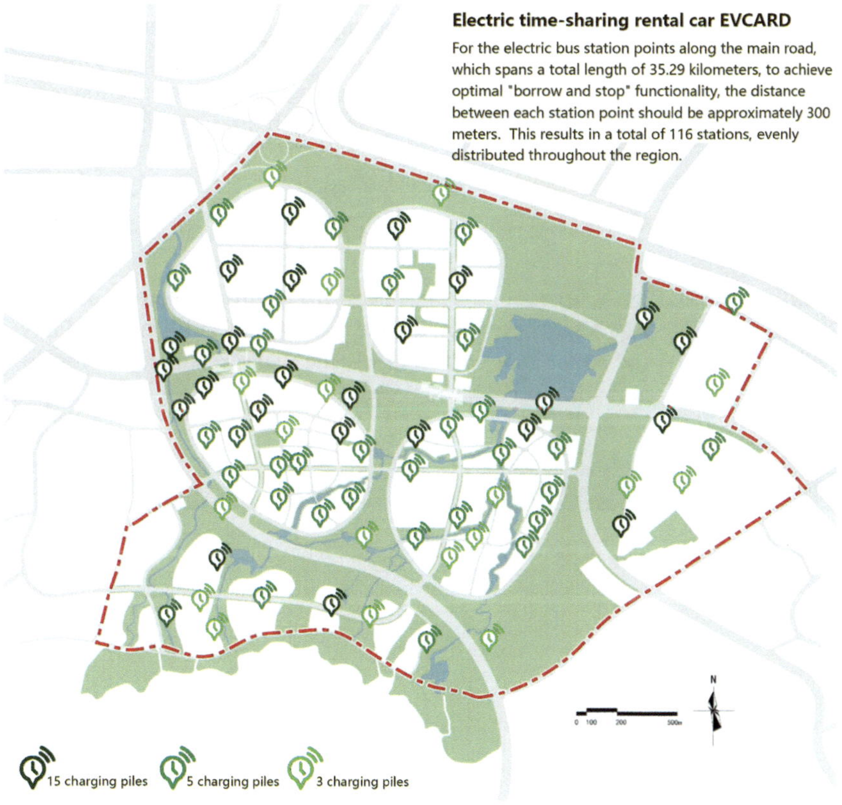

Fig. 9.2 Intelligent charging pile in the public area of the Qingdao Sino German future city

9.3 The CIM Platform of the Qingdao Sino-German Future City

The AI Core of the Qingdao Sino-German Future City, referred to as the AI City Pivot, encapsulates the four fundamental functionalities of a smart city: intelligent perception, decision-making, response, and learning. It possesses the capability for self-updating and continuous evolution (Wu et al. 2018). The cornerstone of this advanced infrastructure is the CIM platform (see Fig. 9.3).

By interfacing with the urban sensory system, the CIM platform of the Sino-German Future City is capable of forecasting the city's status and outcomes. It can mobilize resources in response to scenario analyses, achieving minimal consumption of energy, resources, time, and societal impact. The decision-making system is integrated throughout the city's planning, construction, and operational phases, realizing a sophisticated, precise, and meticulous management and decision-making process that spans four dimensions of time and space across the entire life cycle of the urban environment (Fig. 9.4).

Fig. 9.3 The CIM platform of the Qingdao Sino-German future city

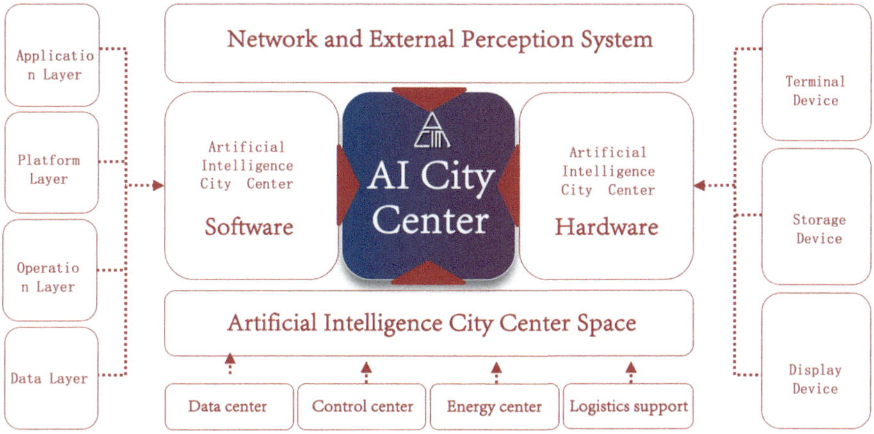

Fig. 9.4 The structure of the AI City Pivot of the Qingdao Sino-German future city

9.4 The Systematic Structure of the CIM Platform of the Qingdao Sino-German Future City

The CIM platform of the Qingdao Sino-German Future City is architecturally structured across three fundamental layers: "data," "computation," and "application." This framework facilitates a comprehensive upgrade targeting the China Biographical Database (CBDB) urban database, a computational platform encompassing three categories and 44 functions, as well as the diagnostic service system (see Fig. 9.5). The system will efficiently interconnect with the park's IoT devices and back-end databases, enabling dynamic data collection and computation. Through the diagnostic system, it will provide precise services for park management, establishing the CIM as a benchmark for urban planning, construction, and management.

The CIM system of the Qingdao Sino-German Future City has been developed in conjunction with system requirements, establishing data standards specifically tailored for surveying, planning, municipal services, landscaping, and three-dimensional modeling. This system comprises three main modules: intelligent planning, intelligent construction, and intelligent governance. It focuses on the research and development of three critical projects: urban development scenario deduction, construction process tracking and management, and dynamic management during the operational phase.

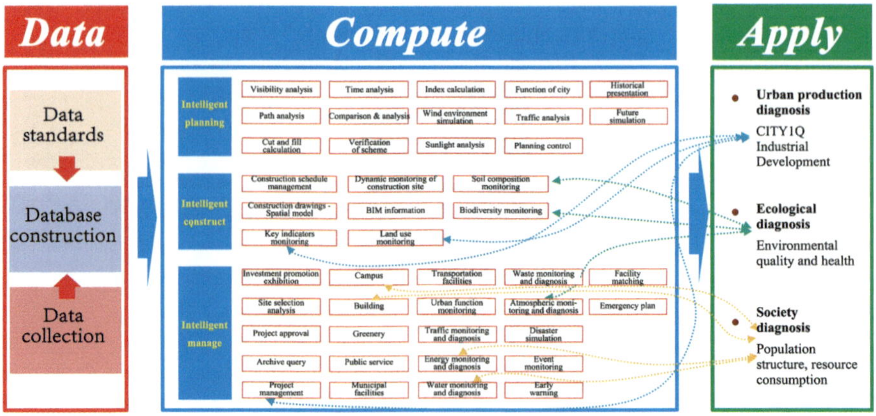

Fig. 9.5 The technology system of the CIM platform of the Qingdao Sino-German future city

Representative expert	Opinions
Wu Zhiqiang Academic of the Chinese Academy of Engineering, Member of the National Academy of Sciences and Engineering of Germany, Fellow of the Royal Swedish Academy of Engineering Sciences, Professor at Tongji University	CIM represents an intelligent system engineering project for urban planning, construction, and management, transcending the mere functionality of software. While BIM focuses on individual buildings, CIM encompasses the entire city. Transitioning from BIM to CIM necessitates the integration of municipal systems to create a comprehensive framework that includes both aboveground and underground components

9.4.1 *Intelligent Planning*

The development goal of the intelligent planning module is to leverage big data simulation and deduction technologies, enabling the visualization of the development trajectory of the Qingdao Sino-German Future City from its past to its future within a three-dimensional system. Its specific functionalities include the presentation of urban historical data, the sequencing of urban development, population distribution, deductions on resource consumption, and the simulation and display of future scenarios. Through a globally managed timeline, spatial and temporal data of the park model are integrated, facilitating the simulation of the urban construction process (see Fig. 9.6).

Fig. 9.6 Intelligent planning application

9.4.2 *Intelligent Construction*

The development goal of the intelligent construction module is to harness IoT technology, enabling real-time monitoring of the construction status of the Qingdao Sino-German Future City within the CIM core. Its specific functionalities include the centralized display of construction progress, inspection of construction status, monitoring of key indicators, and integration of BIM models. This module also connects to park management cameras, covering construction sites of ongoing projects within the park, and achieves the functionality of aggregating BIM model data (see Fig. 9.7).

9.4.3 *Intelligent Management*

The development goal of the intelligent governance module is to utilize big data intelligence for monitoring and analysis technologies, enabling real-time access within the CIM core to critical indicators and data such as urban operational management energy consumption data, environmental statistical data, and data on the allocation of social public service facilities. Additionally, it facilitates monitoring and command decision-making for significant events. Specific functionalities include asset management, operational data management, and event monitoring (see Fig. 9.8).

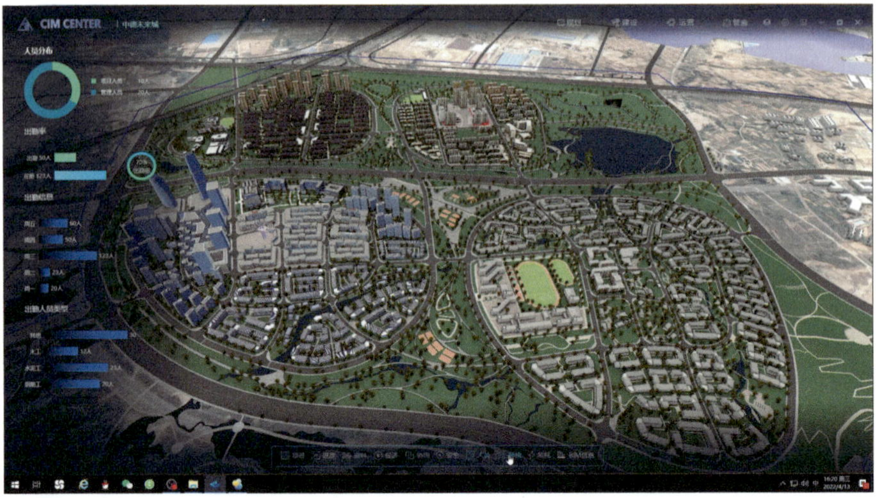

Fig. 9.7 Intelligent construction application

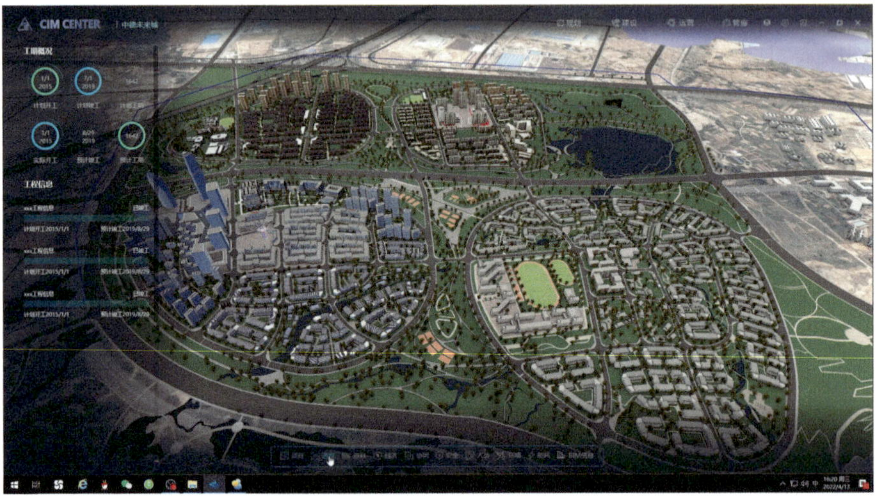

Fig. 9.8 Intelligent management application

9.5 The Environment Development of the AI City Pivot of the Qingdao Sino-German Future City

Leveraging hybrid augmented intelligence facilitates human–machine collaborative decision-making in addressing various urban challenges. Hybrid augmented intelligence focuses on incorporating human roles or emulating human cognitive models in AI systems. Utilizing hybrid intelligence technology, the AI City Core of the Qingdao Sino-German Future City directly imports real-time urban data such as traffic, electricity usage, water supply, and rainfall into the system. It visualizes this data through dashboards and three-dimensional models, providing an interactive control panel that allows for the immediate inspection and adjustment of facilities and resources. This set-up enables human–machine collaboration and decision-making under hybrid augmented intelligence in addressing urban issues.

The AI City Core of the Qingdao Sino-German Future City is located in the Huangdao District of Qingdao, with a building area of 340 m^2 (see Fig. 9.9). The City Core comprises a control center, data center, energy center, and a back-end support system (see Fig. 9.10).

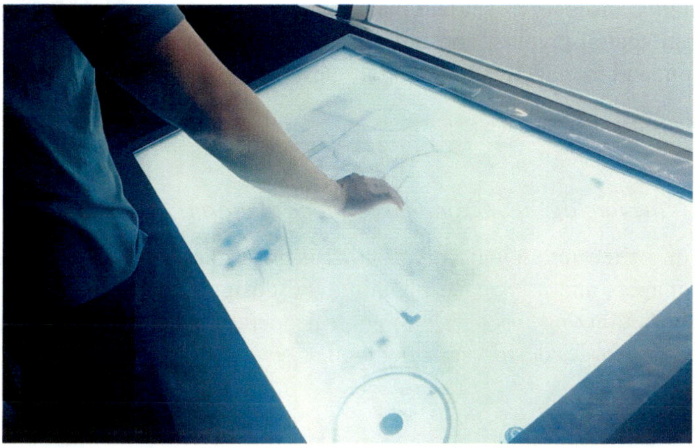

Fig. 9.9 Actual Scene Photo of the AI city pivot in the Qingdao Sino-German Future City

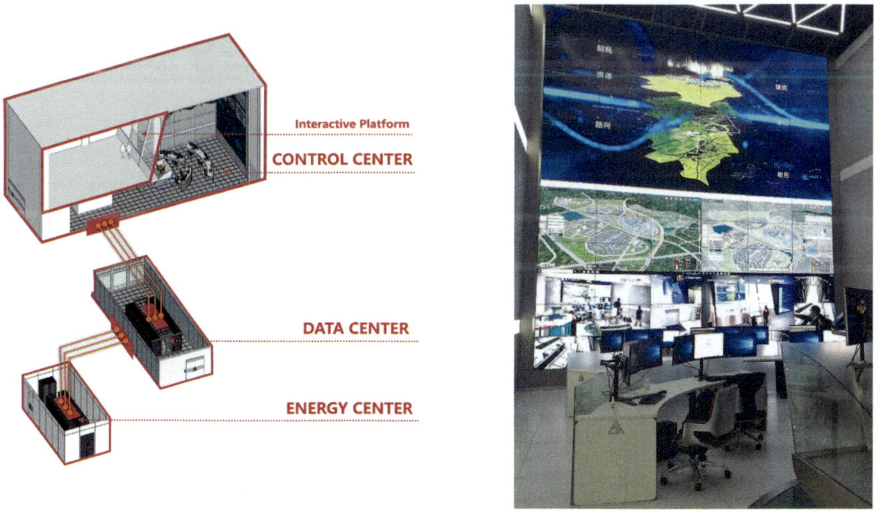

Fig. 9.10 The environment construction module of CIM center

Representative expert	Opinions
Wu Zhiqiang Academic of the Chinese Academy of Engineering, Member of the National Academy of Sciences and Engineering of Germany, Fellow of the Royal Swedish Academy of Engineering Sciences, Professor at Tongji University	The urban core encompasses the city's brain, cerebellum, and central nervous system. Additionally, it is imperative to construct the city's vagus nerve system, thereby establishing a comprehensive three-tiered technological framework for the intelligent city

Significant breakthroughs have been achieved by establishing a hardware infrastructure and the CIM City Intelligence Platform system. These advances facilitate the quantitative discovery of urban patterns, the simulation and deduction of optimized urban spatial layouts, and the creation of intelligent systems for planning, construction, and management methodologies.

Fig. 9.11 The intelligent interactive control panel

Fig. 9.12 Equipment Room in the Operation Command Center of the CIM system in Qingdao Sino German future park

The CIM platform of the Sino-German Future City was officially initiated for research and development in May 2018, with the construction of the accompanying equipment and environment commencing simultaneously. In October of the same year, the construction of the operational command center, referred to as the CIM Center, was completed. The preliminary establishment of the AI core marked a significant milestone in the digital development of the Sino-German Future City (see Figs. 9.11 and 9.12).

References

Wu Z, Han J, Teng Y, Huang Y, Gan W (2018) Qingdao Sino-German Future City: innovating with regulation, devoted to home. Eco-City Green Build 2:27–33

Wu Z, Gan W, Zang W, Ma C, Zhou J, He Z, Zhou X (2021) The concept and development of city intelligence model (CIM). Urban Plann 45(4):106–113+118

Chapter 10
Case Study: The Shanghai Jinding Smart City

Abstract This chapter provides an overview of the development strategy for the Shanghai Jinding Smart City, with a particular emphasis on its advances in digital transformation and the application of AI technologies. Situated in Shanghai's Pudong New Area, Jinding aspires to establish a multi-functional urban environment that is conducive to living, working, and traveling. Leveraging its strategic geographic location and superior transportation infrastructure, Jinding aims to become a leading hub for next-generation communications and innovation. By integrating AI technology and drawing upon global smart city case studies, the Jinding community seeks to develop a replicable and scalable model for future urban development. In terms of intelligent perception of residents' needs, Jinding has identified four levels of requirements through comprehensive analysis, providing a scientific foundation for urban planning. In the realm of intelligent construction, it has adopted an intelligent space model to optimize resource allocation and enhance the efficiency of urban management and services. Through nine AI application scenario demonstrations, Jinding showcases the deep integration and practical applications of intelligent life, business, and transportation, thereby promoting comprehensive smart city development.

Keywords Shanghai Jinding smart city · Digital transformation · AI technology · Intelligent resource allocation · AI application scenario

10.1 The Shanghai Jinding Smart City: Introduction

Shanghai Jinding is located within the inner ring of Shanghai's outer ring road, in the north-central part of Pudong, representing one of the few large-scale integrated development areas in the central city. Situated near the outer ring road and Wuzhou Avenue, with two intersecting rail transit lines, it enjoys excellent external transportation connectivity. Jinding is separated from the Waigaoqiao Free Trade Zone by Wuzhou Avenue, strategically positioned at the north–south center of two nationally designated development zones, Waigaoqiao and Jinqiao, providing a natural advantage for industrial service support. The area, leveraging the pillar industries in the

Z. WU, *The AI City*, The Urban Book Series,
https://doi.org/10.1007/978-981-96-2560-4_10

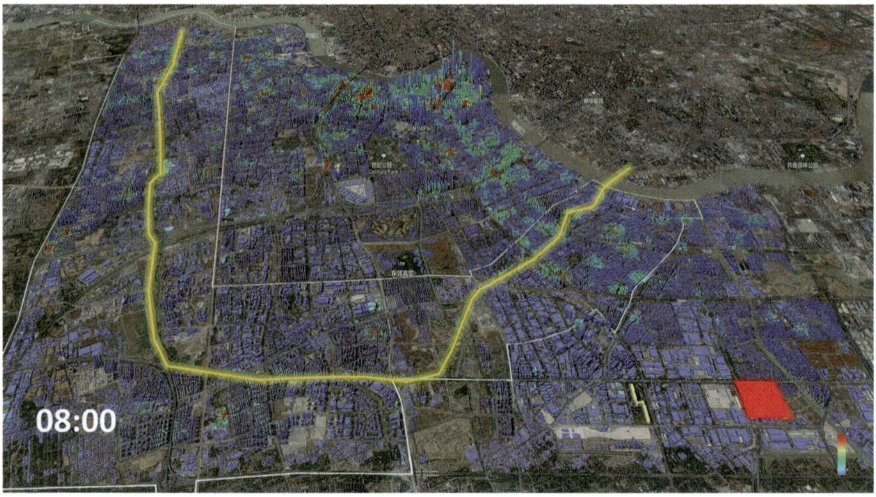

Fig. 10.1 Diagnosis of the current situation in Jinding and the surrounding area

Jinqiao region, aims to become a next-generation hub for communication and innovation, fostering a sustainable and multifunctional urban space that is conducive to living, working, and leisure.

Building upon research achievements in smart city development and a global database of completed urban cases, advanced AI concepts and cutting-edge AI technologies are applied. The Jinding community is envisioned as a new urban unit for the future city. Through top-level design research, it aligns with Shanghai's smart city development strategy, addresses the urban and industrial development needs of the Pudong New Area, Jinqiao, and Jinhui, and utilizes AI technology to enable digital transformation in spatial creation, functional elements, resource allocation, and urban operations. This aims to provide a replicable and scalable model pathway for the future development of urban communities (see Fig. 10.1).

10.2 Intelligent Perception of the Needs of the People

Interviews were conducted with nearly 100 residents in Jinding and the surrounding area, covering questions such as: what is most needed? What do you think is lacking in the current situation of Jinding? The interview results were subjected to intelligent analysis and task profiling through AI, resulting in the distilled identification of four levels of needs, including the following:

(1) Basic life needs: In this category, respondents primarily mentioned the importance of convenient transportation, well-equipped facilities, convenient living conditions, and additionally emphasized basic needs such as healthcare, entertainment, parking, and fitness.
(2) Community vitality needs: The focus in this section is on building a quality, vibrant, and harmonious community. Residents desire access to social and leisure activities, community services, and intelligent facilities, while also emphasizing the importance of maintaining a sense of boundaries and security.
(3) Industrial and economic needs: This section highlights the need for corporate support, available land, complementary industries, and job opportunities. Additionally, it stresses the importance of government understanding management, operational knowledge, and planning.
(4) Spiritual charm needs: Building on a foundation of comfortable living and working conditions, the Jinding area also needs to meet its unique cultural trends, reflecting the characteristics of Shanghai. Unlike other areas in Shanghai, it should showcase distinctive regional appeal and creativity.

These conclusions on needs (see Fig. 10.2) provide a scientific and robust foundation for the subsequent top-level planning and design of Jinding.

10.3 AI-Enabled Space, Function, Allocation, and Operation with Digital Intelligence in Jinding

10.3.1 Highlight 1: Smart Spaces

The urban space in Jinding is undergoing a revolutionary iteration in space development models, transitioning from physical space to social space and further to digitally empowered intelligent space (see Fig. 10.3). The construction of the intelligent three-element urban space emphasizes acquiring the needs of urban residents "from a people-centric perspective." Through means such as policy design, space design, and activity design, artificial interventions are made, maintaining consistency and continuity compared to traditional one-element and two-element urban constructions.

Simultaneously, with the development of ICTs such as the internet and 5G communication, a superimposed digital city appears above the material city. The generation of vast amounts of data provides a novel way of understanding the city, enriching the connotations of the "people" as the design object. This also imposes new requirements on the generation, acquisition, and analysis of data, thereby further enhancing the means of design.

The shaping of intelligent three-element urban spaces involves the integrated connection of people , technology, and design. These three elements mutually support

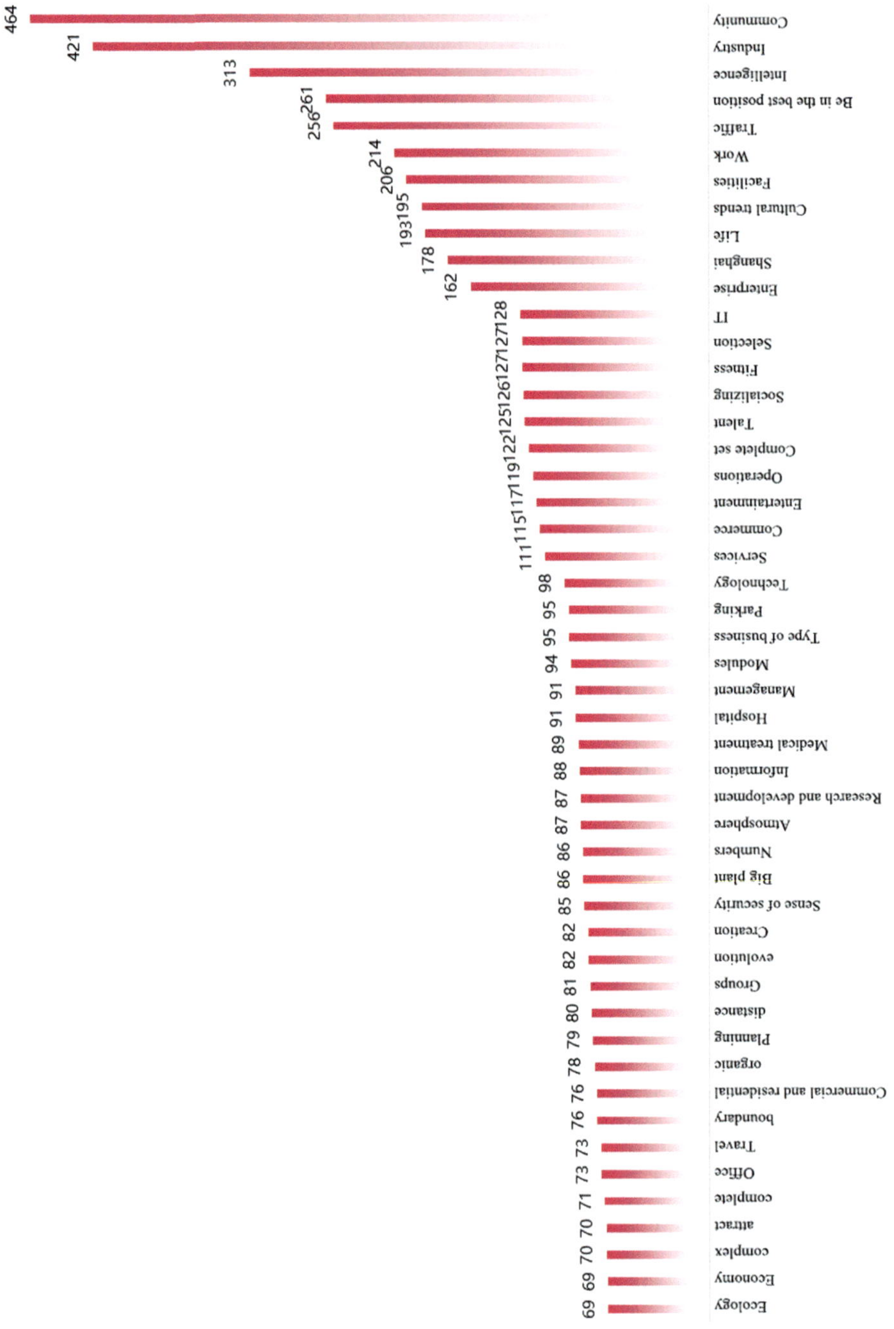

Fig. 10.2 Intelligent perception of citizens' demands

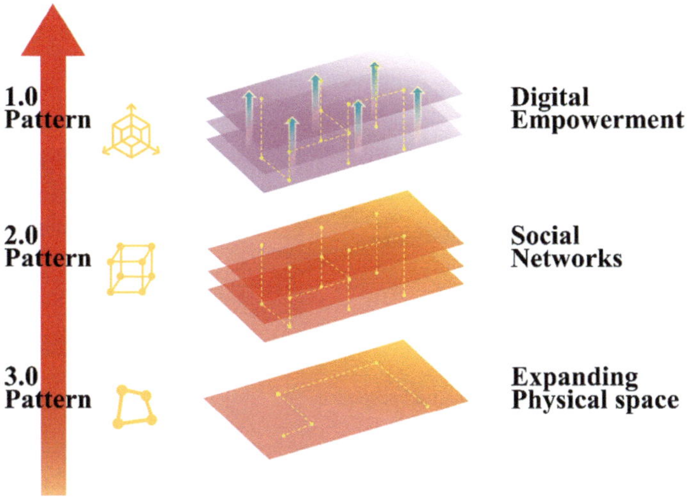

Fig. 10.3 Schematic diagram of the iteration of the urban block development mode

each other, engage in continuous learning, and undergo upgrades and iterations. This integration allows the city to better understand the needs of its residents, providing a more beautiful urban life for the people.

10.4 Highlight 2: Smart Elements Function

Based on in-depth research into Jinding's user needs, the intelligent enhancement is applied to three pyramid-level demands: economic, governance, and industrial economy. This corresponds to the intelligent life, governance, and economic elements (see Fig. 10.4):

(1) Smart economy: Gathers the future development momentum of Jinding's smart community. Intelligent enhancement in the economic domain combines with spatial positioning, including industrial, innovative, and commercial elements. Industrial elements are positioned in productive spaces driving city development; innovative elements are positioned in urban spaces with research and development functions; commercial elements are positioned in urban spaces for residents' shopping, leisure, and consumption.
(2) Smart governance: Gathers the future development resilience of Jinding's smart community. Intelligent enhancement in the governance domain combines with spatial positioning, including natural, traffic, infrastructure, and governance elements. Natural elements are positioned in urban spaces with ecological and green leisure functions; traffic elements are positioned in urban spaces required for daily travel; infrastructure elements are positioned in spaces supporting the

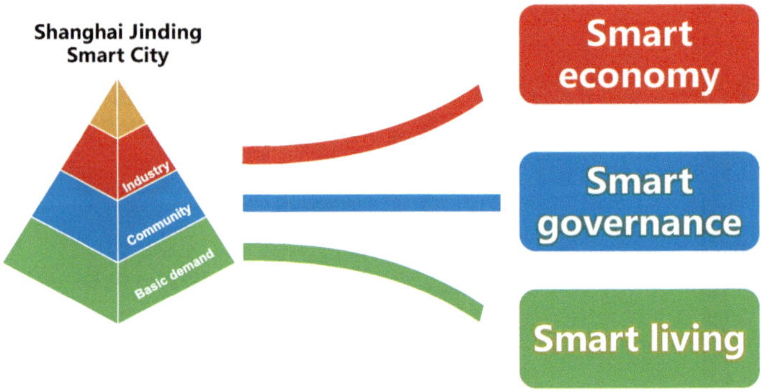

Fig. 10.4 The demand pyramid and smart response

city's life system operation; governance elements are positioned in office areas for urban governance.

(3) Smart life: Gathers the future development vitality of Jinding's smart community. Intelligent enhancement in the life and economic domain combines with spatial positioning, including residential, educational, and medical elements. Residential elements are positioned in the community where citizens live and the city's home; educational elements are positioned in urban spaces providing education and training functions; medical elements are positioned in urban spaces providing various levels of medical services.

10.5 Highlight 3: Smart Resource Allocation

Jinding's smart city block is modeled in three dimensions, depicting the future functional element configuration. The future configuration of functional elements in the Jinding community not only relates to the fairness of facilities and services enjoyed in production and life, but, more importantly, also aims to maximize the utility of services despite limited government investment. It strives to benefit as many residents as possible, attract more people to engage in production and life activities, and gather popularity.

Using AI technology to configure the "Green, Governance, Residence, Transportation, Business, Medical, Education, Production, Infrastructure, and Innovation" ten-element balanced layout model in Jinding, an algorithm for urban element spatial units is employed. This achieves intensive use of construction land, stacking some mutually cooperative public service facilities to achieve functional complexity, and constructing a "one-stop service community complex" (see Figs. 10.5, 10.6 and 10.7).

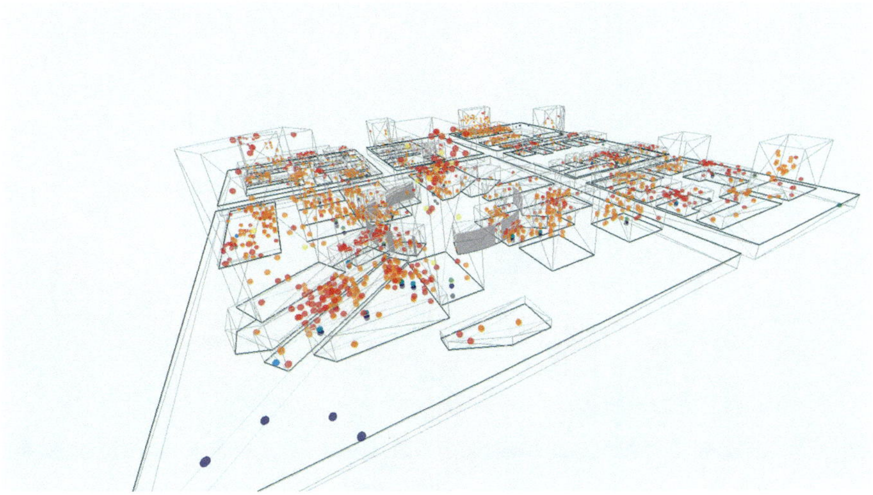

Fig. 10.5 3D Prediction of Points of Interest (POI) for Ten Functions at the Neighborhood Scale in Jinding Smart City

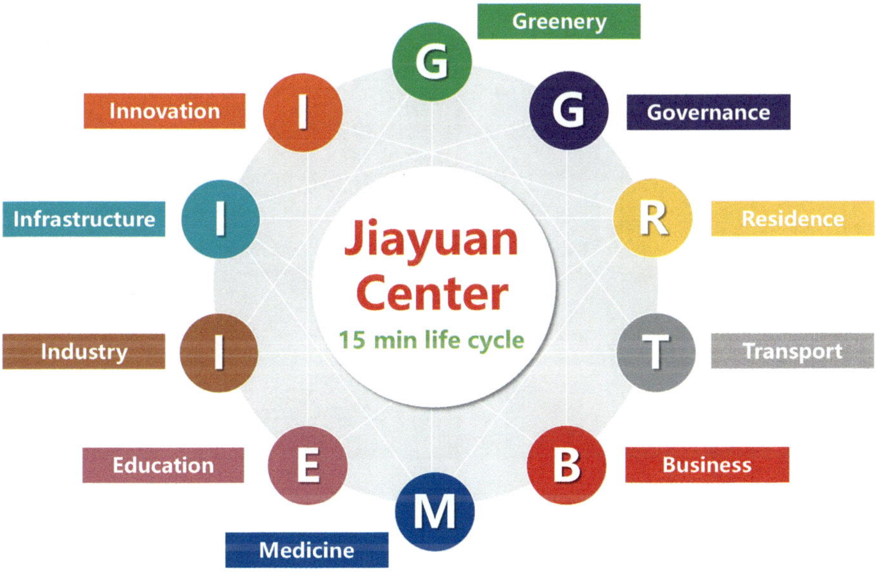

Fig. 10.6 Jiayuan center

Fig. 10.7 Jinding building functional unit refinement

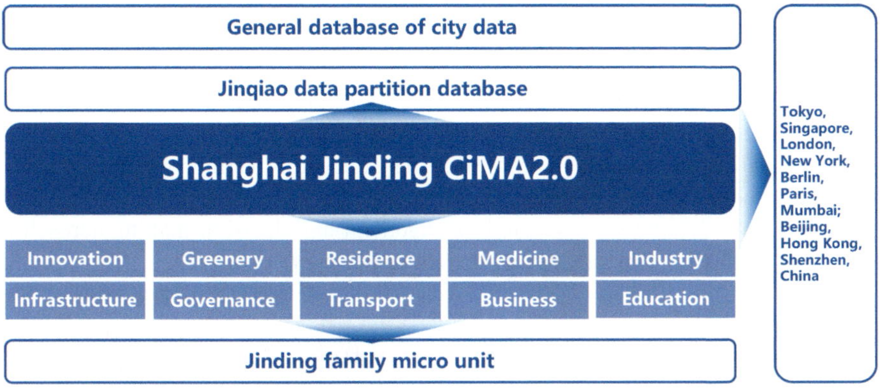

Fig. 10.8 The structure of the Jinding CiMA

10.6 Highlight 4: Smart City Operation

The Jinding database cluster is being established to create a cohesive digital ecosystem that enhances data integration, accessibility, and utilization.

The Jinding database cluster (see Fig. 10.8) connects upwards to the Jin Qiao Town, the Pudong New Area, and the Shanghai Municipal Data Repository. Downward, it establishes internal sub-databases for various systems within the project, integrating micro-units of data for each household.

Shanghai Jinding CiMA2.0 constructs the digital three-dimensional city CiMA model, integrating five categories of elements: buildings, green spaces, roads, rivers, and terrain. It expands to include detailed and comprehensive internal city information such as industry, innovation, greenery, governance, residence, travel, business, medical, education, facilities, and upgrades to CiMA 2.0. Using this as a benchmark, it aligns with international metropolises and leads industry standards.

10.7 AI Scenario Integration Demonstration

Nine major AI scenarios have been selected from a vast range of possibilities for innovative integration demonstrations in Jin Ding. These include Smart Living Services (Residential Services), Smart Business Matching (Commerce), Smart Eating and Drinking (Catering), Local Smart Learning (Education), Inclusive Smart Healthcare (Medical), Smart Transportation and Travel (Transportation), Green Smart Homeland (Ecology), Smart Energy Management (Energy), and Intelligent Security and Disaster Prevention (Security) (see Fig. 10.9).

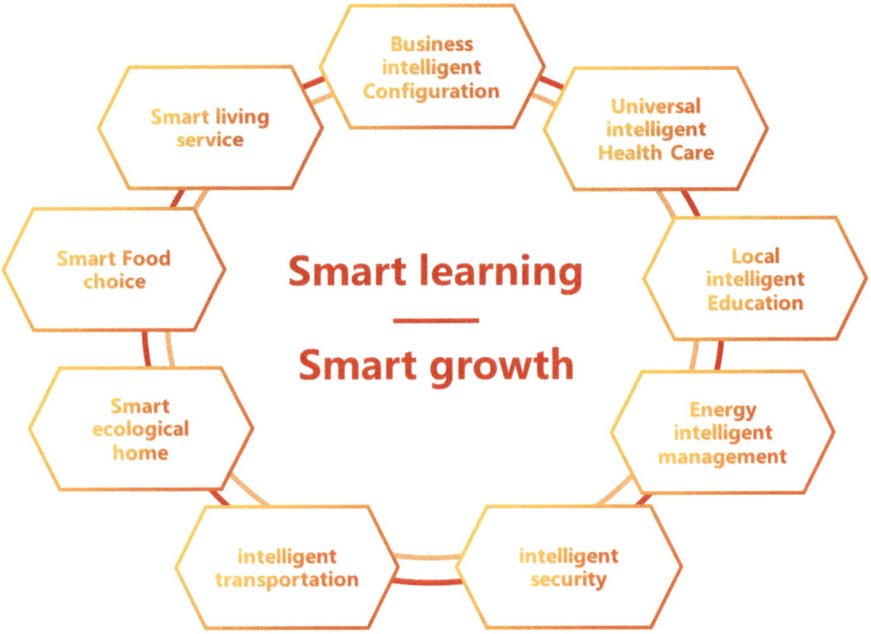

Fig. 10.9 AI scenario integration demonstration

10.7.1 Scenario 1: Smart Living Services

Jin Ding addresses various aspects of community life, such as residence, parking, logistics, environment, and sports, relying on AI algorithms like smart image recognition, natural language recognition, customer preference learning, and scheduling. It continuously optimizes customized learning for the life needs of community residents, gradually improves individual user preference profiles, enriches and simplifies resident interactions with the community, and provides comprehensive intelligent life services (see Fig. 10.10).

10.7.2 Scenario 2: Smart Business Matching

Jin Ding's AI Business Space Matching Center (see Fig. 10.11) includes user-side, merchant-side, and management-side components, constructing a complete online ecosystem, accurately capturing changes in customer flow, funds, and logistics, and continuously optimizing the utilization of commercial space.

Fig. 10.10 Customized life smart service

Fig. 10.11 AI business smart allocation

Fig. 10.12 Smart eatery street

10.7.3 Scenario 3: Smart Eating and Drinking

Jin Ding's AI canteen has functionalities such as cooking, dish recognition, temperature sensing, freshness recognition, display matching, visual recognition settlement, and more. The entire production process is automated, digitized, and traceable, combining storage, order processing, production, packaging, energy saving, and other functions. The AI system can also recommend nutritionally balanced meals and provide customized meal choices for different groups, such as the elderly and white-collar workers (see Fig. 10.12).

10.7.4 Scenario 4: Local Smart Learning

Jin Ding achieves convenient teaching services covering online and offline through the construction of a smart cloud information system platform (see Fig. 10.13). It expands the learning scenes for students through intelligent means, implements intelligent teaching support, behavior assessment, emotional assistance, and enhances the level of educational intelligence using AI technology. Leveraging the WUPEN World Planning Education Organization platform, it collaborates with globally renowned institutions, establishes a network for mutual recognition of educational qualifica-

Fig. 10.13 Study-in-Place AI Lab for Innovative Learning and Research

tions, and provides a convenient experience of reading worldwide books locally, forming Jin Ding's unique education brand and resource advantages, attracting talents worldwide.

10.7.5 Scenario 5: Inclusive Smart Healthcare

Leveraging the Jin Qiao 5G+ Ultra HD Video Industry Demonstration Base, Jin Ding establishes a "Smart Healthcare Cloud Platform" covering the entire region (see Fig. 10.14). The platform, relying on advanced technologies such as the internet, 5G communication, and AI, connects various advanced specialized hospitals domestically and internationally. It enables remote pathological diagnosis, real-time high-definition video guidance for specimen collection, and AI-assisted diagnosis. Residents of Jin Ding can enjoy the expertise and care plans of internationally renowned medical experts without having to travel far.

On the other hand, the cloud platform can establish health records for Jin Ding residents. Residents can monitor and self-assess their health continuously using home perception devices and personal intelligent health assistants.

10.7.6 Scenario 6: Smart Transportation and Travel

Leveraging the future car research and development base in Jin Qiao and the 5G industrial ecosystem, Jin Ding is dedicated to creating an intelligent transportation system integrating perception, communication, and computation.

The intelligent transportation system extends beyond unmanned vehicles on city roads and includes unmanned shuttle vehicles, smart buses, smart parking, and

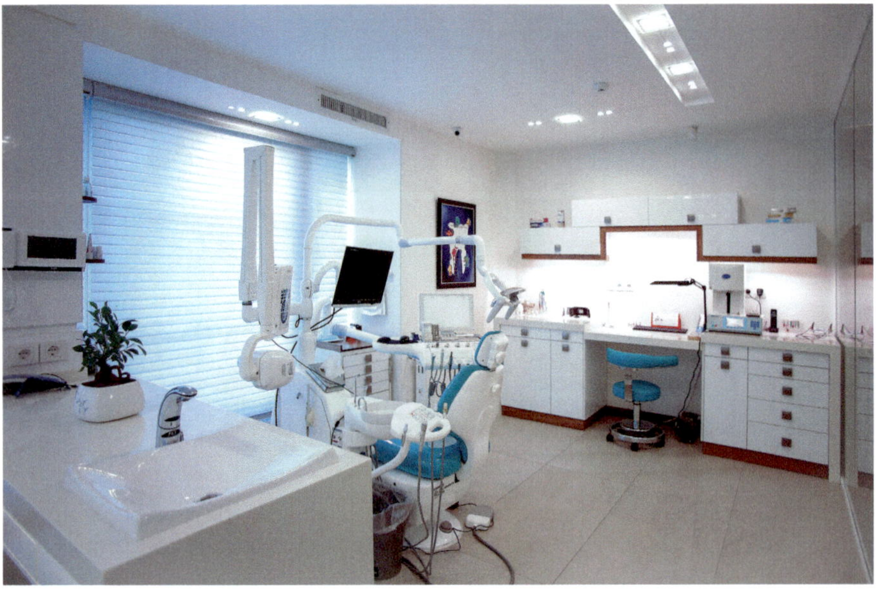

Fig. 10.14 Smart medical applications

smart slow-moving transportation in multiple dimensions. It integrates various technologies, including smart parking, intelligent network supervision, and ubiquitous connected intelligent roads, to connect various aspects of transportation. It achieves the integrated development of 5G communication, edge computing, AI, intelligent connected vehicles, and intelligent transportation. Building an integrated and all-encompassing intelligent transportation system, it realizes the organic fusion of infrastructure, traffic management, vehicles, pedestrians, and roads, constructing a city traffic system that is perceptive, learning, and responsive (see Fig. 10.15).

10.7.7 Scenario 7: Green Smart Jiayuan

Jin Ding is constructing a carbon–neutral community, optimizing energy use with the support of green technologies. By deploying comprehensive sensing of human activities, industrial activities, and natural activities, it establishes a carbon–neutral green homeland platform. This platform achieves real-time calculation of carbon emissions and carbon sinks within a 1 km^2 area. It scientifically assists in carbon–neutral urban design layout optimization, urban energy balance, and urban activity guidance (see Fig. 10.16).

Fig. 10.15 The smart transportation system

Fig. 10.16 The carbon–neutral green Jiayuan platform

Fig. 10.17 Smart energy management operation and maintenance platform

10.7.8 Scenario 8: Smart Energy Management

Jin Ding's intelligent energy management and operation platform (see Fig. 10.17) establish a comprehensive perception system based on the actual environment, combining diverse data to form a self-aware, self-diagnosing, and self-decision-making system. It promptly detects and predicts network issues, assisting managers in decision-making to achieve precise matching and efficient low-carbon goals.

10.7.9 Scenario 9: Intelligent Security and Disaster Prevention

Jin Ding, through a complete platform system, reduces the difficulties of repetitive manual work and inadequate law enforcement forces. It aims to achieve goals such as emergency responses at any time, high-frequency operations, and intelligent management. This satisfies the development needs of urban comprehensive governance in terms of automation, intelligence, and refinement (see Fig. 10.18). In addition, it serves as a representative applied scenario for the innovative landing of the Jin Ding robot industry base.

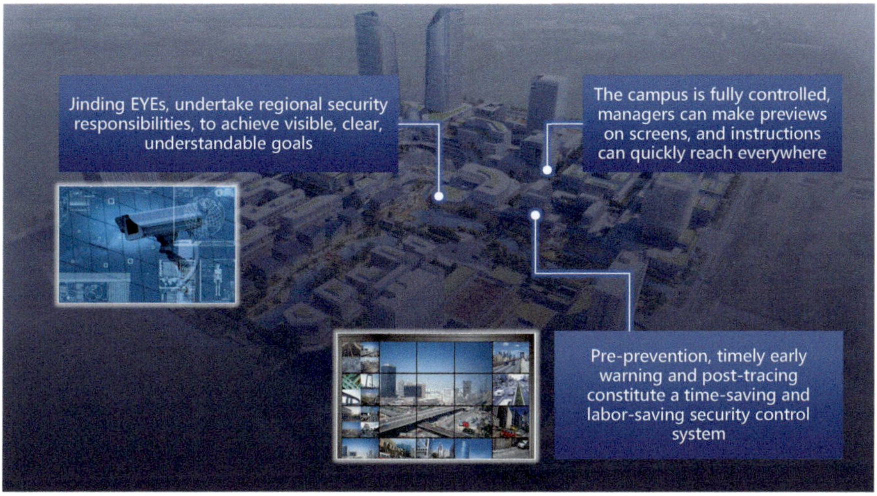

Fig. 10.18 The smart city safety warning platform

Chapter 11
Case Study: Taizhou Innovation Park

Abstract This chapter explains the significance of Taizhou Innovation Park as a leading Industry 4.0 demonstration city and outlines its strategic development framework. Situated in Huangyan District, Taizhou, Zhejiang Province, the park is committed to facilitating the transformation and upgrading of traditional industries through advanced technologies such as AI, big data, and the IoT. The park employs three core strategies—intelligent network applications, talent aggregation, and innovative ecosystem development—to address key challenges in industrial upgrading and environmental sustainability. With the support of a team led by academician Wu Zhiqiang from Tongji University, the park has formulated the "Yongningjiang Science and Technology Innovation Belt" initiative, aiming to become China's premier Industry 4.0 demonstration city. By integrating intelligent spatial design, digital twin platforms, and smart park management systems, the park achieves dynamic monitoring and real-time updates. Additionally, it combines ecological restoration with the preservation of original industrial heritage, creating distinctive landscapes and functional areas that serve as a model for industrial upgrading and sustainable development.

Keywords Taizhou Innovation Park · Industry 4.0 · AI and the IoT · Digital twins platform · Industrial transformation · Ecological restoration

11.1 Introduction

11.1.1 *Taizhou: A Smart City in the Era of Industry 4.0*

In response to future industrial transformation, Taizhou is actively developing an Industry 4.0 city by leveraging AI, big data, and the Internet of Things (IoT) to drive innovation and smart urban development.

The intelligent integration of networks and other advanced technologies in both industry and urban development, along with the creation of a conceptual plan for

Z. WU, *The AI City*, The Urban Book Series,
https://doi.org/10.1007/978-981-96-2560-4_11

Fig. 11.1 The Taizhou Industry 4.0 urban strategic system

Taizhou as an Industry 4.0 city. By conducting methodical investigations into developed nations and regions, and tailoring them to the specific circumstances of Taizhou, the strategy aims to comprehensively comprehend the "Industry 4.0" standard. It will establish a framework that enables the development of an Industry 4.0 benchmark city in Taizhou, explains the overarching concept, establishes strategic objectives and operational trajectories, and suggests a strategic system for the Industry 4.0 benchmark city (see Fig. 11.1).

Three breakthrough strategies—intelligent network, talent aggregation, and innovation ecology—are proposed at the highest level; three brand strategies—modern governance, cultural development, and brand building—are suggested at the brand strategic level; and intelligent space, science and innovation home, and intelligent infrastructure are suggested as supporting strategies at the supporting strategic level. By integrating AI technology with industrial park scenarios and future innovation requirements, this study employs machine learning to intelligently design new industrial space scenarios in accordance with the new Industry 4.0 urban space model (see Fig. 11.2).

11.1.2 The First Construction Area of Taizhou Industry 4.0: Taizhou Innovation Park

Huangyan District is situated in Taizhou City, Zhejiang Province. It is 908 km^2 in size and is situated in the center of the province's golden coastline. Over the past half-century, the district has undergone rapid development and has been awarded numerous accolades, including being recognized as one of the top 100 districts of

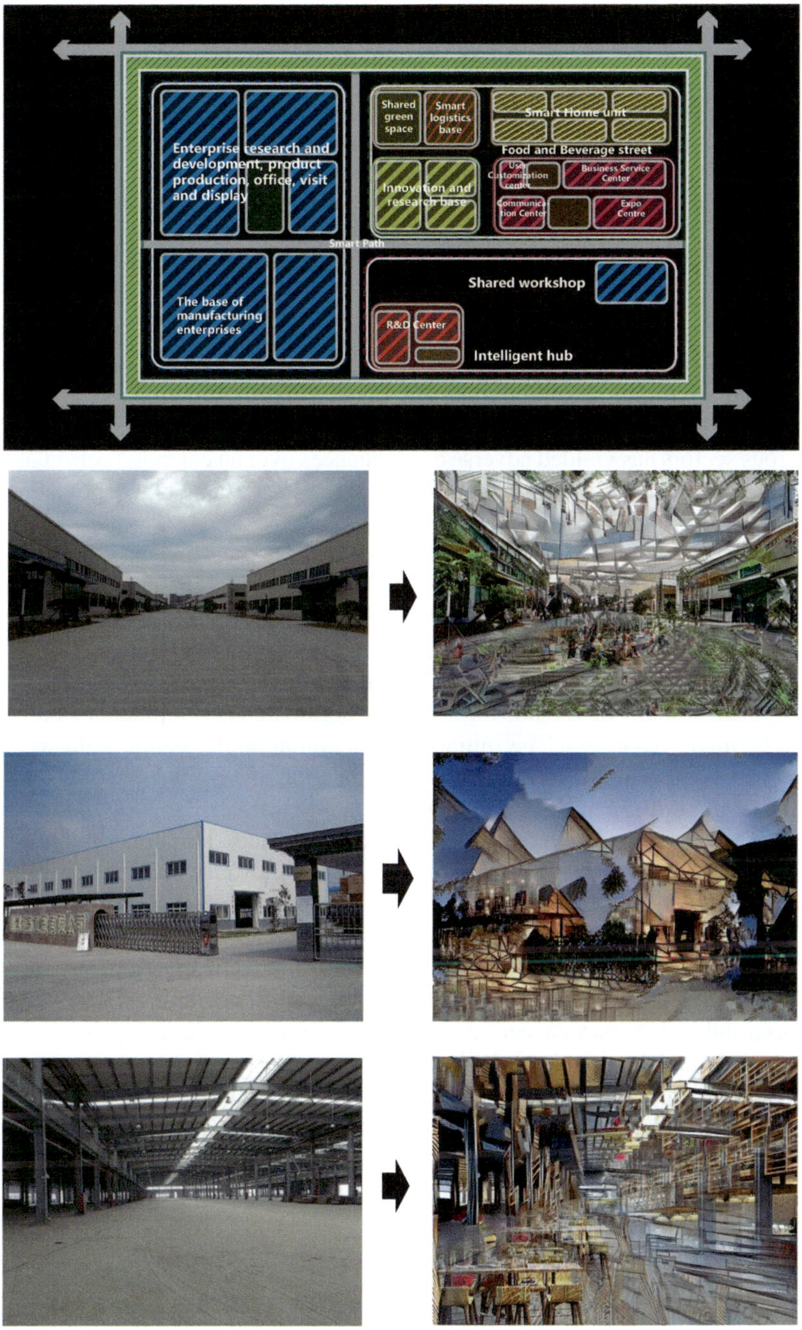

Fig. 11.2 Taizhou Industry 4.0 new urban industrial space model

China. Furthermore, its mold industry has experienced significant growth, expanding from a few isolated small workshops to over 3,000 enterprises at present. With an annual output value exceeding 10 billion yuan, it has emerged as the most intensive sector for domestic mold enterprises. Additionally, it has been designated as one of the 20 industrial block economic transformation and upgrading demonstration zones in Zhejiang Province and is regarded as the "hometown of mold."

However, with the accelerated development of the Huangyan industry, concealed hazards are also beginning to emerge. At present, the most significant obstacle confronting the Huangyan industry is its awkward position at the conclusion of the sector. Due to its status as an intermediary manufacturer devoid of independent brands, direct consumer contact, and minimal industrial agglomeration, the establishment of economies of scale is arduous. Consequently, this deficiency undermines the internal driving force behind industrial transformation and hinders the organization's ability to advance such processes. The protracted and disorganized progress of numerous sectors has yielded adverse consequences over an extended period of time, including significantly diminished output values and environmental degradation that has severely compromised the local ecosystem.

Under the direction of the Taizhou Municipal Government and with the support of the Huangyan District Party Committee and the district government, the academician Wu Zhiqiang's team at Tongji University proposed "the overall strategy of Yongning River Science and Technology Innovation Belt" as a solution to the major problems presently afflicting Huangyan District. The strategy firmly grasped the crucial urban development strategy of Taizhou during the "Coordinated development on both sides of the Jiaojiang river" era. The initial construction area of Taizhou Industry 4.0 is designated as the window of external communication, the confluence of history and the future, the estuary of the Yongning and Jiaojiang Rivers, and the old industrial zone of Taizhou replete with numerous industrial artefacts. This area symbolizes the city's proactive and forward-thinking approach to innovation, positioning it as the prototypical "Industry 4.0" center of the nation. To accomplish the "overall strategy of Yongning River Science and Technology Innovation Belt" and address the fundamental challenges confronting the Huangyan industry, the team led by academician Wu Zhiqiang implemented a reform in the Huangyan Wharf Industrial Zone, which had been dubbed "urban cancer" due to its severe urban issues, lagging industrial development, and deplorable ecological conditions. The location has been designated for decades to accommodate industrial transformation of cement products processing facilities, characterized by a solitary industrial mode, a sluggish increase in output value, and severe environmental pollution.

11.2 Industrial Transformation

11.2.1 Overview of the Industrial Transformation in Taizhou

In accordance with Taizhou's overarching urban development goal of becoming an "Industry 4.0 city," the first Industry 4.0 construction zone, Taizhou Innovation Park, was ingeniously constructed in Huangyan District. Academic Wu Zhiqiang of Tongji University led a team that altered the aspect of this heavily industrialized, contaminated riverside area within 100 days (see Figs. 11.3, 11.4 and 11.5).

Taizhou Innovation Park facilitates the coordination of factory hardware and software activation with innovation sources, emphasizes the organic connection between industrial parks and communities, while developing the organizational structure and spatial form of an Industry 4.0 city, and realizes the link between industrial parks and communities. Develop AI Park 4.0 with a stronger focus on the integration of cross-border collaboration and industrial ecology, while establishing an interconnected and mutually beneficial ecological platform network. Simultaneously, at the level of community 4.0, in support of the latest information technologies including mobile internet, the IoT, and big data, isolated communities, and independent living

Fig. 11.3 Taizhou Innovation Park before regeneration

Fig. 11.4 Taizhou Innovation Park during regeneration

space are becoming more prevalent. The ubiquitous network re-establishes connections between spaces, thereby constructing a circle mode of living that transcends the limitations imposed by familial and communal boundaries.

This type of innovation source power emphasizes the comprehensive accessibility of data, objects, and people in relation to the three dimensions of production, ecology, and life. Demand is directly connected, and design and production are therefore driven.

Taizhou Innovation Park is located in Jiaojiang Cement Factory, Huangyan District. The first construction area was completed after 100 days of accelerated reconstruction and construction. It revitalized a new scene by integrating the functions of a fashion show, office, communication, and life. Concurrently, Taizhou Innovation Park constructs a digital twin platform and incorporates a smart park management system in order to enable dynamic surveillance and real-time updates of the park.

The implementation of AI technology at the Taizhou Innovation Park site enables the intelligent perception of human emotions and behaviors, as well as the establishment of a real-time connection between individuals and physical elements such as fountains and lighting. In order to foster future scene experience and accomplish sustainable innovation, intelligent perception is employed.

Fig. 11.5 Taizhou Innovation Park after regeneration

11.2.2 Design Innovation Highlights

The following key initiatives are being implemented to advance the development of an Industry 4.0 city in Taizhou:

(1) Transform the initially disorganized and dilapidated factory malignancy into an environment that fosters positivity and stimulates creativity.
(2) Beautify natural landscapes with industrial heritage through ecological restoration.
(3) Conduct intelligent and future emotional perception, as well as real-time observation and feedback on the park's happiness index for the first time.
(4) The structure preserves a substantial portion of its historic industrial character and establishes air corridors.

(5) Integrate digital art installations using the original mechanism and relics. In addition, intuitive nudge and face recognition capabilities.
(6) Utilize an application to facilitate the creative interaction of multiple composite spaces, establish integrated online and offline connections, and emerge as the future innovation engine of Taizhou.

11.2.3 Technology Innovation Highlights

(1) Landscape enhancement

The precursor to Taizhou Innovation Park was a cement product processing plant characterized by sluggish growth and a singular purpose; the native ecology surrounding the park had been significantly impacted and polluted, and the park's odor was foul and offensive as a result of improper waste disposal and treatment. As a result, the primary objective of the park's hardware innovation was to enhance the overall landscape. To restore it through natural water management practices using both aquatic and autobiotic plants, reeds (84,495 m^2), *persicaria orientalis* (118,555 m^2), *zizania latifolia* (72,043 m^2), and *lythrum salicaria* (33,437 m^2) were strategically incorporated into the waterfront ecosystem, constructing 31.6 hectares of green planting ecology while showcasing Huangyan Bund's breathtaking scenery.

The aim of Industry 4.0 is not to completely disregard past practices, but rather to maintain their fundamental qualities, strike a balance between break and build, emphasize its valuable historical origins, and preserve its original key attributes. Taizhou Innovation Park retains and renovates the historic buildings and structures of the original cement products processing facility, following meticulous site arrangement. The road guide belt, which represents the "Silk Road" of Taizhou, is traversed as depicted in Fig. 11.6. These surviving components originated from the original cement factory plant and plant elements with distinct functions and structures. They were then organically incorporated with the park's lighting multimedia and green vegetation to form distinctive park blocks, including the shady square, time disc, creative harbor, future portholders, dream path, and cement forest. It exemplifies the ideal blend of the new and the old, thereby emphasizing the distinctive allure of Taizhou Innovation Park.

(2) Interior renovation

Assembling a dynamic and intricate innovation space from a solitary functional factory area is the paramount concern of this project. To accomplish this goal, Taizhou Innovation Park has constructed the following: an Industry 4.0 catwalk capable of showcasing industrial products; a digital interactive exhibition area showcasing the historical and prospective industrial development of Huangyan; a panoramic interpretation forum hall that amalgamates knowledge and innovation; an ecological restaurant featuring a bamboo-and-steel framework that harmoniously merges ecology and industry; and an open office box community

Fig. 11.6 Taizhou Innovation Park

comprising various boxes, each having a distinct purpose. These functions vary from area to area as an answer sheet. They unite the functions of the entire park and integrate the exhibit, interaction, investigation, interpretation, leisure, office, and other components in an organic manner, transforming the park from a simple to a complex link. The process by which Taizhou Innovation Park brings a product from the factory to the stage not only exemplifies the attributes associated with Industry 4.0, but also demonstrates the park's vitality.

11.3 AI-Enabled Space Innovation

11.3.1 Framework Innovation

Taizhou Innovation Park deviates from the traditional approach of commencing solely with space design by integrating technology and operation, as well as offline and online components, in an innovative manner. In addition to the facets of factory, park, and community, multidimensional reforms are implemented, and innovative approaches are employed to expedite the park's transition from the sluggish growth and singular function of Industry 1.0 to Industry 4.0. By effectively implementing a framework for the composite of Industry 4.0 elements, constructing an industrial data center within the park, and organically renewing regional three-life integration, this endeavor has established itself as a pre-eminent Industry 4.0 benchmark park in Taizhou, which is distinguished by its regional characteristics. As aspirations give rise to innovation and as creation brings visions to fruition, the Taizhou Innovation Park Industry 4.0 zone was established.

11.3.2 Operational Innovation

An ecological platform network is a critical component of Industry 4.0. Taizhou Innovation Park accomplishes this by constructing a resource sharing platform, a market-oriented display and trading platform, and a public service platform using e-commerce technology, big data technology, and cloud computing technology. These platforms serve to connect people, technology and the industry.

(1) Online platform

The online platform of Taizhou Innovation Park strengthens the connection between the park and its consumers. The provision of expeditious information regarding the park on the application is contingent upon the platform, while feedback regarding the functionality of each block can be obtained in a timely fashion. On the platform, masters' inspiration and ideas can be discussed and shared. Offline forums for reserving meeting rooms can be organized directly through the platform. It incorporates the user and the park as a whole, increases the effective utilization rate of the park, and introduces a novel concept regarding the relationship between Industry 4.0 individuals and intelligent parks.

(2) Industrial doctor

Taizhou Innovation Park has expanded the notion of the "industrial doctor," has integrated the technological and human resources of Huangyan, and has served as a conduit for the development of cross-industry industrial production scenario solutions by utilizing the online platform. The online portal conducts an in-depth analysis of the requirements of Huangyan businesses, caters to a broad user base, and offers offline-and-online industrial technical consulting services to resolve production-related issues encountered by businesses. Offline diagnosis services to resolve complex issues on the ground, strengthen the connection with the park, and tailor technical solutions to the specific requirements of businesses.

11.3.3 Updated Effect

The online system is fully functional, while the offline environment remains dynamic and vibrant. The park reasonably arranges the planting of autogenous plants and aquatic plants near the waterfront, and controls the water resources to restore the waterfront ecology and reproduce the ecological landscape (see Figs. 11.7 and 11.8).

Fig. 11.7 Indoor scenes in Taizhou Innovation Park after regeneration

Fig. 11.8 Light show in Taizhou Innovation Park after regeneration

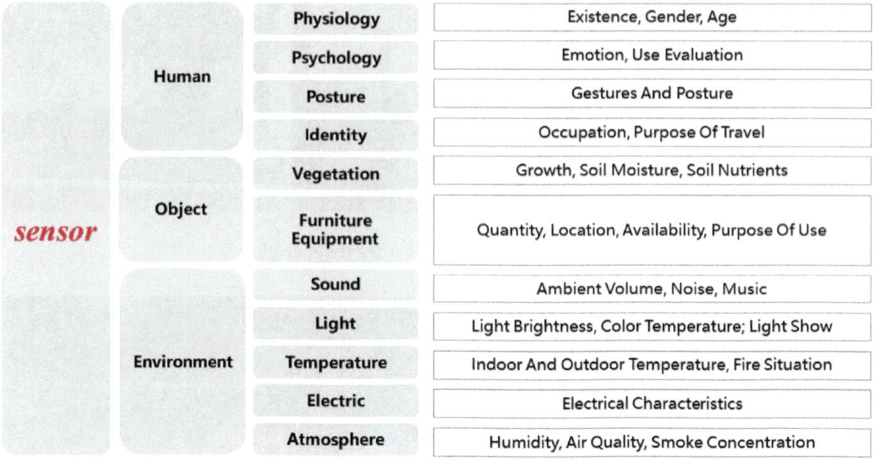

Fig. 11.9 The sensing network of Taizhou Innovation Park

11.4 Demonstration of AI Scenario Integration

"All things can be felt, all laws can be followed, and all things can be renewed" quote from the book of Dao by Laozi or Lao-Tze, the sacred text of Daoism. By leveraging various intelligent perception technologies and incorporating AI intelligent algorithms, the IoT, 5G, and other technologies, this approach aims to harness the energy of the urban populace and uncover the functional attributes of the space, thereby facilitating sustainable urban innovation (see Fig. 11.9).

Taizhou Innovation Park creates both an "interactive park" and a "learnable park" through the multi-dimensional perception of park space and users. Attaining a multi-level surge step-by-step, Taizhou Innovation Park inspires vibrant park activities, encourages the discovery of innovation laws, further encourages the iterative update of scene construction, and the final product is pertinent to the promotion of global experiences.

11.4.1 An Interactive Park

Scenario 1: music recommendation based on feature and emotion recognition

This project identifies the gender, age, clothing characteristics, and likelihood of seven emotions (calm, joyful, melancholy, furious, fear, astonishment, and disgust) associated with an interaction in the park hall using a face recognition algorithm. In consideration of the day's weather, festivals, park activities, and other pertinent factors, it is advisable to select an exclusive backdrop music selection to activate the park hall's interactive ambiance (see Fig. 11.10).

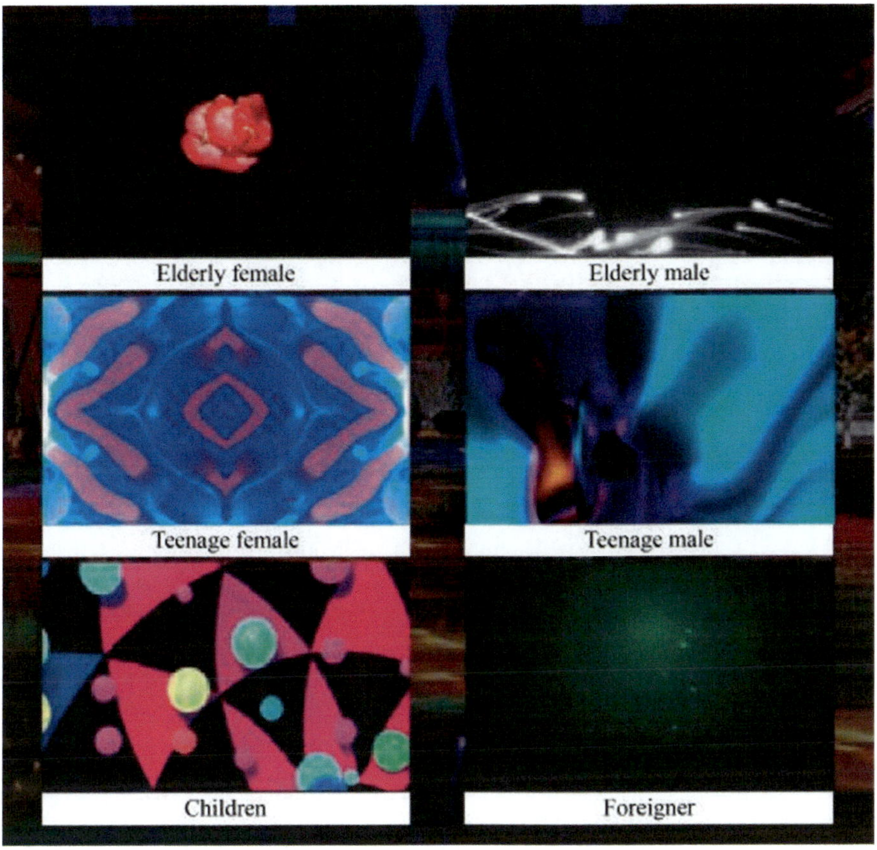

Fig. 11.10 Feature recognition with camera

Scenario 2: sports field based on motion recognition

Based on the motion recognition algorithm, the interaction can get the corresponding light and voice stimulation by completing the specified fitness action in front of the camera, and after attaining a certain achievement, the user can trigger a special light or spray effect. The technology determines the interlocutor's age and presents a range of challenging action requirements. Also permitted is collaborative interaction between multiple people, which encourages both the entrepreneurial community working in the park and the tourists visiting the park to increase their activity and interaction levels (see Fig. 11.11).

Fig. 11.11 Sports field based on action recognition

Scenario 3: water curtain light show based on feature recognition

The majority of the nighttime visitors to Taizhou Innovation Park are locals, tourists, park personnel, and business travelers. By identifying the composition of the population surrounding the venue, the light show will be able to intelligently assess the performance weight of multiple sets of light show programs in order to respond more effectively to the audience's requirements (see Fig. 11.12).

11.4.2 A Learnable Park

Scenario 1: the intelligent management platform

The intelligent management platform aggregates and retains data from various sources, such as the park environment, visitor attributes, activities, and more, in order to facilitate the visual administration of the entire park management process,

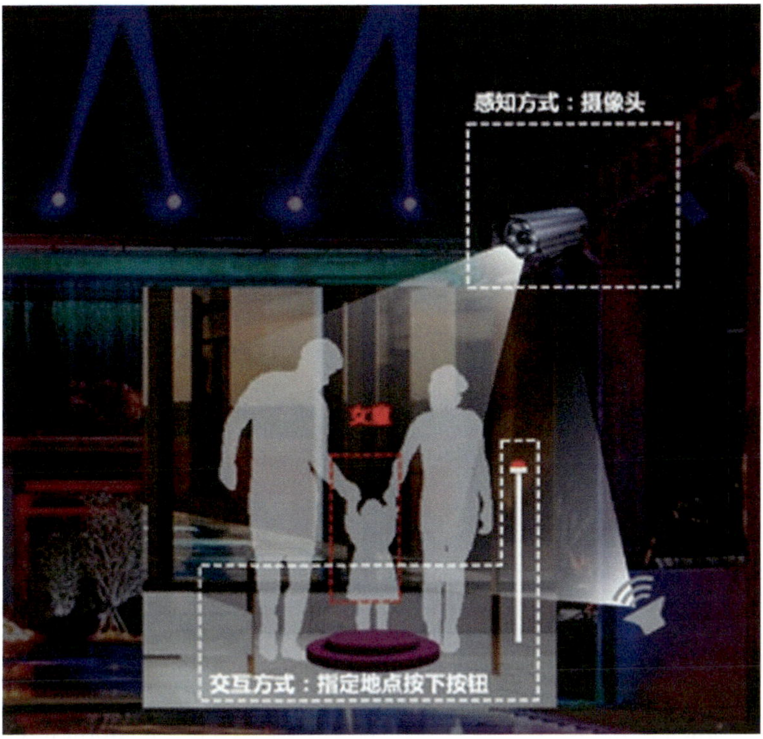

Fig. 11.12 Light show schemes that match the preferences of different groups of people

encompassing parking, security, space utilization, energy conservation, and asset administration (see Fig. 11.13).

By conducting an extensive examination of this data over an extended period of time, Taizhou Innovation Park can enhance the efficacy of its management and utilization of various resources (e.g., personnel, assets, and space), gain profound insights into user requirements, and establish a future park that is sustainable in nature.

Fig. 11.13 Intelligent sensing devices

Scenario 2: the intelligent operation assistance platform

The mission of the intelligent operation assistance platform is to provide support to park managers and associated planning and design teams with the intention of consistently optimizing the park's long-term operational trajectory and providing guidance for its future design and operation.

By continuously gathering activity planning and functional configuration data for the micro-spatial units of the park in time segments, the platform assesses the economic, innovation, and vitality benefits that result from space utilization. In doing so, it simulates the spatio-temporal combination of the park's spatial units, functions, and activities. Ultimately, recommendations are generated regarding the configuration of the park's functions, activity types, frequency, and spatial carriage (see Figs. 11.14, 11.15 and 11.16).

Fig. 11.14 The intelligent management platform of Taizhou Innovation Park

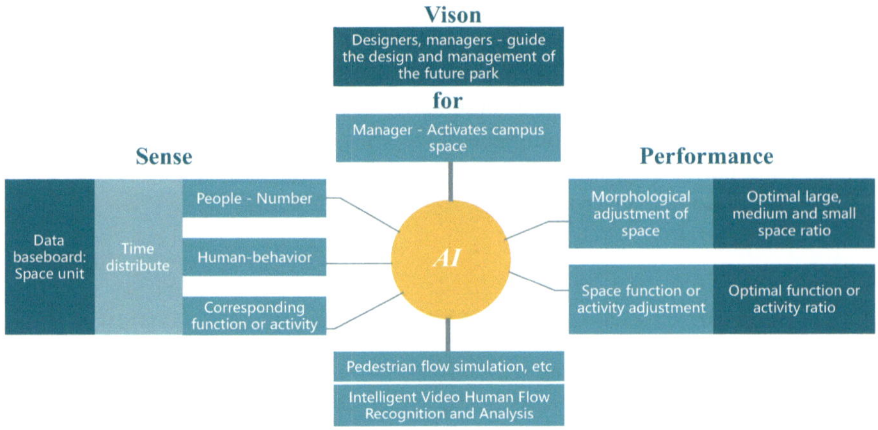

Fig. 11.15 The structure of the smart operation platform

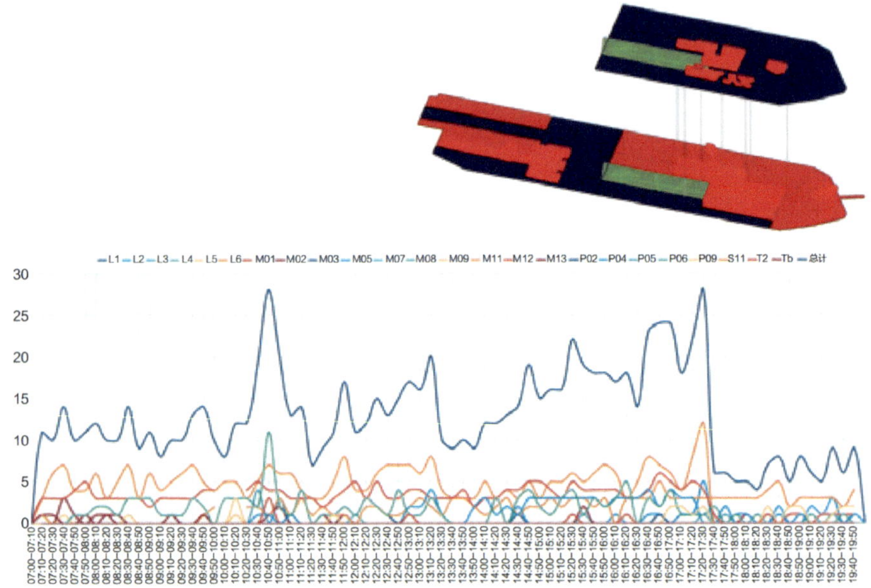

Fig. 11.16 3D visualization of operational data of micro-units in Taizhou Innovation Park

Chapter 12
Shanghai Maqiao: AI Innovation Experimental Area

Abstract Shanghai Maqiao AI Innovation Pilot Zone stands as China's pioneering new city fully embracing AI technology, with the objective of catalyzing regional transformation through innovation and aspiring to become a global leader in AI urban development. Situated in the southwestern part of Shanghai's Minhang District, this pilot zone encompasses the entire lifecycle of AI applications—from planning and design to construction and operation—exploring the integration of intelligent production, living, and ecological systems. By establishing an urban brain system, the Maqiao District achieves intelligent urban governance, enhancing residents' quality of life through AI-driven scenarios while ensuring sustainable green development. Furthermore, the pilot zone has attracted numerous enterprises and academic institutions, fostering the aggregation and technological advancement of the AI industry. Shanghai Maqiao not only serves as a model for AI innovation in China but also offers valuable insights for global smart city initiatives.

Keywords Shanghai · Maqiao · AI city · Urban brain system · Intelligent governance · Industrial agglomeration

12.1 Shanghai Maqiao: The First AI Innovation Experimental Area in China

The Shanghai Maqiao AI Innovation Pilot Zone is located in the southwestern area of Minhang District, Maqiao Town, adjacent to Shanghai Jiao Tong University and the Zizhu Science Park, with a 30 min reach to the Shanghai Hongqiao Hub (see Fig. 12.1). The total area of the pilot zone is approximately 15.7 km^2, divided into two major sections: the applied practice area and the industrial development area.

Since 2019, the local government has actively promoted the construction of Shanghai Maqiao Artificial Intelligence Innovation Pilot Zone, creating a highland for artificial intelligence development and promoting the overall transformation of the region. It aims to create a distinctive leading industry to drive overall regional development in the innovation pilot zone, integrating Maqiao into the city's

Z. WU, *The AI City*, The Urban Book Series,
https://doi.org/10.1007/978-981-96-2560-4_12

Fig. 12.1 Aerial view of the Maqiao AI innovation experimental area

"3 + 5 + X" key areas for comprehensive transformation. Through insights into the application scenarios of the AI industry and continuous iterations, the plan seeks to enhance the ecosystem of intelligent manufacturing industries in Minhang.

In August 2019, the Maqiao AI Innovation Pilot Zone was designated as a national-level innovation development pilot zone and a national-level innovation application leading area. It was included in the "4 + X" innovation integration carrier action plan for Shanghai, along with Pudong Zhangjiang, Xuhui Binjiang, and Lingang New Area.

Maqiao is the world's first pilot project for an AI city, providing numerous test scenarios for the application of AI technology. It aims to become a comprehensive AI future city, combining application demonstrations, research and development innovation, training demonstrations, consumer experiences, and product manufacturing. Additionally, Maqiao is the world's first new city to apply AI technology throughout its entire lifecycle, from planning, design, and construction to operation. In the future, it is expected to achieve full-scale intelligence in various urban systems, making it a globally leading AI city.

12.2 Maqiao to be a World-Class AI City

The positioning of Maqiao is as the world's first city in terms of AI. "First" not only reflects the fact that the project was established earliest, but also requires seizing the latest high ground in the global field of practical applications of AI cities at the fastest pace. It aims to gather together world-class AI industry clusters, research and development personnel, and teams to jointly explore the possibilities of developing an AI city. Maqiao will be dedicated to exploring and creating a series of experiential prototypes for smart city living, including transportation, healthcare, leisure, education, and more. From the operational management of the entire city to the intelligent systems for ecological maintenance, and hardware and software integration, Maqiao will establish an integrated operating platform. Through this, it aims to integrate

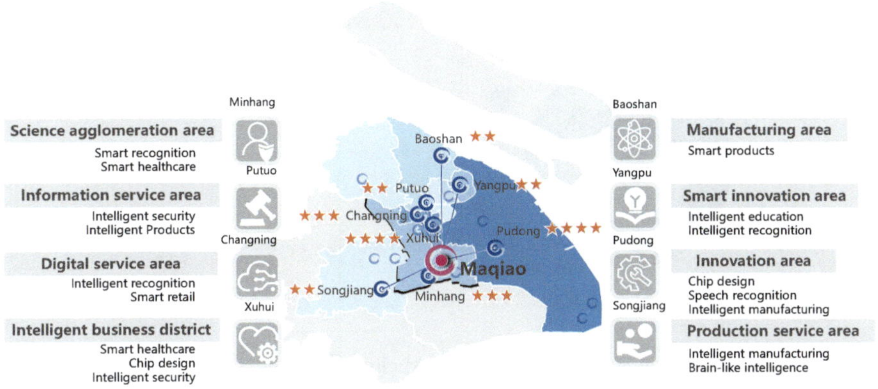

Fig. 12.2 Maqiao: the centre of Shanghai's AI strategy

intelligent production, smart living, and intelligent ecology in the world's first AI city, leading the way in achieving breakthroughs from non-existence to existence, and from existence to excellence. This aligns with the goal set by the General Secretary, as depicted in Fig. 12.2, to achieve success in production, convenience in life, and pleasant ecological environments through AI.

12.2.1 Planning Concept: Shared Home, Intelligent Production, Smart Living, and Smart Ecology

In the field of a shared home, the planning concept introduces three concepts, including Maqiao cultural elements, urban homes, and happy neighborhood relationships. Regarding intelligent production, Maqiao will align with the latest international technological standards, dynamically configuring intelligence, complete cloud sharing, and applications. After completing research and iteration, products will be promoted nationwide and even globally.

In terms of smart living, the planning concept emphasizes ecological communities, the intelligentization of focused scenes, and the integration of diverse networks. As for the smart ecology aspect, the planning concept emphasizes ecological awareness, low carbon, and safety, using these three aspects to coordinate the entire city (see Fig. 12.3).

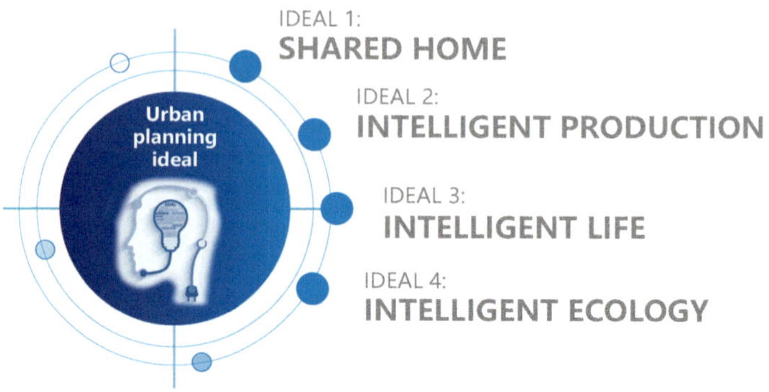

Fig. 12.3 The urban planning concept of Maqiao AI city

12.2.2 Planning and Construction Model Highlights: Application of AI Technology Throughout the Entire Urban Life Cycle

Highlight 1: During the strategic planning phase, leveraging cross-media intelligence achieved city intelligent evaluation based on multi-source massive data

Cross-media intelligence aims to comprehensively perceive, learn, and reason across various senses such as vision, language, and hearing. Based on collaborative intelligence technology, over 100,000 pieces of text, images, and video information from major cities worldwide are automatically collected weekly. These data from various sources are integrated and extracted into four dimensions of the city: economic industries, management services, environmental construction, and hardware facilities for diagnosis, identifying shortcomings in smart city construction (see Fig. 12.4).

Representative expert	Opinions
Wu Zhiqiang Academic of Chinese Academy of Engineering	Maqiao brings together seven major innovative elements: place, reception, land, industry, government determination, schools, and ecology. It has sufficient conditions to support the development and construction of the AI Innovation Park, attracting startups in the AI-related field In the future, Maqiao will serve as a global model, contributing to the prototype of the world's AI city and the operating model of Industry 4.0 cities. It aims to become a benchmark for the world-class experience in AI living, an industrial cluster for world-class AI production, and an integrated innovation ecosystem for world-class AI towns

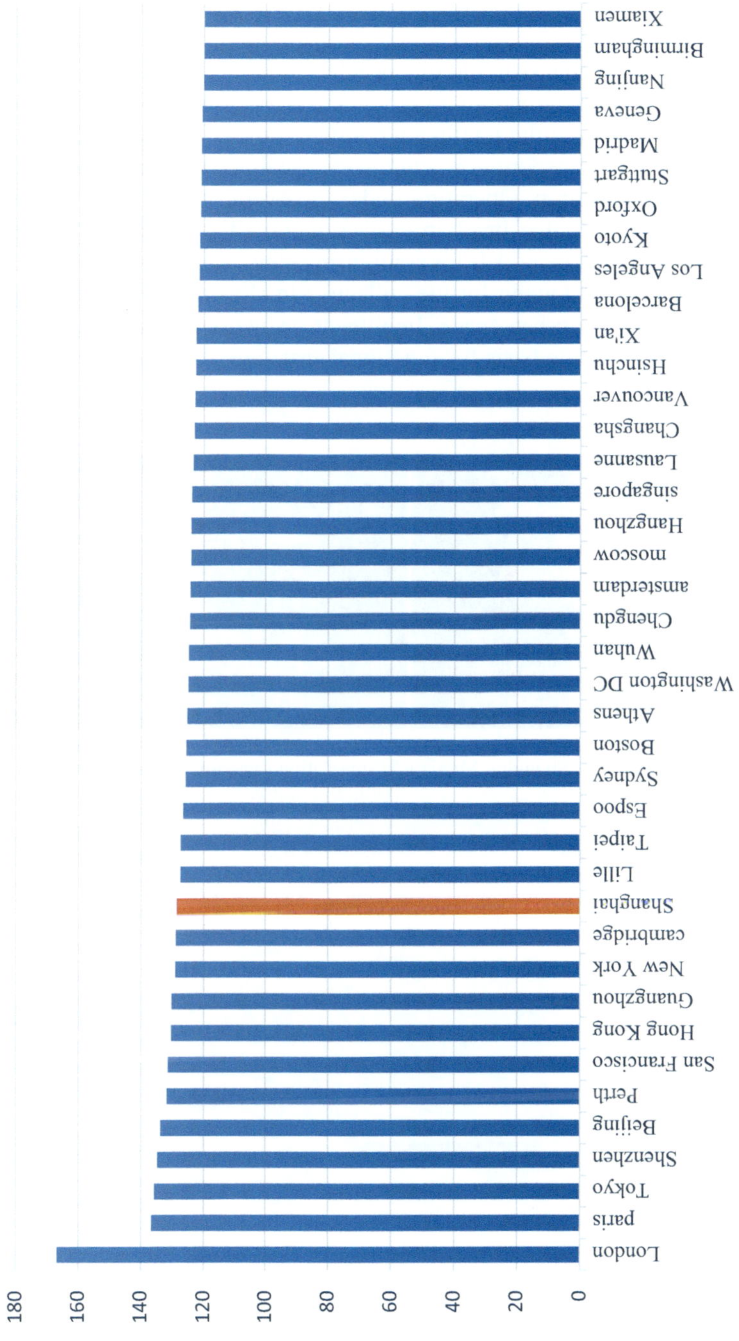

Fig. 12.4 Real-time comparison between Shanghai and other cities

Highlight 2: During the spatial design phase, utilizing collective intelligence achieved the collaborative development and optimized configuration of various elements within the city

Collective intelligence emphasizes intelligence that goes beyond individual capabilities, formed by large-scale autonomous participants. Using swarm intelligence technology, Maqiao has realized the intelligent configuration of ten elements: ecology, governance, residence, transportation, commerce, healthcare, education, industry, infrastructure, and innovation. Operating under the overall rules of the 15-minute community, a four-party game involving government, citizens, capital, and planning is established. Decision models for configuring elements and game subjects are established and refined, allowing for the collective intelligent allocation and planning of these elements in urban space. Intelligent deduction is employed for land layout, providing a scientific basis for functional structure planning (see Figs. 12.5 and 12.6).

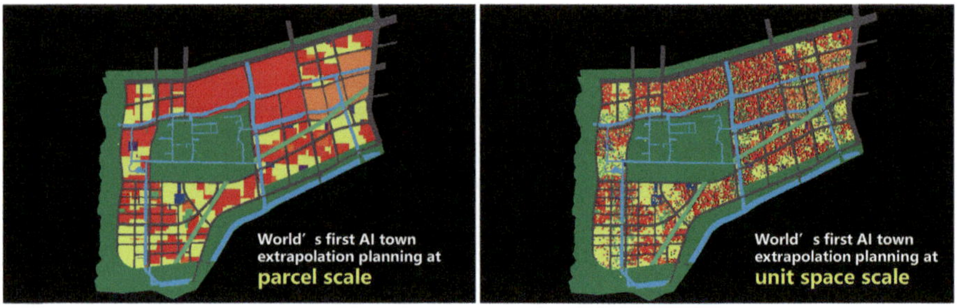

Fig. 12.5 AI prediction of the Shanghai Maqiao AI innovation experimental area

Fig. 12.6 Theme planning of each district based on AI prediction

Highlight 3: Urban demands driving technological development

The Maqiao AI Innovation Demonstration Zone focuses on addressing three major urban needs in its planning: urban governance, urban living, and urban production. It constructs a series of intelligent scenarios, utilizing AI technology for autonomous sensing, judgment, response, and learning, comprehensively enhancing the operational capabilities of various city functions to meet urban demands. In this process, the city's needs determine which technologies will be applied in the city, consequently driving technological development.

In the future, cities need to undergo a transformation in governance, shifting from passive reactions to proactive anticipation. For instance, effective prevention and handling of urban emergencies, and predicting the outcomes of governance and decision-making before implementation are essential. This ensures satisfaction among various stakeholders and meets the requirements of refined, accurate, and efficient urban governance, thereby reducing urban operational costs. As a result, future urban governance will be fully intelligent, utilizing AI technology for information collection, decision-making, execution, and more. This necessitates making the decision-making process in urban governance explicit and algorithmic, thereby enhancing decision efficiency, accuracy, and reliability. Through AI technology simulation and demonstration, the final implementation effects of urban decisions are showcased, ultimately improving urban governance efficiency.

The future pattern of urban living will also undergo a transformation, further meeting emotional needs on the basis of fulfilling basic human requirements. To achieve this, cities must shape an emotionally connected urban ecosystem, becoming an omnipresent giant AI entity. Supported by intelligent technology, the ability to engage in dialogue will no longer be limited to humans or specific living entities. Any system within the city will be capable of real-time response to individual needs, progressing from "everything connected" to "everything conversing."

A significant feature of future urban production will be customized manufacturing, requiring automatic analysis, reasoning, judgment, conceptualization, and decision-making during the production process to achieve precision and efficiency. Therefore, future urban production will transition from interconnected automation to industrial intelligence. Intelligent products produced will universally incorporate intelligent technology systems with high adaptability, interference resistance, predictability, and user-friendliness. These products will seamlessly fit various application scenarios in the future city. The AI enterprise ecosystem cluster in the future development of Maqiao includes VANKE, sensetime, iflytek, HUAWEI, Tongji University and Alibaba.

12.3 AI Technology Application in Maqiao

12.3.1 AI Empowering Urban Governance

In the field of urban governance, Maqiao has established the AI City Pivot (see Fig. 12.7), which is a decision-making system for an AI city based on technologies such as cloud computing, urban three-dimensional mapping, machine learning, and augmented reality.

The AI City Pivot includes the urban brain, cerebellum, and central nervous system in the intelligent city system. It integrates the four major functions of an intelligent city: perception, judgment, response, and learning. Moreover, it has the capability for self-updating and continuous evolution. The decision-making system permeates through the entire process of urban planning, construction, operation, etc., realizing intelligent, precise, and sophisticated management and decision-making across the four spatio-temporal dimensions and the entire life cycle of the city.

Fig. 12.7 AI City Pivot tower in Maqiao

12.3.2 AI Empowers a Better Life

In urban life, AI will comprehensively empower the residents of Maqiao in various aspects, including entertainment, social interactions, cultural celebrations, business activities, traffic management, education, healthcare, etc., forming a series of AI application scenarios.

Scenario 1: The AI square

Through AI technology, the square can recognize and analyze crowd characteristics. It enables the creation of personalized audiovisual works for visitors through intelligent interactions, transforming the square from a simple space for leisure and gatherings to meeting higher-level spiritual needs. Additionally, it further promotes urban innovation and economic activities (see Fig. 12.8).

Scenario 2: The AI park

The AI Park is the core area of Maqiao's AI innovation trial zone and serves as a showcase for the achievements in building an intelligent city in the Maqiao District. On the one hand, it implements intelligent, finely managed, and scientifically decision-oriented operational models for park services. On the other hand, it gathers the world's cutting-edge AI technologies at the urban level, showcasing China's leadership in intelligent urban development (see Fig. 12.9).

Scenario 3: The AI customized tourism service system

In this project, we developed a customized travel service application, through which tourists can easily use public transportation, make online payments, apply for tax refunds, purchase tickets, and obtain information about various attractions, etc. (see

Fig. 12.8 The future AI square in Maqiao

Fig. 12.9 The future AI park in Maqiao

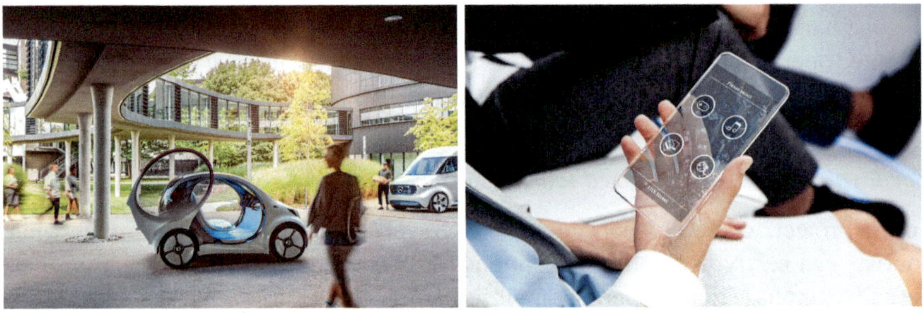

Fig. 12.10 An app customizes guided tours in the future AI park of Maqiao

Fig. 12.10). Additionally, within the demonstration area, autonomous electric vehicles are deployed to provide tourists with sightseeing guidance, city tours, interactive experiences, and carriage gatherings.

12.3.3 AI Empowering Innovation and Entrepreneurship

The groundbreaking projects in AI technology in the urban tech sector transcend the traditional boundaries of planning and design, construction engineering, innovative research and development, and industrial production, impacting a wider range of societal, environmental, or urban decision-making processes (see Fig. 12.11).

The role of Maqiao AI Innovation Park is to encourage more research activities to move beyond the confines of idealized laboratory environments and into practical applications in order to increase their impact. The innovation park will play a

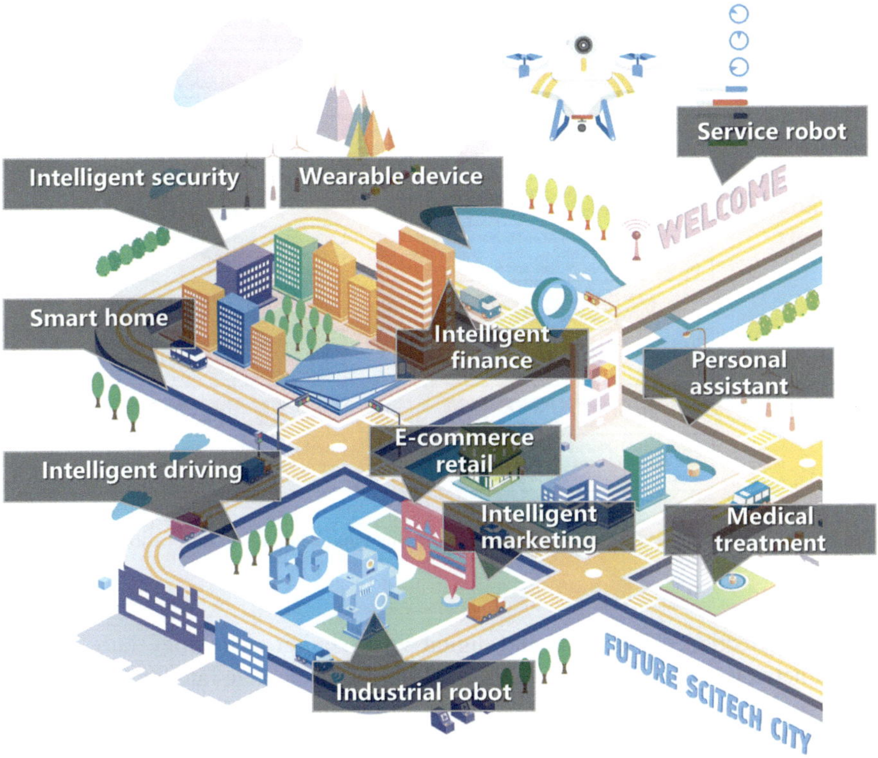

Fig. 12.11 AI application in specialized industries

crucial role as an "AI Urban Laboratory," serving as a venue for experiments and practical applications. It will connect AI technology applications from research and development departments to the market, providing AI developers with a realistic and controllable urban environment and testing ground. Simultaneously, it will offer residents and visitors a cutting-edge experience of AI technology products. Through this, it aims to explore the challenges faced in the development of smart cities and provide more possibilities and new visions for more cities to move toward intelligence (see Fig. 12.12).

12.3.4 AI Empowers Green Ecology

The intelligent city comprehensive environmental monitoring system in the Maqiao AI Innovation Trial Zone integrates computer network technology, air quality

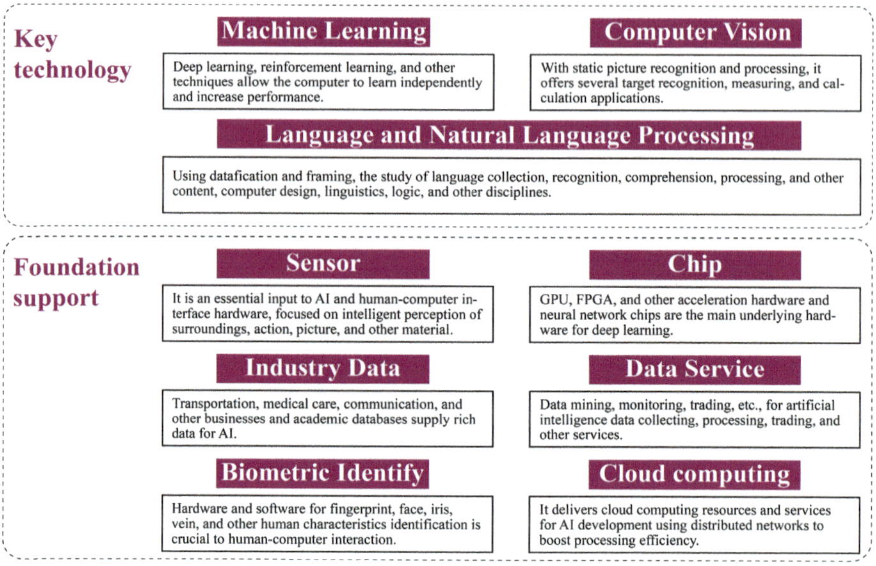

Fig. 12.12 The unmanned industrial system in the Shanghai Maqiao AI innovation experimental area

-sensing detection technology, and digital visualization technology into an intelligent, networked, and automated system. It forms a complete intelligent air quality monitoring system. The system collects real-time air quality monitoring data from various regional monitoring points, and after computational analysis, it transforms the data into visual announcements, multimedia touch screen queries, or smartphone queries through wired and wireless networks. This allows everyone to access the real-time quality of the air environment in their city area, ensuring the public's right to know.

Residents can use a unified mobile app to view the environmental monitoring indices for the entire trial zone, indoor environmental indices for residential and office spaces, as well as personal carbon footprint indices. Additionally, the system provides recommendations based on these indices, such as whether it is suitable for outdoor activities, and integrates with smart homes to promptly adjust indoor environments by activating corresponding devices (see Fig. 12.13).

Representative expert	Opinions
Wu Zhiqiang Academic of Chinese Academy of Engineering	We aim to achieve the following in Maqiao (1) Establish the core of the AI industry, a regional highland, and an internationally leading hub (2) Comprehensive coverage in various domains of intelligent living, becoming an AI innovation park that encompasses intelligent production, innovation, residence, care, health, and leisure

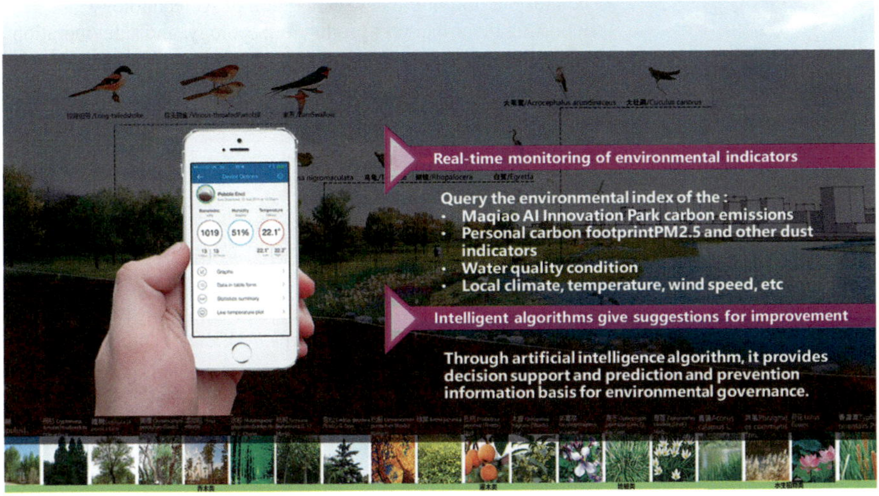

Fig. 12.13 Real-time environmental monitoring index via a mobile app

Chapter 13
The Iteration Mode of the AI City

Abstract The future of AI city construction is grounded in a five-element advancement model, encompassing citizen needs, AI 2.0, infrastructure, governance models, and professional talent. These elements interact synergistically to form a robust urban development framework. Citizen needs serve as the cornerstone for driving urban intelligence, fostering technological advances and innovative applications by addressing fundamental requirements such as survival, health, and personal fulfillment. The development of intelligent infrastructure, including information systems, 5G networks, and IoT technologies, provides critical support for efficient urban operations. Governance models have evolved from traditional top-down approaches to collaborative frameworks, leveraging AI technology to enhance urban management capabilities and boost the overall competitiveness of urban clusters. Furthermore, policy support and risk mitigation mechanisms are essential components in ensuring technical safety and social stability within AI cities. This chapter's proposed model offers a comprehensive framework and strategic insights for the planning and implementation of future AI cities.

Keywords AI city · Citizen demand · Artificial Intelligence 2.0 · Intelligent infrastructure · Urban governance

13.1 Urban Demand Iteration

For the construction of future AI cities, a five-element advancement model is proposed: citizen demand, AI 2.0, infrastructure, governance model, and professional talents. These elements interact with each other and are closely related, collectively forming a stable structure resembling a "pentagram" (see Fig. 13.1).

Z. WU, *The AI City*, The Urban Book Series,
https://doi.org/10.1007/978-981-96-2560-4_13

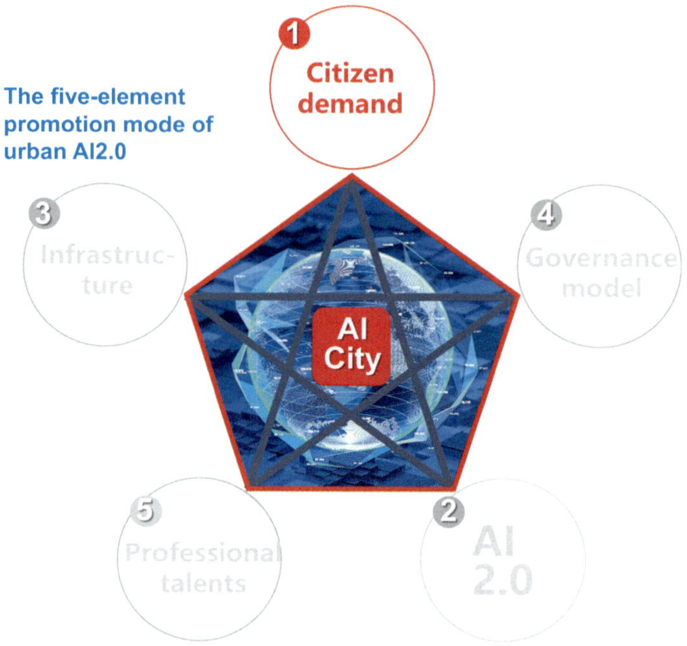

Fig. 13.1 Five-element promotion mode of AI city 2.0 dimension 1: citizens' needs

13.1.1 Urban Demand Sources

(1) Citizen demands constitute the fundamental basis of urban needs. As individual entities, citizens have diverse needs, and these needs vary based on factors such as gender, age, and geographic location. Citizens are the microscopic basic units that make up the city. However, these basic units do not directly form the whole; instead, they form a unique urban ecosystem through certain structures and hierarchical relationships, progressing through the stages of "individual—group—system" (see Fig. 13.2).

(2) Urban needs are the external manifestations of citizen demands. As an aggregate of the population, the city may not express the needs of each individual, but it accommodates them internally. When the number of people with demands in certain aspects increases or when the demands become urgent, this will be reflected in some way on the whole, such as capital flow, media promotion, group emotions, or social trends.

Fig. 13.2 The further promotion of AI requires the city to provide a compound development scenario

13.1.2 Urban Demand Drives Urban Intelligence

Starting from the basic unit, human needs bring about the desire for a good urban life. Human needs can be divided into three advanced levels: existence basics, existence states, and existence meanings. These three levels coexist. Correspondingly, the demands for a good urban life are survival (safety, housing, food), health (physical and mental well-being), and pursuit (culture, profession) (see Fig. 13.3).

The original purpose of technology is to use tools to accomplish tasks that humans cannot achieve on their own. Human intrinsic needs always exist and, while being satisfied, continually generate higher needs. Therefore, technology is constantly advancing with no endpoint. The urban environment concentrates a variety

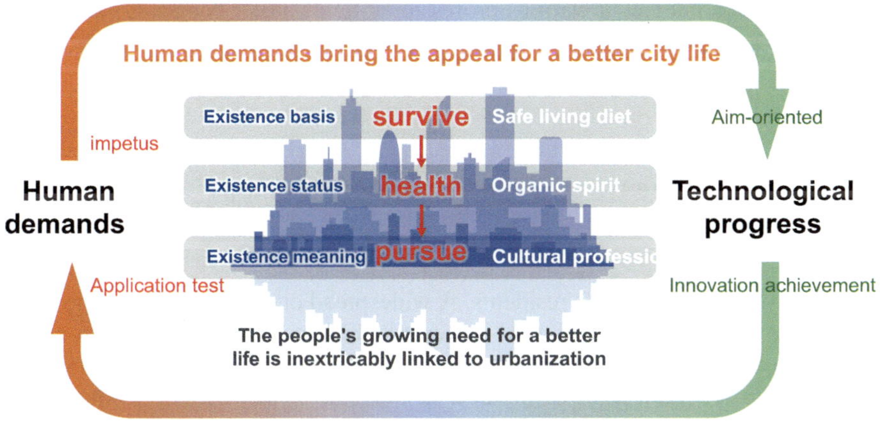

Fig. 13.3 Better city life provides the goal for AI 2.0

of human needs, providing continuous impetus for technological progress. Goal-oriented technological research and development produce innovative results, which are then applied to cities, forming application markets and undergoing practical testing. Through continuous adjustment and interaction with actual human needs, optimization spaces are created, forming a new cycle of dynamic forces.

In the current stage of technological development, human needs increasingly drive urban intelligence. On the one hand, this involves promoting the horizontal dimension of smart city systems, including smart production, smart living, smart ecology, and smart sharing. On the other hand, it involves promoting the vertical dimension of the urban life process, including smart planning, smart design, smart construction, and smart operation. Through the interaction of these two dimensions, ten major physical spaces are identified for intelligence: occupational space, residential space, educational space, medical space, commercial space, recreational space, road network space, river network space, green network space, and heritage space.

The intelligence of these ten major physical spaces provides the foundation for the formation of the prototype architecture of an AI city. In these ten types of spatial scenarios, AI technology can form a pattern of supporting technology research and development to conceptual implementation, ultimately leading to the practical application of scenarios.

13.1.3 The Impact of AI on the Transformation of Urban Life in the Future

At present, AI technology has been widely applied in many professional fields such as image recognition and semantic recognition. In the future, the cutting-edge technologies of AI 2.0 will further integrate human needs and spatial evolution (see Fig. 13.4). Technologies in various professional fields are no longer isolated. They can be interconnected in both the temporal and spatial dimensions when needed by humans.

13.1.4 Comprehensive Enhancement of Residents' AI Literacy

As the city evolves, so do its residents. A widespread civic foundation is the fertile ground for the development of an AI-driven city. Figure 13.5 summarizes the advantages brought about by enhancing residents' AI literacy. Participation in social activities requires a certain level of literacy. In the past, it was literacy in the written language, and those lacking it were called "illiterate." Later, with the ubiquity and penetration of the internet, it became an indispensable tool in daily life, and those who couldn't use the internet were referred to as "internet illiterate." Looking to the

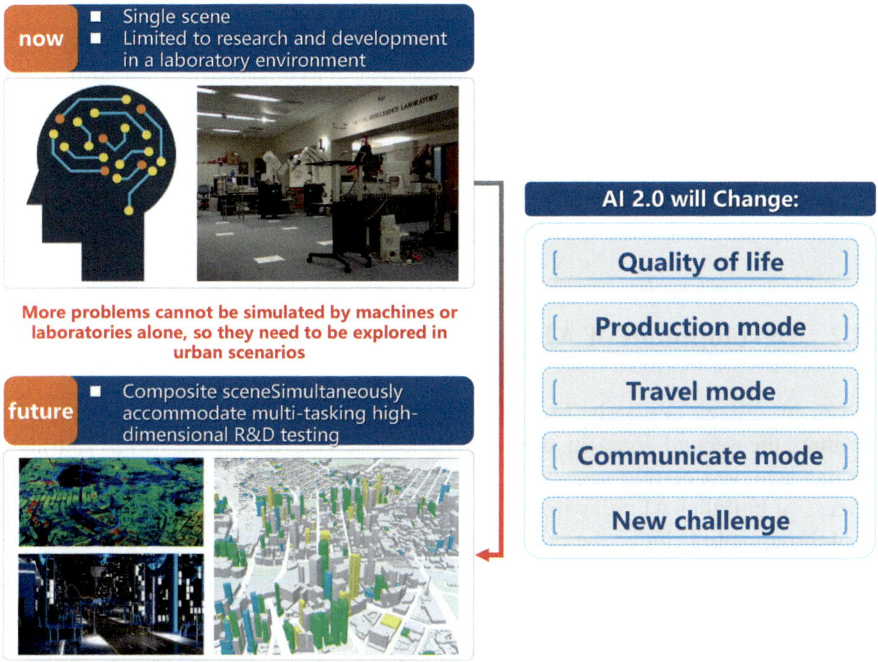

Fig. 13.4 Two major stages in the integration of AI technology and cities

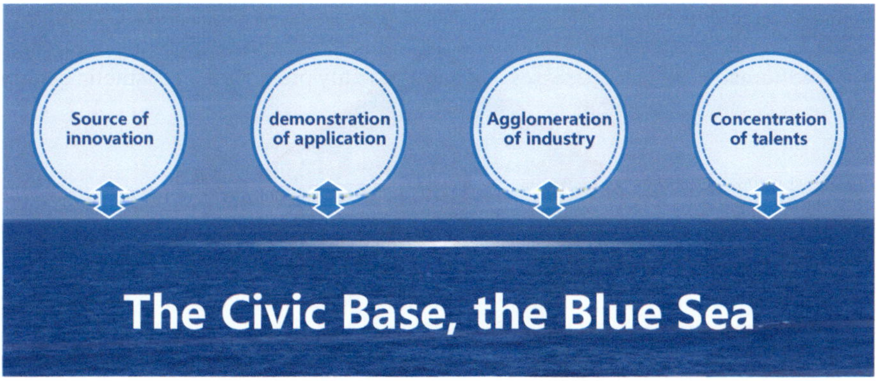

Fig. 13.5 The broad civic base is the blue sea that breeds AI city development

future, as AI becomes an omnipresent assistant, acquiring the necessary "AI literacy" becomes essential to better harness this tool for human use. This involves a return to the ethical and responsible use of technology, avoiding situations where technology undermines human instinctual judgment or assumes superiority over human decision-making.

Representative expert	Opinions
Wu Zhiqiang Academic of Chinese Academy of Engineering	The urban habitat serves as the core fundamental unit of the urban organism, and the metropolis can be viewed as a collective phenomenon of life. The residents of the urban habitat, in their everyday utilization of AI, reflect the sustained capacity, immune capability, and resilience of the habitat, thereby influencing the vitality of the city

13.2 Development of AI Technologies

Driven by citizen demands, the introduction of AI 2.0 as the technological core becomes the second force in the five-element driving model (see Fig. 13.6). AI 1.0 has achieved certain successes in current urban applications. However, in the process of building AI cities in the future, there is a need for further technological breakthroughs to achieve the comprehensive popularization of AI 2.0, forming the necessary support.

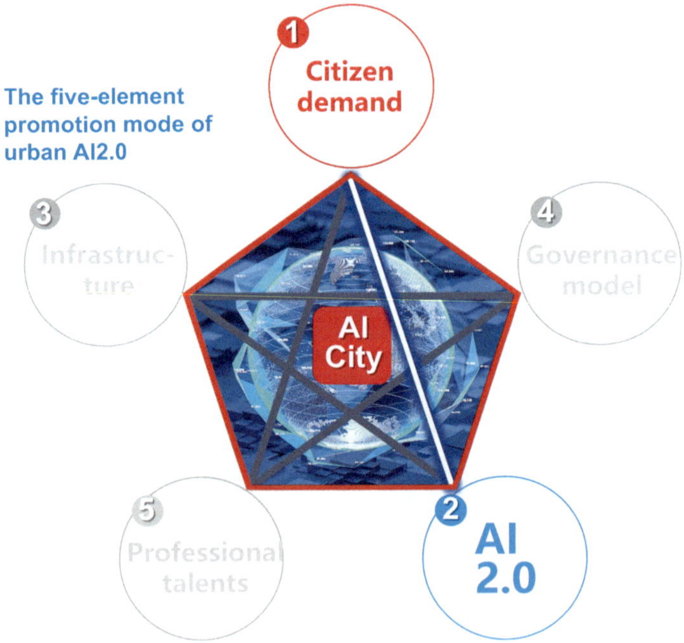

Fig. 13.6 Five-element promotion mode of AI city 2.0 dimension 2: AI 2.0

13.2.1 The New Situation of AI

The development of AI has now entered a new stage (see Fig. 13.7). On July 8, 2017, China issued the "New Generation Artificial Intelligence Development Plan," which stated: "Currently, the overall advancement of disciplines related to the new generation of AI, theoretical modeling, technological innovation, software and hardware upgrades, and so forth, is triggering breakthroughs across the board, accelerating the transformation of various fields of the economy and society from digitization and networking to intelligence." In the current and future periods, AI will become a new focus of international competition, a new engine for economic development, bringing new opportunities to social construction, while its uncertainties will also pose new challenges (see Fig. 13.8).

13.2.2 The AI Technology Maturation Curve

The market research firm Gartner released its annual "Hype Cycle for Emerging Technologies" report in 2019, which highlighted the significant development trends in advanced AI technology during that year.

Advanced analytics under the assistance of AI is a tool that goes beyond traditional business insights, autonomously or semi-autonomously inspecting data or content. This involves the integration of new capabilities brought about by novel algorithms and data science, such as transfer learning, which uses previously trained machine learning models as advanced starting points for new technologies. Advanced analytics capabilities provide deeper insights, predictions, and recommendations. Other technologies in this trend include adaptive machine learning, edge intelligence, edge analytics, explainable AI, AI Platform as a Service (AI PaaS), generative adversarial networks, and graph analytics.

As AI technology continues to mature, it becomes more adept at rapidly and effectively analyzing massive amounts of data, making better decisions, and partially replacing human labor, while also driving the development of other technologies. Undoubtedly, AI will have a tremendous impact on urban development.

Currently, most advanced AI technologies are still in the research and experimental stages, and society as a whole is intensely focused on and discussing them. It will take some time before these technologies are truly implemented. During this period, society is expected to go through a phase of declining interest from its peak, moving toward stabilization. Simultaneously, this will be a valuable phase for effective urban planning and design for the future.

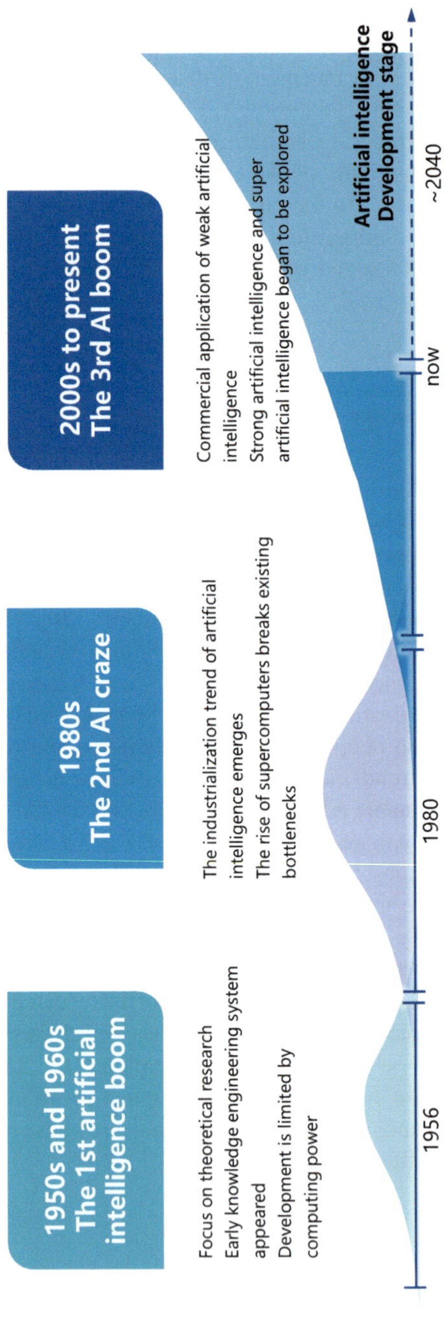

Fig. 13.7 Schematic diagram of the AI development stages

Fig. 13.8 National AI plans of China, the United States, France, and the United Kingdom

13.2.3 *The Development Direction of the Global AI Industry*

At present, the development direction of AI can be classified into two dimensions: vertical by technical types and horizontal by application areas, forming a two-dimensional chart (see Fig. 13.9).

Vertically, technical types can be categorized into the foundational layer, data layer, computing layer, and technological layer. The foundational layer primarily involves intelligent hardware, serving as the tangible carrier of AI technology. This includes chip manufacturing, chip servers, and computing devices. The data

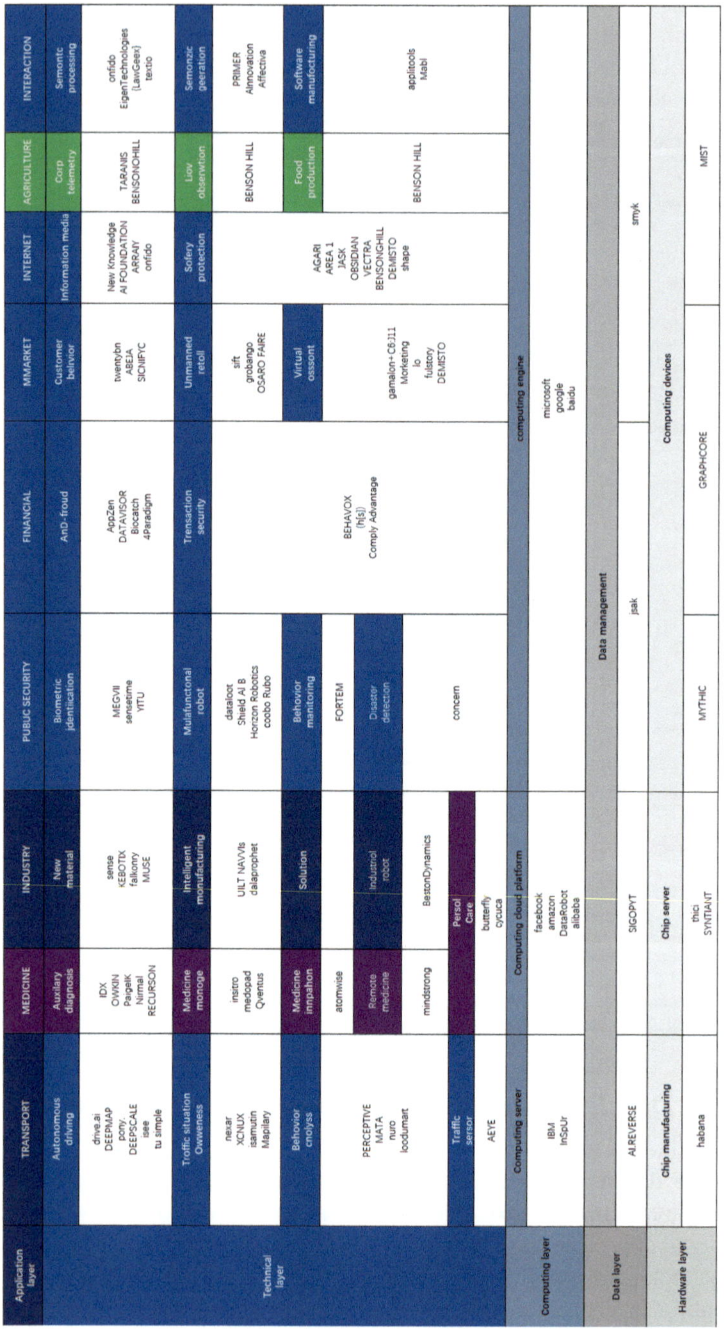

Fig. 13.9 Development direction map of the global AI industry in 2020

layer focuses on management applications, centering on data management. The computing layer pertains to computing platforms, encompassing computing servers, cloud computing platforms, and computing engines. The technological layer serves as the main provider for products, applications, and solutions, constituting the most diverse aspect of the industry.

Specific application areas include transportation, healthcare, industry, public safety, finance, market and retail, cybersecurity, agriculture, and human–computer interaction. Additionally, each domain has its own hotspots and subfields.

13.3 Construction of Intelligent Infrastructure

The technological development of AI 2.0 requires advanced infrastructure as its carrier. The requirements for this carrier are multi-faceted, needing not only to meet the high-dimensional computational support for massive data but also requiring fast, real-time, scenario-linked, and intelligent processing. Consequently, the demands on the infrastructure extend beyond the physical hardware support and become more pressing for the software environment.

As the third element in the five-element advancement model, infrastructure shoulders the requirements of AI 2.0 technology, forming the cornerstone of the entire model (see Fig. 13.10).

13.3.1 Construction of New Infrastructure

From a traditional perspective, infrastructure primarily refers to engineering facilities that provide public services for societal production and residents' daily lives. These are essential for ensuring the normal functioning of social and economic activities at the national or regional level, forming the material foundation upon which society relies for survival and development.

As societal production and lifestyles continue to evolve, traditional infrastructure increasingly fails to meet the demands for efficient social operations, giving rise to the need for new infrastructure.

In December 2018, the Central Economic Work Conference mentioned new infrastructure at the central level for the first time. Subsequent central conferences and work deployments continuously developed and strengthened the concept of new infrastructure. By April 2020, the National Development and Reform Commission (NDRC) clarified the scope of new infrastructure construction. New infrastructure, guided by new development concepts, driven by technological innovation, and based on information networks, aims to meet the needs of high-quality development by providing infrastructure systems that facilitate digital transformation, intelligent upgrades, and integrated innovation.

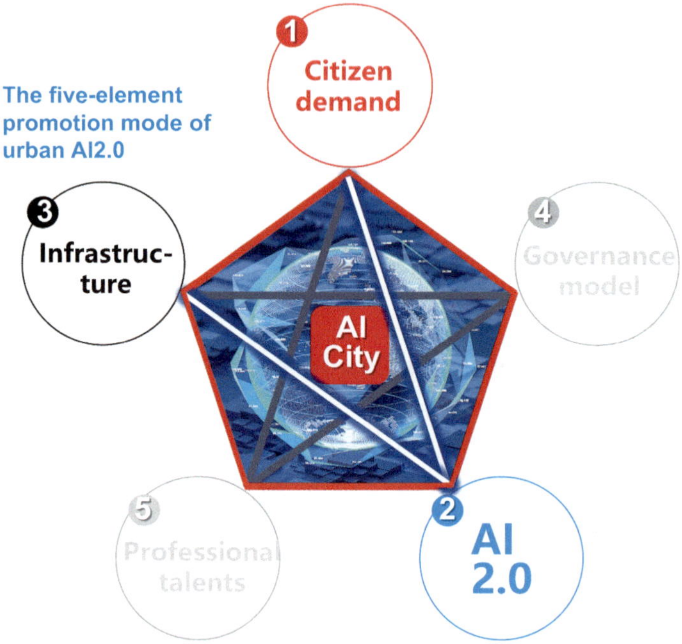

Fig. 13.10 Five-element promotion mode of AI city 2.0 dimension 3: infrastructure

According to the authoritative definition by the NDRC, new infrastructure mainly includes three aspects: information infrastructure, integrated infrastructure, and innovative infrastructure (see Fig. 13.11):

(1) Information infrastructure encompasses communication networks represented by 5G, the IoT, industrial internet, and satellite internet; new technology infrastructure represented by AI, cloud computing, blockchain, etc., and computing infrastructure represented by data centers, intelligent computing centers, etc.
(2) Integrated infrastructure mainly refers to the deep application of internet, big data, AI, and other technologies, supporting the transformation and upgrade of traditional infrastructure, thereby forming new forms of upgraded infrastructure, such as intelligent transportation infrastructure, and smart energy infrastructure.
(3) Innovative infrastructure mainly refers to infrastructure with public welfare attributes that support scientific research, technological development, and product development, such as major scientific infrastructure, science and education infrastructure, and industrial technology innovation infrastructure.

New infrastructure will comprehensively enhance the efficiency and sustainability of societal production and life, promote overall evolution and upgrade, and lay a solid foundation for AI cities with higher intelligence forms.

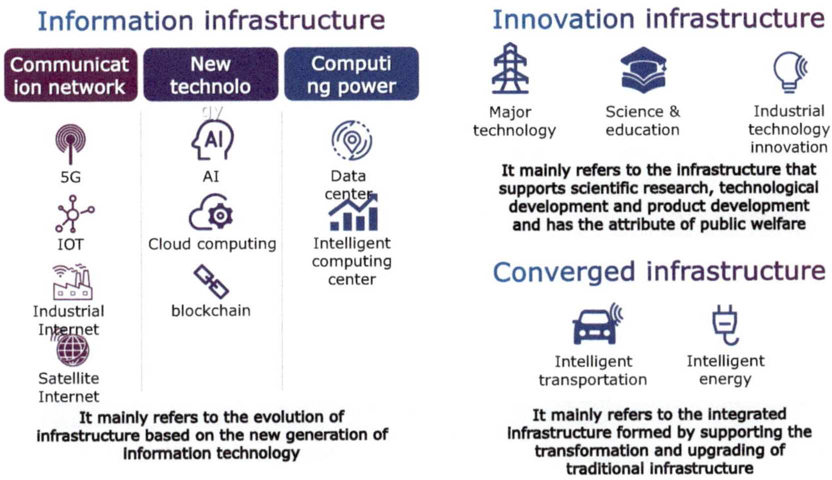

Fig. 13.11 Content of new infrastructure construction

13.3.2 Smart Infrastructure

Smart infrastructure serves as the "hardware" foundation for smart cities. The current architecture of urban infrastructure networks is well established, capable of supporting the normal operation of cities against the backdrop of current technological developments. Infrastructure content primarily includes power supply facilities, water supply facilities, gas supply facilities, sewage facilities, waste disposal facilities, transportation facilities, and ICT facilities.

However, at present and in the foreseeable future, technology is expected to advance significantly. The existing infrastructure systems will increasingly face challenges in adapting to technological developments, necessitating a thorough transition to intelligent solutions.

Currently, the development of 5G technology shows significant potential for application in the infrastructure domain. Optimizing the hardware of infrastructure systems, integrating with 5G base station application programming interfaces, and combining sensor systems in underground, ground, and near-space composite spaces can create a ubiquitous connected network. This facilitates decentralized regulation and central control (see Figs. 13.12, 13.13 and 13.14).

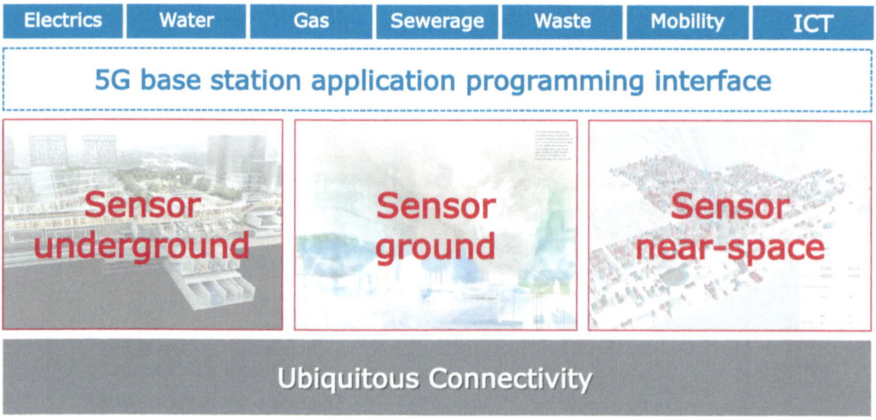

Fig. 13.12 5G-connected three-dimensional urban sensing system

Fig. 13.13 A city sense smart street lamp

13.3.3 Smart Social Service Facilities

On the basis of intelligent infrastructure, it is necessary to improve smart social service facilities to better align with the urbanization of cities. Smart social service facilities need to be supported by urban big databases, upon which diverse functional systems can be constructed.

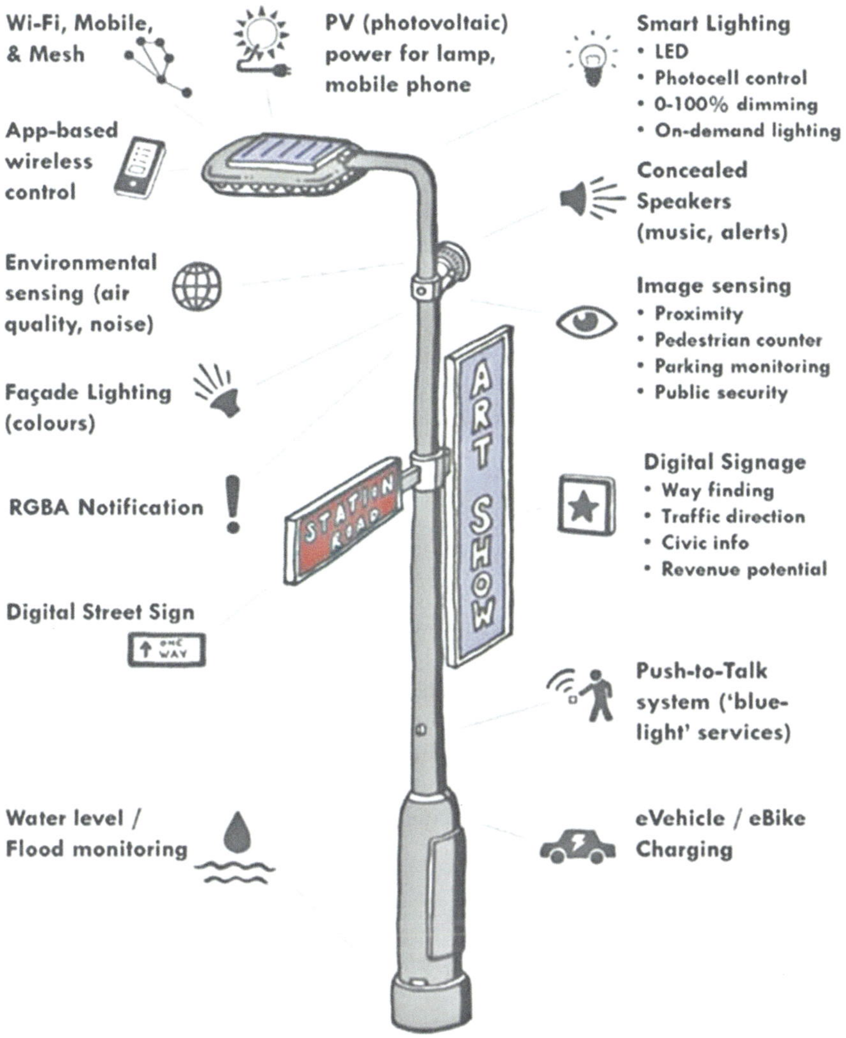

Fig. 13.14 Function diagram of a smart street lamp

(1) Cloud computing center

A cloud computing center is an organization or unit that provides external services such as computing resources and storage resources. It relies on high-performance computers to offer high-performance computing services to various sectors.

(2) Data trading center

    The data trading center, with its comprehensive functions such as member registration audit, de-identification ID recognition, autonomous listing control, and unified settlement and clearing platforms, achieves the aggregated circulation of commercial data-derived products.

(3) Data asset center

    The data asset center facilitates the registration and confirmation of data assets. It values and prices data assets based primarily on market demand intensity and user satisfaction.

(4) Special data consultation center

    The special data consultation center conducts analysis and consultation on specific data, such as the quality level of communities where consultants reside (educational background, personal credit records, etc.), and forecasts trends in housing prices.

13.4 Improvement of the Governance Mode

The urbanization process not only involves technological advances but also continuously presents new challenges that will demand higher standards for urban governance models. The past top-down approach to urban governance will gradually shift toward greater collaboration with participatory governance. Technological advances represented by AI 2.0 will create an intelligent "nervous system" for cities, fostering an environment conducive to collective intelligence. This will lead to more effective clustering of intelligence among cities, enhancing the overall competitiveness of urban clusters (see Fig. 13.15).

13.4.1 Urban Governance Capability

Urban governance capacity is categorized into five levels based on functions:

(1) Baseline Capacity (UG1): The city's ability for secure survival, primarily focused on disaster defense, ensuring the city's safety baseline. This includes capabilities for urban disaster warning, emergency response, and post-disaster recovery.
(2) Mid-lower level capacity (UG2): The city's ability for healthy learning, ensuring the orderly operation of daily production and life, meeting the basic needs of residents, and providing a livable environment.
(3) Mid-upper level capacity (UG3): The city's efficient operational capability, mainly providing unobstructed mobility and efficient economic and social interactions for urban residents.

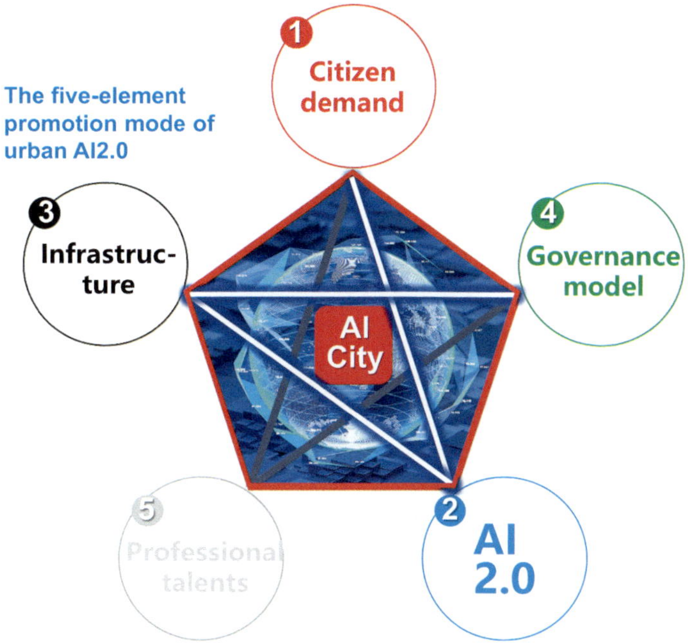

Fig. 13.15 Five-element promotion mode of AI city 2.0 dimension 4: governance mode

(4) High-level capacity (UG4): The city's capability for happiness and innovation, aiming to stimulate residents' innovative abilities in knowledge, technology, industry, culture, and civilizational systems. This involves gaining social respect, individual liberation, and community happiness through multi-dimensional innovation.

(5) Community capacity (UG5): The collaborative governance capability between a city and surrounding community cities. This involves achieving the safety, order, efficiency, and happiness of individual cities through community collaboration (see Fig. 13.16).

13.4.2 AI 2.0 is the New Engine for the Transformation and Development of Intelligent Urban Governance

The increasingly prominent roles of foundational technological resources such as big data, cloud computing, the IoT, and AI indicate a trend toward intelligent innovation driving urban transformation and upgrading. Currently, China's urban development is facing challenges in three major aspects: "dissonance," "disharmony," and "discontinuity" (see Fig. 13.17).

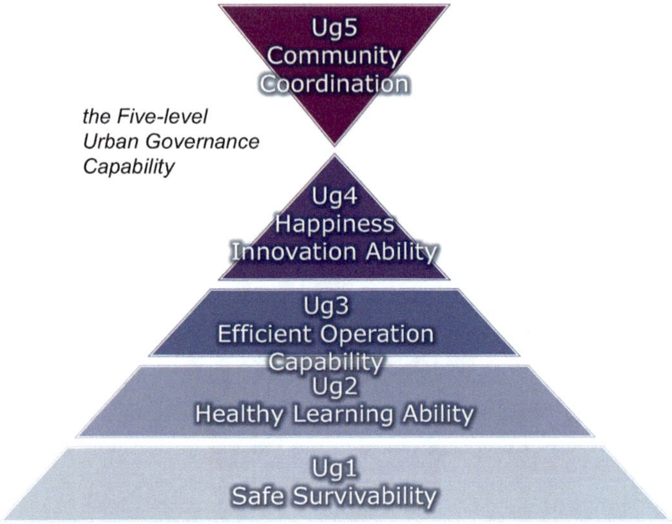

Fig. 13.16 The five levels of urban governance capacity

Simultaneously, the insufficient urban governance capacity is rooted in three aspects—arbitrary decision-making, policy randomness, and information silo management:

(1) The intelligent hardware infrastructure system of point, network, and flow. Intelligent information systems rely on the basic architectural elements of point, network, and flow to support the underlying hardware foundation of smart governance. Within this framework, it can accommodate massive information access, storage, processing, connect to extensive communication networks, and support real-time dynamic data exchange and circulation (see Fig. 13.18).
(2) Constructing the iGOVERNCE (intelligent governance) platform to enhance the city's strategic formulation and policy execution capabilities. Vertically, it integrates government, enterprises, citizens, and other urban governance entities, while horizontally connecting urban economic, social, and environmental governance objects (see Fig. 13.19).
(3) Establishing balanced governance units modeled on the home, serving as the prototype for governance (see Fig. 13.20).
(4) Prioritizing human needs, employing AI prediction technology to enhance urban residents' well-being and jointly create a better city (see Fig. 13.21).
(5) Constructing a collaborative and innovative intelligent network. Globally, urban agglomerations have become growth poles for competitiveness. In the future, China needs to further develop regional urban clusters, aggregating capital, intellectual resources, and talent to generate world-class competitiveness. On December 1, 2019, the Central Committee of the Communist Party of China and the State Council issued the "Outline of the Plan for the Integrated Development

Fig. 13.17 Problems of urban development in China

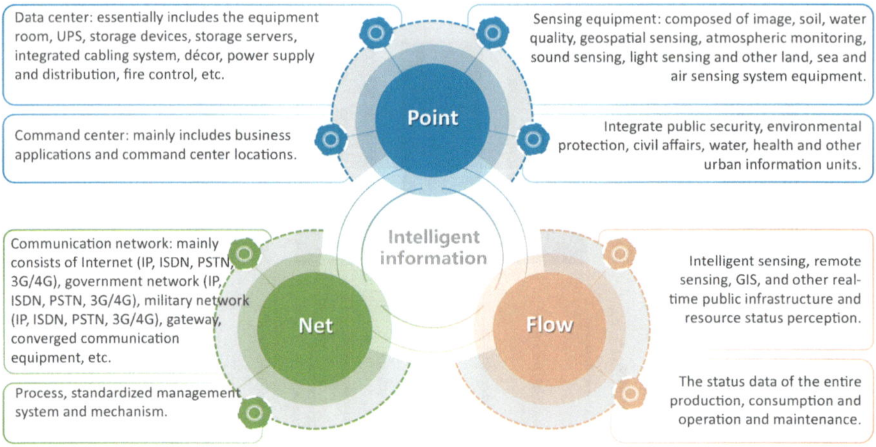

Fig. 13.18 Composition and characteristics of the intelligent information system

	Economy	Society	Environment
Government	Industrial development Employment situation and policy Transportation facilities and policies Infrastructure construction	Development of population Cultural services Public security situation and management Emergency warning response	Resource utilization status Utilization of energy Environmental status and protection Ecological environment construction
Enterprise	Market information Market development trend Industrial policy Location possibility	Labor and social security policies Labor Market conditions Social security and security	Environmental policy provisions The Energy Situation Urban ecological carrying capacity
Citizen	Housing prices and comparison Urban traffic conditions The Job Market Prices of daily necessities	Health care system Safety of blocks Transparency of government management Private property security	Water and air quality Food safety Status of public green space Traffic jams

Fig. 13.19 The urban intelligent governance (iGOVERNCE) platform system

of the Yangtze River Delta Region," clarifying the strategic positioning of the Yangtze River Delta as "one core, three zones, and one high ground," making its position in the national reform and opening up layout clearer. Shanghai, focusing on the goal of high-quality integration in the Yangtze River Delta, will adhere to the development concept of openness, inclusiveness, cooperation, and mutual benefit, leading the Yangtze River Delta region to create a multi-level, all-round, and globally coordinated urban area, becoming a global benchmark for cross-regional infrastructure and shared ecological environment construction (see Fig. 13.22).

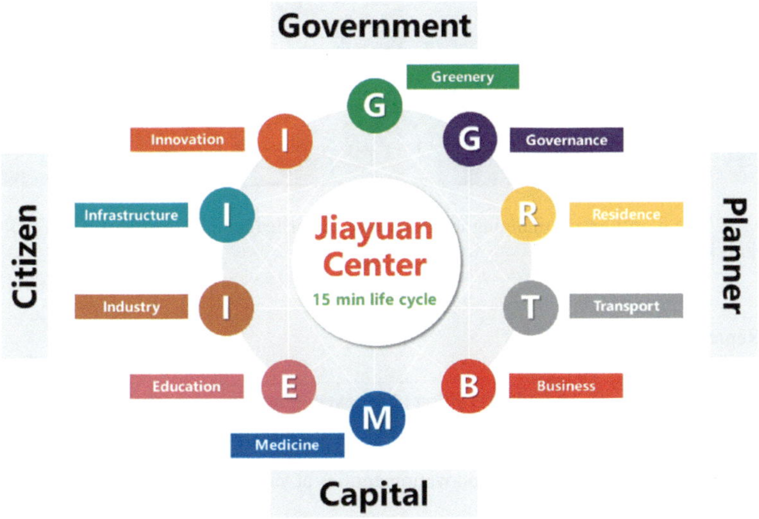

Fig. 13.20 The game model of function layout deduction of meta-space

Fig. 13.21 Functional composite diagram

Fig. 13.22 The world urban planning artificial intelligent league founded at the 2017 Global AI (Shanghai) innovation summit

Representative expert	Opinions
Wu Zhiqiang Academic of Chinese Academy of Engineering	The intelligentization of innovative modes refers to the intelligentization of collaborative innovation modes among people in the workplace. This involves globally searching for, matching, and collaborating with the most sophisticated innovation entities at various professional points

13.4.3 Policy Support and Risk Response

AI cities, although fully integrated with AI technology, are not merely a matter of technical application; rather, they can be explored as a strategic issue in urban development. The future global power will stem from the comprehensive strength of different city clusters, making the internal and external coordination of city clusters increasingly important. The strategic development led by AI cities will escalate from urban development strategies to city cluster strategies and national strategies, and will subsequently influence the rise and fall of global regional power.

(1) The structured policy formulation path

The current urban development has undergone digitization and informatization, entering the era of intelligence, with the advanced stage being AI-equipped cities, or AI cities. Cities in this form are prone to develop higher comprehensive capabilities. AI cities not only have intelligent hardware but also crucially rely on intelligent software. This determines that the construction of AI cities has high requirements for complexity and precision. Policy makers need to coordinate deeply in various important areas and guide the progress appropriately at different stages: building on new infrastructure, establishing a more advanced hardware system improvement path, using urban clusters as a basis to optimize the interaction mechanism of funds, technology, and talent, cultivating a favorable development environment, and enhancing regional competitiveness.

(2) Establishing effective internal and external risk prevention mechanisms

Security in the field of technology is a crucial component of national security. With the accelerated advancement of technological revolution and industrial transformation, new technologies and industries are developing rapidly, significantly impacting economic and social development. Global competition relating to technological innovation is intensifying, and the risks in the field of technology are increasingly significant, necessitating heightened vigilance and effective measures for mitigation. AI cities involve a highly forward-looking conception of future urban states and social forms. Therefore, special attention needs to be given to potential risk factors impacting the core elements of AI cities, including but not limited to the technological and financial sectors.

According to relevant central theoretical research from *People's Daily Online*, the major risks in the current technological field in China that deserve attention include the following:

(i) Risks arising from the tense external environment of technological development.
(ii) Risks of being constrained by others due to inadequate self-capacity in technological development.
(iii) Vulnerability risks generated by technological research and its application.
(iv) Social risks and other risks triggered by technological progress.

(3) Risks of not achieving expected goals in technological development due to factors like economic structural adjustments and insufficient resource allocation.

Cities belong to the people, and any form of risk, if not prevented and mitigated, will ultimately be borne by each individual. Advancing the construction of AI cities requires, as a core starting point for establishing preventive mechanisms, a focus on human-centric risk concerns based on a thorough consideration of the risks in the technological field mentioned above.

13.4.4 The AI City: Exploring Ethical Values Standards in a City

Reviewing the development process of modern cities, in the past six rounds of technological innovation waves (see Fig. 13.23), each technology has faced the issue of "technological benevolence" during its development and application. When technological waves disrupt the existing social order, people's responses usually fall into two categories: one is "making mistakes first and then setting rules," where technology precedes legislation, forcing society to form regulatory mechanisms, while the other is anticipatory, anticipating and establishing guiding mechanisms when certain developments that may have significant future impacts are still in their nascent or potential stages.

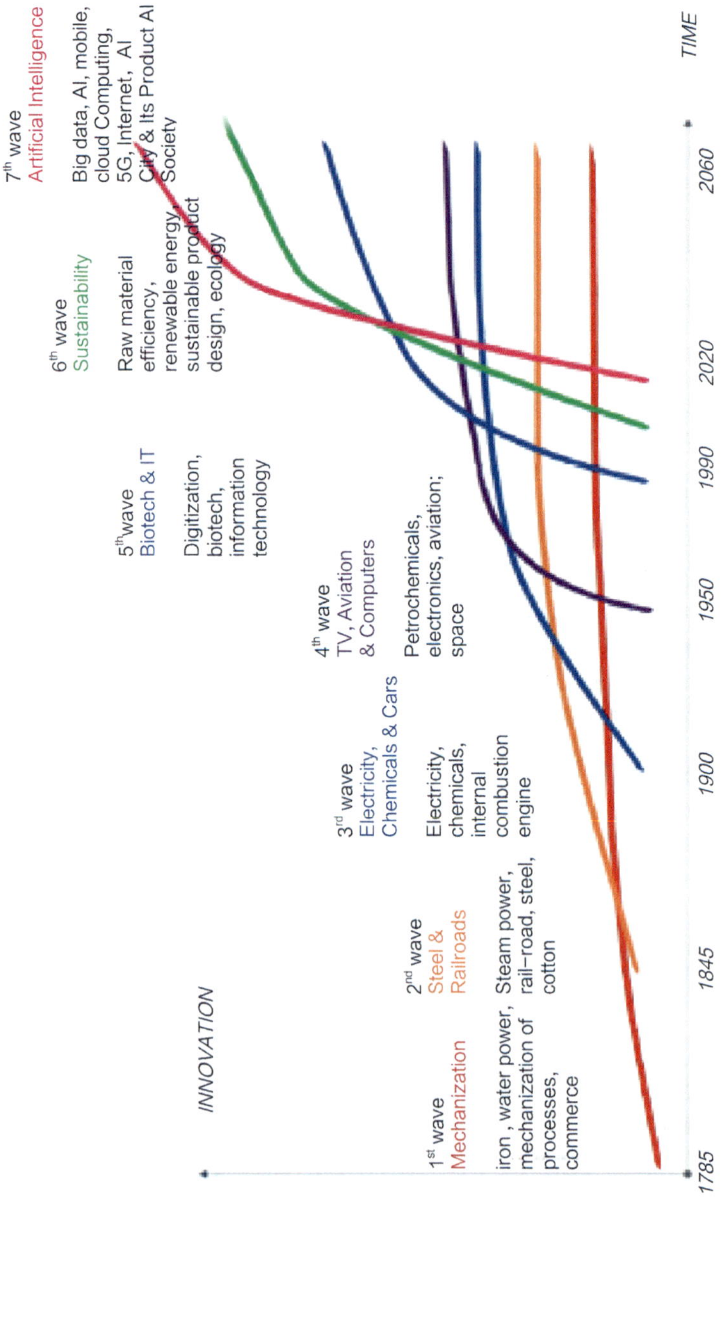

Fig. 13.23 Technological innovation waves

Evidence shows that over the past 150–200 years, modern technology has significantly increased the efficiency of social production and life during its integration into cities, and has also greatly satisfied human desires. However, this process has also been accompanied by crises and the resolution of crises. Today, the potential dangers of AI are greater than they were in the past, because a society constructed with the participation of AI is more prone to impacting individuals' mental and intellectual well-being. Therefore, the fundamental boundary of assessing the involvement of AI in urban construction should be whether it contributes beneficially to a better quality of life or has destructive effects.

Currently, the introduction of AI can generate new functions, assist society in undertaking important tasks such as elderly care and childcare, improving service efficiency and medical standards, and promoting industrial development. However, it is also evident that the improper use of AI may infringe on individuals' privacy, leading to job displacement as companies reduce their reliance on human labor, and reducing people's instinctive judgment of natural disasters (such as fires and earthquakes) as they become accustomed to relying on AI. The potential destruction caused by AI systems in the future could lead to urban paralysis, as well as risks such as data breaches and AI misjudgments. These issues are likely to occur in the near future, and we need to make adequate preparations in advance to address them seriously.

Returning to the benevolence of technology, with a focus on making life, production, and ecosystems better, we should reduce our demands on natural resources, time resources, and social and cultural spiritual resources. This should serve as the baseline standard for our values.

13.5 Cultivation of Innovative Talents

Professional talent is the final link in the five-element advancement model, thus completing the entire "pentagram" structure (see Fig. 13.24). As an intellectual resource for societal development, talent is a crucial requirement at every stage.

13.5.1 AI Education

The "2016 China Internet Education Industry Trends Report" pointed out that internet education will transition from "knowledge output" to integration with "opportunity output," thus meeting the societal demand for talent. It also proposed that leveraging advanced technologies such as big data, cloud computing, and AI on the internet can enhance learning and content production efficiency. By connecting individuals with educational services through efficient platforms, an education ecosystem with the goal of improving efficiency will be formed.

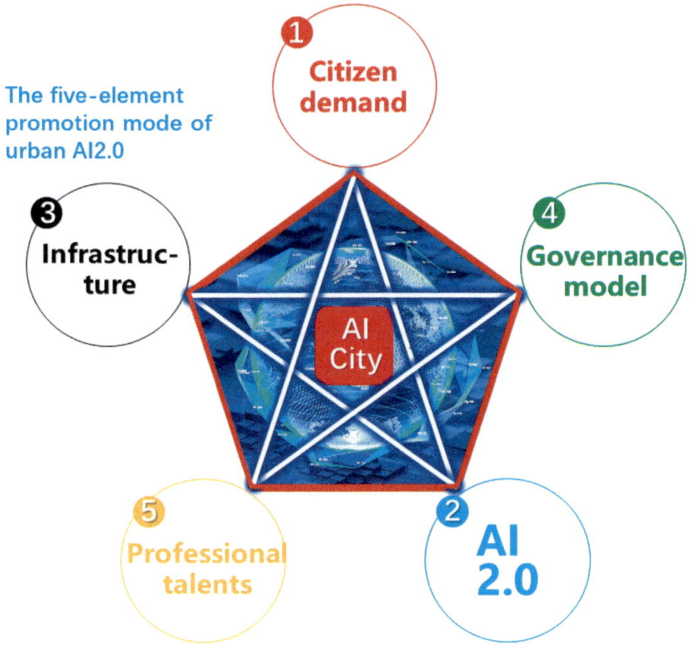

Fig. 13.24 Five-element promotion mode of AI city 2.0 dimension 5: talents

In the future, AI will have a significant impact on the education system, primarily in the following three areas.

(1) Impact on teachers: disruption in teaching methods.

    Any task that involves repetition and has a significant amount of accumulated data can potentially be replaced by AI, posing a challenge to the status of teachers.

(2) Impact on students: disruption in learning methods.

    People's time will become increasingly fragmented, and sources of knowledge will become extremely diverse. Additionally, customized learning will emerge.

(3) Impact on schools: disruption in the education system.

    The value of schools lies not only in imparting knowledge or fostering abilities but also in shaping values. The shaping of values and the cultivation of abilities are often not achievable within the confines of the classroom. The purpose of education is to cultivate a new generation of talents with sound personalities, innovative thinking, global perspectives, and a sense of social responsibility. The efficient services and assistance brought by AI will support the realization of this goal (see Figs. 13.25, 13.26 and 13.27).

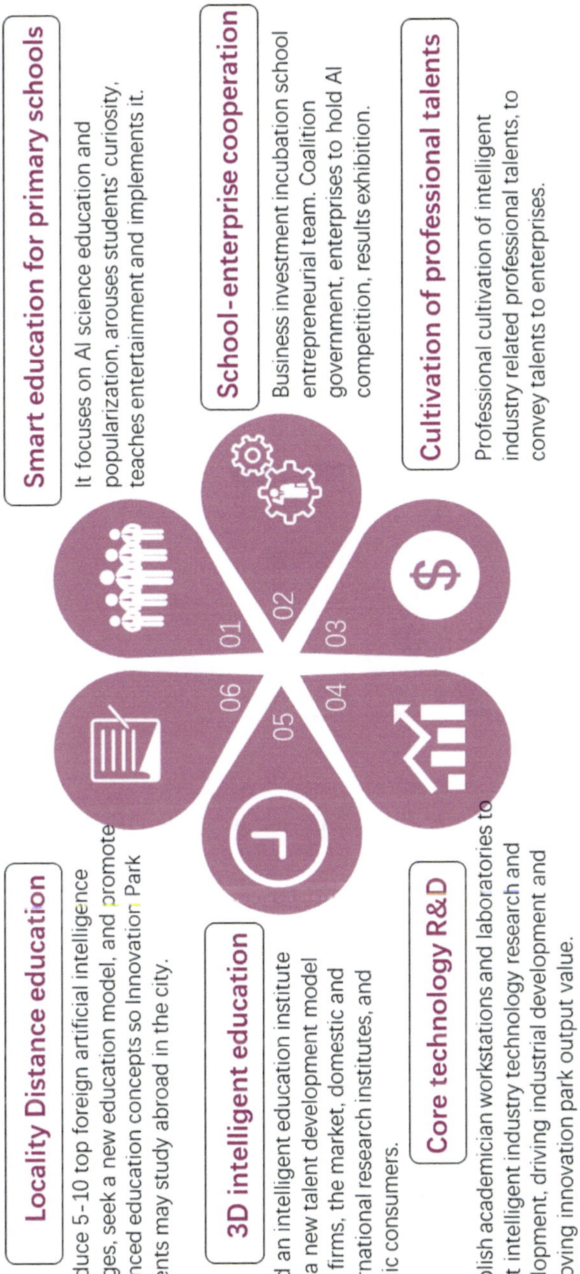

Fig. 13.25 The realization of AI education

Fig. 13.26 The conception of the AI entrepreneur street

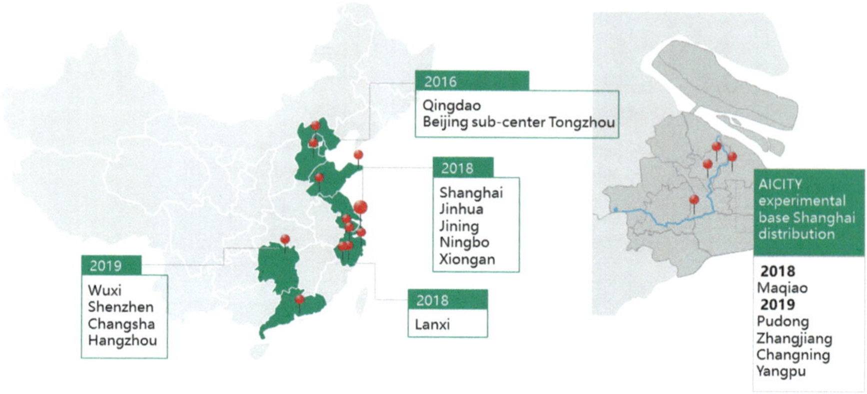

Fig. 13.27 Distribution of the AI city experimental base (as of July 2019)

Representative expert	Opinions
Wu Zhiqiang Academic of Chinese Academy of Engineering	Globalization hasn't ended; rather, a more advanced form of globalization has begun. In the past, it was globalization of material goods, but in the future, globalization will be about the dissemination of ideas and educational strategies

13.5.2 Practical Applications of AI Talent Services

Innovation talents are strategic resources for China's future proactive international competitiveness and are also fundamental conditions for building AI cities. Therefore, efforts should be made to attract and gather excellent talents around the core, focusing on strengthening the cultivation of elements such as the production and living environment, policies, etc., required by innovative talents, and emphasizing the creation of vibrant work and living spaces. Starting from three aspects—the construction of innovation and entrepreneurship spaces, the housing needs of innovative talents, and the quality of life requirements for young talents—optimizes the production and living environment of innovative talents in cities and provides them with a comprehensive spatial security system. The following sections elaborate on the key technologies and foundational support required to implement these talent services effectively.

(1) Key technologies for the implementation of talent services. Under the current conditions of technological development, the key technologies that can be applied mainly include machine learning, computer vision, and natural language processing. Depending on different sub-application scenarios, these technologies have strong adaptability and penetrability. Compared to the past, the most significant improvement brought by AI technology is the direct interaction between humans and the environment, and these interactions are developing in more complex and advanced directions (see Fig. 13.28).
(2) Basic support for the implementation of talent services. The core of basic support lies in the ability to provide data and computing power. Achieving these two goals involves cooperation in areas such as sensors, chips, industry data, data services, biometrics, and cloud computing.

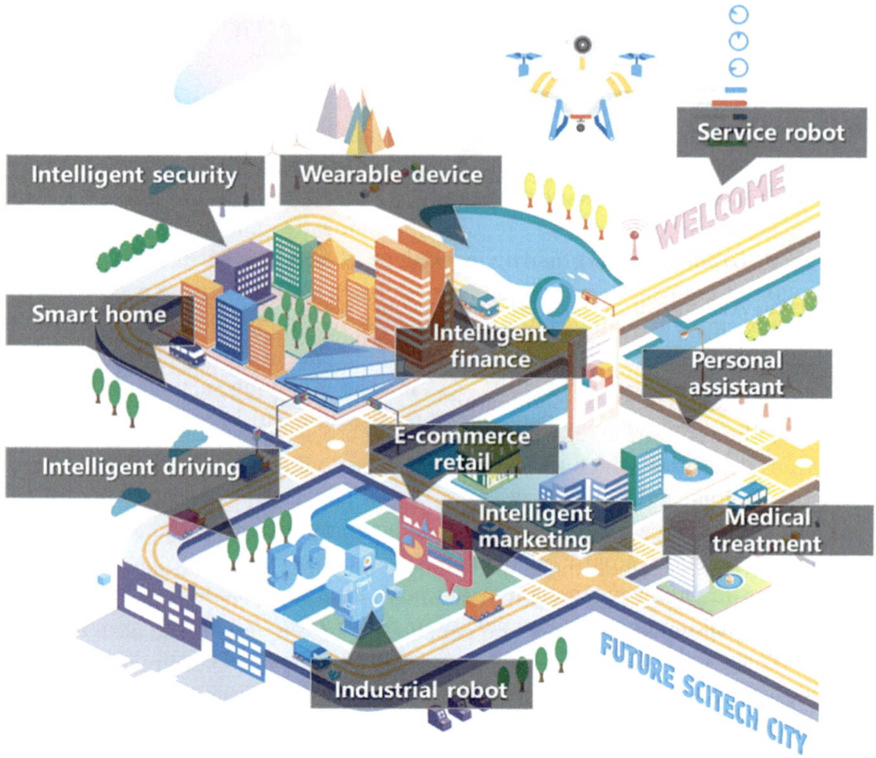

Fig. 13.28 The application of AI talent services in specialized industries

Chapter 14
The Opportunities and Challenges of Constructing AI Cities in China

Abstract China's urbanization process has entered its advanced stages, marked by a rapid increase in the urbanization rate and the maturation of urban agglomerations, which provide a robust foundation for the development of AI cities. By 2023, the urbanization rate of permanent residents had reached 66.2%, while China's AI market is experiencing exponential growth. The core industry is projected to reach 400 billion yuan by 2025 and surpass 1 trillion yuan by 2030. Despite these advances, the construction of AI cities still encounters significant challenges, such as the absence of efficient hierarchical decision-making systems and highly intelligent self-organizing capabilities. Additionally, intelligent infrastructure remains in the early stages of addressing data silos and model development. As technology continues to evolve and market demand expands, the development of AI cities should prioritize human-centric, demand-driven approaches, fostering positive interactions between technological innovation and social progress, and breaking down barriers to both technological and societal advances.

Keywords AI city · Urbanization · Data island · Technology and social innovation

14.1 China's Foundation for the Development of AI Cities

14.1.1 Urbanization and City Construction

China's urbanization development can be divided into four stages, and it is now in the second half of urbanization construction (see Fig. 14.1). From 1978 to 2023, the urbanization rate of China's permanent residents increased from 17.9 to 66.2%. Throughout the world's urban development process, the urbanization rate of 65% is the key point to determine the urbanization road to "intellectual" or "physical" development, and China is currently standing at the fork of the two urbanization roads. At this stage, China has completed the urbanization of most areas quantitatively, and can explore the existing experience in urban construction to assist the top-level design of AI cities. At the same time, before the urbanization rate eventually reaches

Z. WU, *The AI City*, The Urban Book Series,
https://doi.org/10.1007/978-981-96-2560-4_14

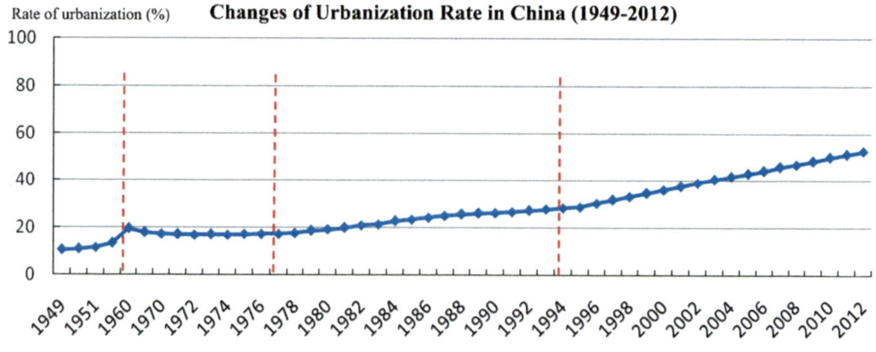

Fig. 14.1 The trend of China's urbanization rate from 1949 to 2021

80–90%, China can explore, develop, cultivate, apply, feedback, and optimize the development ideas and construction technologies of AI cities.

In addition, at present, the pattern of urban agglomerations in China is gradually taking shape, and the importance of connections between and within urban groups is becoming increasingly significant. Cities are no longer homogenous, but have distinct positioning, unique characteristics, and complement each other. At present, China has at least three world-class urban agglomerations: the Beijing-Tianjin-Hebei, Yangtze River Delta, and Pearl River Delta urban agglomerations. Such rich urban community resources are rare in other countries in the world. AI cities have the characteristics of continuous self-learning, and the stratification and diversification of Chinese cities are conducive to the sustainable development of AI city concept.

14.1.2 Industrial Development

At present, China's AI market is growing rapidly, and the industrial application of AI is booming. According to the national plan launched by the Chinese government, the scale of China's core AI industry will increase to 400 billion yuan in 2025 and is expected to exceed one trillion yuan in 2030. AI innovation and entrepreneurship are also increasingly active, and a number of leading backbone enterprises are growing rapidly. According to statistics, the number of AI enterprises, the number of patent applications and the scale of financing in China are second only to the United States in the world. Among the world's 100 most noteworthy AI enterprises, there are 27 in China, among which Tencent, Alibaba Cloud, Baidu, and iFlytek have become global leaders in the field of AI. The accelerated accumulation of technical capabilities combined with massive data resources, huge application demands, and open market environment has formed a unique advantage in the development of AI in China. Many scientific and creative enterprises are rooted in the urban environment, and their technology research and development and application form a virtuous circle of "from the city to the city," which continuously provides a source of vitality for the bottom-up vigorous growth of China's AI city construction.

14.1.3 Scientific and Technological Talents

Universities and scientific research institutions are the main carriers of AI talents, and China attaches great importance to the cultivation of talents in the field of AI. According to statistics, from 1998 to 2018, China published a total of 134,000 papers in the field of AI, ranking first globally, while the United States ranked second with 106,000 papers. China surpassed the United States in the number of highly cited papers to become the world leader in 2013. As of 2017, the number of AI talents in China reached 18,232, accounting for 8.9% of the world's total, second only to the United States (13.9%). In March 2019, the Ministry of Education officially issued a notice that the AI major was included in the list of newly approved undergraduate majors, and a total of 35 universities across the country obtained the first batch of construction qualifications. China is gradually strengthening forward-looking basic research on AI, actively cultivating talents in the field of AI with international influence, and gathering scientific research strength to provide scientific research strength guarantees for the further deep integration of AI and related cross-fields. As a highly intelligent urban development form, AI city needs a gradual construction process, and talents in related professional fields can be promoted as the backbone to achieve rapid development.

14.2 The Challenges of Constructing AI Cities in China

14.2.1 The Construction of AI Cities is Still in Its Infancy

China's smart city system architecture is a centralized structure; all urban operation data and sensor data will be sent to the city's big data and cloud computing center for collection and analysis, and unified scheduling of the entire city's operations. However, due to the lack of a hierarchical decision-making system, the city does not have the ability to conduct comprehensive regulation and management.

At the same time, China's urban intelligent construction is in its early stages, focusing on the elimination of data islands, data perception collection, and data analysis model construction, which is far from the self-organized, learnable and iterable highly intelligent urban development form (see Fig. 14.2).

In addition, looking back at the development process of urban intelligence in China, the construction of new cities has almost universally served as the carrier. The advantages of this method are similar to creating on a piece of blank canvas, which can fully realize the original intelligent design concept (China Academy of

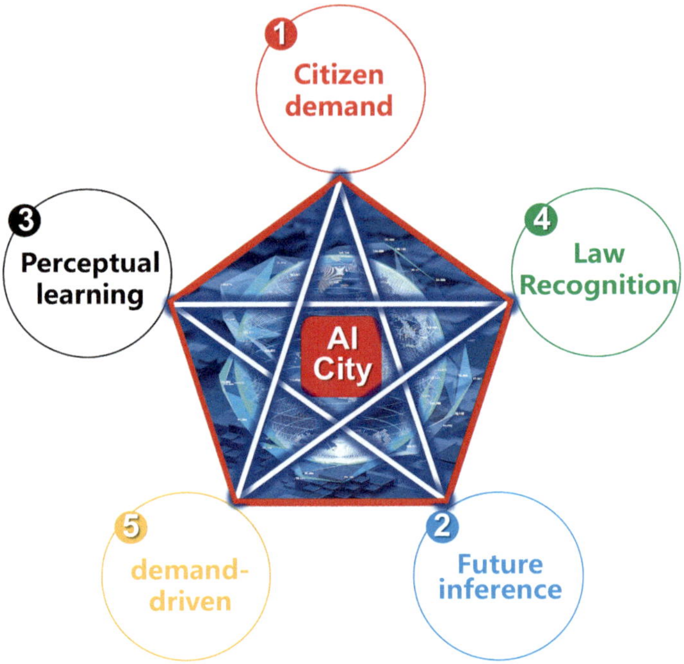

Fig. 14.2 Five elements of the AI city

Sciences Key Laboratory of Big Data Mining and Knowledge Management 2020). The disadvantage is also on this blank canvas, the lack of human needs as a driver, intelligent design is easily divorced from the actual situation. When adjustments need to be made after large-scale implementation, it is easy to face the dilemma of high sunk costs.

14.2.2 AI Cities Need to Be Able to Continuously Adapt to the Rapid Iteration of Technology

At this stage, the innovation cycle of science and technology is short and efficient, and it has entered an era of continuous outbreak of new technologies. The construction of the AI city will involve integrating technologies at various developmental stages: embryonic-phase innovations like the metaverse, generative AI, and autonomous systems; expectation-expansion technologies such as super APP and basic models; and trough-phase technologies including. All of these will be progressively incorporated alongside rapid technological updates. In the future, technological change will continue, so AI cities cannot be static; they must have the ability to continuously and effectively absorb new technologies. Yet, at the same time, AI cities also need to be robust, able to selectively screen and optimize AI technology, and make it fully integrated into human society. Managing the rhythmic interaction between AI cities and AI technologies is a key challenge.

14.2.3 The Construction of AI City Needs the Collaboration of Industry, Education, Research, and Government

The development process of China's smart city is oriented by the technology supply of enterprises, focusing on the input of information software and hardware, and implementing the design concept "top-down" without feedback from the demand level of the city itself. In the future, AI cities need to be jointly built by the whole society; it is not a project, or a series of projects, but involves all aspects of urban development and needs to be integrated with the overall strategy of urban development. The construction of AI cities cannot only rely on the execution of the "top-down" top-level design, but must also stimulate the collaborative innovation of scientific and technological enterprises, universities, scientific research institutions, and local governments, and promote the intelligence of the whole life cycle of planning, construction, management, and operation from the bottom up.

14.2.4 The Needs of AI Cities and People Are not yet Connected

The development of AI cities can learn lessons from the construction of smart cities. In the past, smart city development followed a product technology supply-oriented approach, prioritizing hardware and software investments and the development of various platforms, while public communication and participation remained inadequate. This resulted in passive public acceptance of smart applications and services, deviating from the fundamental needs of cities and citizens.

The development of the AI city is a new path to solve a series of problems such as people's production, life, economy, society and environment, which will be a long-term and complex large-scale systematic work. However, relying solely on technology-oriented and project-driven approaches is insufficient to establish fundamental driving forces. The development of the AI city in the future will be driven by the needs of people, giving each part of the city the vitality of self-perception, self-diagnosis, and self-optimization. Urban demand is the concentrated embodiment of human needs; unlike the past technology "equipped" city, the AI city can spontaneously be based on different levels of urban needs for technology selection, effectively optimize the development of science and technology pattern, and promote the complementary relationship between social progress and technological advancement.

Representative expert	Opinions
WU Zhiqiang Academic of Chinese Academy of Engineering	The construction of the AI city plays an important role in the development and evolution of cities. AI cities can realize the self-organization evolution process of continuous learning and iteration to provide a better life for people; they can break through the governance model that is difficult to complete by a single system of traditional smart cities and combine top-down and bottom-up, thus improving the efficiency of social organizations. The introduction of the new generation of AI technology supporting the urban life, production, ecology, and safe operation has broad possibilities, and requires more research and participation of social subjects in the future

Reference

China Academy of Sciences Key Laboratory of Big Data Mining and Knowledge Management (2020) 2019 artificial intelligence development white paper. https://pdf.dfcfw.com/pdf/H3_AP202001171374280695_1.pdf

Chapter 15
Emerging Next-Generation AI Techniques

Abstract This chapter delves into the application of next-generation AI technologies in smart city design, with a particular focus on advances in intelligence, emotional intelligence, and aesthetic intelligence. Intelligence creation fosters innovation in urban design by leveraging machine learning to support human creativity and enhance intelligent design through the integration of physical and digital analog technologies. Emotional intelligence emphasizes the emotional dimension of city life, utilizing AI to perceive citizen emotions and establish feedback mechanisms that provide more personalized services. Aesthetic intelligence investigates how machines can understand and create beauty, driving new breakthroughs in art creation via computational aesthetics and image-generating models such as OpenAI's DALL·E2. Additionally, this chapter explores innovative approaches to future smart city design, highlighting the integration of physical and virtual simulation technologies, the application of AI algorithms in design processes, and the significance of emotion and aesthetics in urban development to offer comprehensive optimization and personalized services for smart cities.

Keywords Creative intelligence · Emotional intelligence · Aesthetic intelligence · Smart city design · AI and urban innovation

15.1 Creative Intelligence

15.1.1 The Intelligentization of Future Creation

Unlike animals' creativity, a city is the product of people's creative efforts at every stage, a form of innovative construction. The creative process for a city is an intentional act of creation by humans for their own world, encompassing living, production, and the ecological environment. The current development of AI technology emphasizes intelligent assistance, learning from humans, helping humans, and supporting humans, rather than artificially created intelligence. The most promising area for the next generation of AI is creative intelligence, which is the opposite of

Z. WU, *The AI City*, The Urban Book Series,
https://doi.org/10.1007/978-981-96-2560-4_15

AI. In the past, results were known through deduction, but now, any result that can be deduced is deemed unnecessary. Instead, we train the machine's creative intelligence and empower people in the creative process of their own urban life.

For example, Google proposed the Video Diffusion Models, which significantly outperform the previous state-of-the-art (SOTA) models for unconditional video generation. This model is an extension of the standard image diffusion model, Unet. Unet is a neural network architecture that consists of a spatial downsampling pathway and an upsampling pathway, connected through residuals.

15.1.2 City Creation

(1) *Physical form*

The intelligent simulation's physical approach is based on the design of tangible models. When one or more blocks in the model are altered or rotated, it provides a visual feedback on the accessibility, the shadow coverage, and other environmental adaptability indicators. The application of modern technology has further enhanced this design-based physical approach. An experimental product known as the "Smart Simulation Desk" has been utilized in research projects at the Urban Simulation Laboratory of the Polytechnic University of Milan in Italy and other research institutions. The concept of the simulation desk originates from the most primitive design methods, manipulating models to explore solutions. The "Simulation Desk" working principle involves placing a tangible planning model on a real desk and evaluating the environmental impact on the model through movable light sources, small fans, and other micro-environment simulation devices. As the model evolves, the outcomes generated by the simulation device also change accordingly. These changes are visually presented to the designer through feedback, allowing them to refine solutions more accurately based on environmental influences.

(B) *Digital form*

In digital form, the simulation table serves as an interactive creative platform for design proposals. Using computer software, virtual models of the proposed design are created, with real-time simulation and analysis of environmental indicators conducted concurrently. In contrast to physical methods, digital intelligent simulation replaces tangible models with virtual two-dimensional or three-dimensional models. It also substitutes real-time analytical images for the visual feedback of physical models, reducing the need for small-scale simulation devices and introducing computer-assisted software technology. Moreover, digital methods enable the calculation of comprehensive indicator systems through relevant software, providing insights into the attributes behind the material space of the urban environment.

MIT Media Lab integrates LEGO models with computer-assisted systems in the development of the CityScope platform. This platform embodies the concept of shared and interactive urban planning, utilizing a tangible digital platform to address challenges in spatial design and city planning. This includes quantifying simulations of interventions on urban impacts and collaborative applications in the planning process.

The ideal model for future intelligent simulation methods involves a combination of physical and virtual approaches. On the one hand, designers can shape spatial models (either physical or virtual) through manual manipulation. On the other hand, digital methods can simulate environmental indicators and provide feedback on evaluation results. Two key technologies support this intelligent simulation in a comprehensive approach. The first technology is the IoT sensor technology, which establishes a connection between real models and virtual information through sensing devices, collecting tangible information into the computer in a data-driven manner. The second technology is Holographic 3D projection technology, which enables human–machine interaction by interchangeably converting real and virtual information through holographic projections.

15.1.3 Future Intelligent Urban Creative Platforms

Urban design creation is a complex iterative process involving stages such as current situation analysis, case references, design conceptualization, solution validation, feedback collection, and outcome production. Future AI algorithms can play a more significant role in the urban design process, breaking free from the limitations imposed by the designer's cognitive inertia and enhancing design outcomes (see Fig. 15.1).

For instance, in current situation analysis, algorithms incorporating deep learning and cross-media data fusion can be employed to explore local data features. In the process of design conceptualization, AI can autonomously propose solutions to designers, fostering collaborative creativity between humans and machines. Consequently, AI algorithms have the potential to introduce a fresh perspective to urban design.

Building on AI algorithms, the author envisions an intelligent platform for urban design. Future AI algorithms can assist in the creative process on a spatio-temporal platform, transitioning from creation supported by a small amount of information to that supported by vast details. This evolution includes the shift from low intelligence to human-AI interaction, from individual offline wisdom to online collective intelligence, and from goal-oriented to process innovation in the urban design creation process.

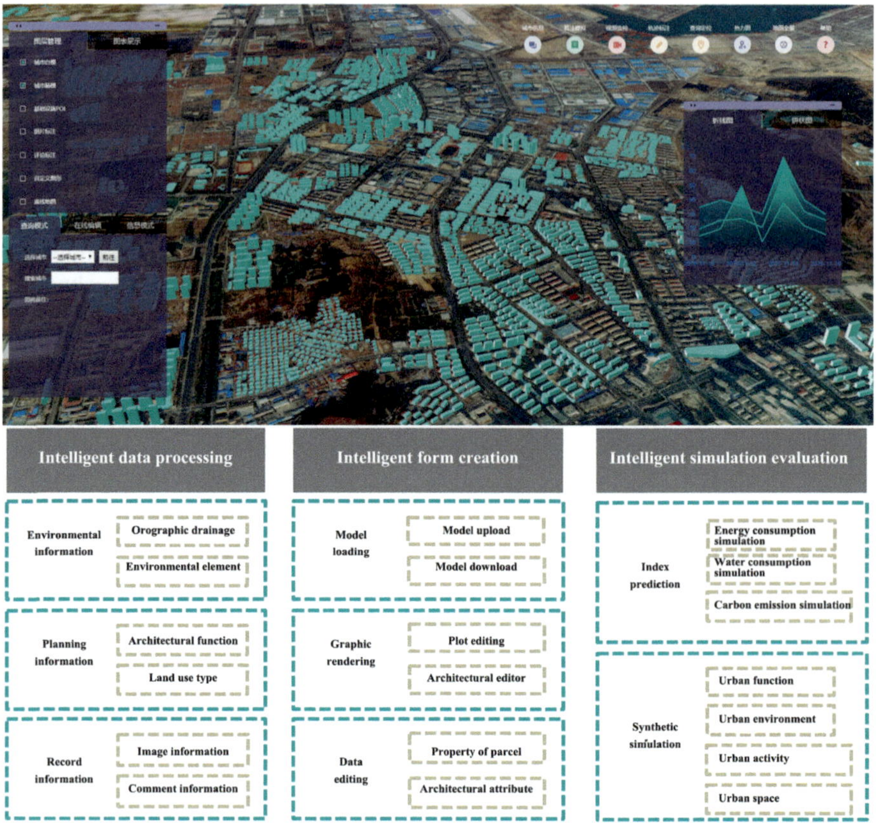

Fig. 15.1 The prototype of future intelligent planning

Representative expert	Opinions
WU Zhiqiang Academic of Chinese Academy of Engineering	In the creative process of urban design, the most fundamental philosophical question lies in the distinction between "planning" and "design." Anything that lacks innovation and has already been done by predecessors cannot be called design. This differentiation hinges on the essential elements of the two; design, in contrast to planning, prioritizes uniqueness before considering factors like rationality and acceptability. Conversely, planning follows established patterns—what others have done and validated as reliable and repeatable—but design cannot be replicated

The essence of creating intelligence involves breaking established rules after learning them. It represents a form of AI that goes against the grain. Creative intelligence does not adhere to set rules; anything with a rule is rejected by the computer. It relies on case-based reasoning, learning from a global pool of cases to assess and eliminate design proposals that replicate existing cases. The core focus lies in using

AI to assist designers in eliminating globally documented cases, emphasizing that true design involves something that has not been done before.

15.2 Emotional Intelligence

For a smart city, having only "IQ" (intelligence quotient) is not enough; "EQ" (emotional quotient) is equally essential. Without either, the abundant data generated and accumulated in urban life may either remain dormant and isolated or be used solely for data management without truly serving the people. In the concept of an AI-driven city, emotional intelligence refers to utilizing technological means to better perceive the emotions of citizens in the era of the "Big Wisdom Cloud." This involves actively expressing urban sentiment, self-driving and motivating the emotions of citizen communities, empathizing with the vulnerable in the city, and establishing a comprehensive sentiment feedback mechanism. This is the fundamental measure for the future development of Chinese cities, which is focused on the people.

A study from Imperial College London and Samsung introduces a generative adversarial network (GAN) with temporal characteristics. This network can generate a video by using a static facial image and a speech recording. It captures changes in the speaker's emotions, reflecting them in facial changes through the movement of lips and muscles.

Representative expert	Opinions
LI Shipeng	AI can be defined at six levels: common intelligence, computing intelligence, sensory intelligence, cognitive intelligence, predictive intelligence, and decision intelligence. The most crucial core is data to achieve intelligence from the foundational to the advanced levels. Currently, iFlytek has achieved maturity in foundational intelligence, including technologies such as speech synthesis, speech recognition (including dialect recognition), facial recognition, scene recognition, and medical image analysis, earning high awards in various competitions

Speech synthesis is a potent yet potentially risky technology, and iFlytek includes its watermark in the synthesized speech to distinguish between human and machine-generated voices. AI can help break language barriers by facilitating human–computer interaction and overcoming communication barriers between people.

In breaking barriers in human–computer communication, iFlytek collaborated with Haidilao to introduce robot customer service. In breaking barriers in human–human interaction, iFlytek introduced the iFlytek Translator to overcome language barriers during travel. In meetings, speech content can be converted into text with real-time Chinese-English translation. iFlytek's intelligent recording pen can convert real-time recording into text within 8–10 s, with real-time translation capability. Intelligent office tools can convert audio to text.

Minsky suggests that by studying various forms of mental activities, we can explain the reasons behind our thinking being sometimes analytically cautious and at other times emotionally influenced. This illustrates how our minds evolve from simple instinctive thinking to more complex forms, such as consciousness and self-awareness. He believes that because we tend to view our thinking as a step-by-step process, we fail to appreciate how exceptional thinkers we are.

In fact, if thinking can be understood as a step-by-step process, we can construct a kind of machine (AI) that not only assists us in thinking similarly but also has the potential to develop consciousness similar to ours.

15.3 Aesthetics Intelligence

15.3.1 Computational Aesthetics

If machines can begin to understand and influence our perception of beauty, it is crucial to find better methods in the design process to actualize these aesthetic perceptions. When machines learn to design, collaboration with AI should enrich urban development practices through aesthetic and creative thinking. Beyond enhancing productivity, this collaboration can also reconsider residents' lifestyles and the shaping of the architectural environment.

In the study of computational aesthetics, enabling computers or robots to "discover beauty" and "understand beauty" is currently the most active research topic and the first step in aesthetic intelligence research. Since visual aesthetics is a subjective attribute often involving emotions and personal taste, automatically assessing aesthetic quality becomes a highly subjective task. However, consensus can often be reached that certain combinations of features are visually more attractive than others. This is one of the principles of the emerging research field—computational aesthetics. Computational aesthetics explores how to use computational techniques to predict emotional responses generated by human perceptions, allowing computers to mimic human aesthetic processes and automatically predict urban aesthetic quality using computational methods.

15.3.2 Graphic Art: OpenAI DALL·E2

OpenAI is a non-profit organization founded by several Silicon Valley and Seattle technology tycoons. In 2015, after continuous discussions between Elon Musk and other tech giants in Silicon Valley and Seattle, they decided to jointly establish

OpenAI with the goal of preventing catastrophic impacts of AI and promoting its positive role.

DALL·E 2 is a remarkable cross-modal generation model with independent creativity. Unlike previous AI technologies like CycleGAN, which can switch to cartoon style with a single click, or Partialconv, which automatically repairs images, these technologies could only generate and imitate either images or text in a single mode. However, the ability of DALL·E 2 to convert text into images or even modify pictures based on text, showcasing a form of "imagination," represents an innovative breakthrough.

The results from DALL·E 2 indicate that its associative ability is approaching that of a six-year-old child, and its artistic processing, especially its Photoshop (PS) capabilities, has reached the peak level of human designers. With the continued expansion of parameter scales in the future, DALL·E 2 hints at limitless possibilities for DALL·E 3, prompting further exploration of the boundaries of AI.

15.4 The Intelligent Creative Cluster

15.4.1 Intelligent Automation of Common Issues

Distinguished from narrow AI that can only handle specific tasks, general AI emphasizes the capability to deal with common problems. The exploration of general AI makes optimizing and solving various issues possible using the same model. For instance, a study from Google Brain introduced a neural architecture search technique to construct neural networks capable of directly performing various reinforcement learning and supervised learning tasks without the need for training and tuning.

In an urban context, continuous collection of real-time data on the complete state of the city and the human-defined definition of urban problems could enable AI cities to utilize general AI technology to build a new generation of city models with general intelligent behaviors. These models could record and learn from massive urban data, predict various problems emerging in city operations, and autonomously adjust and optimize the city's "form" and "flow" states. The ultimate goal is to optimize the overall operation of the city, achieving spontaneous exploration and automatic fulfillment of human needs in an AI city.

15.4.2 Case Study: The iCity Intelligent Urban Knowledge Service System

iCity, short for "Intelligent City Knowledge Service System," is a part of the International Knowledge Centre for Engineering Sciences and Technology (IKCEST), jointly initiated by the Chinese Academy of Engineering and the United Nations

Educational, Scientific and Cultural Organization (UNESCO). Focused on the realm of smart city development, iCity provides data knowledge services for global professionals in the field of smart cities and plays a crucial role in supporting the construction of smart cities in China.

The overarching goals of iCity are as follows:

(1) Database resource construction: To establish a world-class database resource library related to intelligent cities. This database includes, but is not limited to, urban basic data, practical cases, CityIQ databases, planning industry news, scholar networks, research hotspots, and planning education courses. The aim is to provide information and updates on smart city construction for the public, students, scholars, and experts.
(2) Smart city knowledge application services: Leveraging the construction of various resources such as databases and the support of talents from planning institutions and research organizations, iCity aims to provide services such as discovering urban patterns, diagnosing urban issues, and offering methods for urban planning and future city scenarios. This long-term vision aims to provide scientific and robust support for the future development of smart cities.
(3) Popularizing smart city knowledge education: Building on existing educational resources, faculty expertise, and academic and technological achievements, iCity collaborates with various resources to establish a platform for systematic learning of smart city knowledge. This platform aims to serve engineering and technical professionals, students, as well as practitioners and researchers in related fields from Third World countries. iCity aspires to become a global leader in promoting smart city knowledge.

The overall structure of iCity comprises two main components: the World Observatory of Cities (WOC) and World Knowledge for Urban Planning and Education (WUP), as depicted in Fig. 15.2.

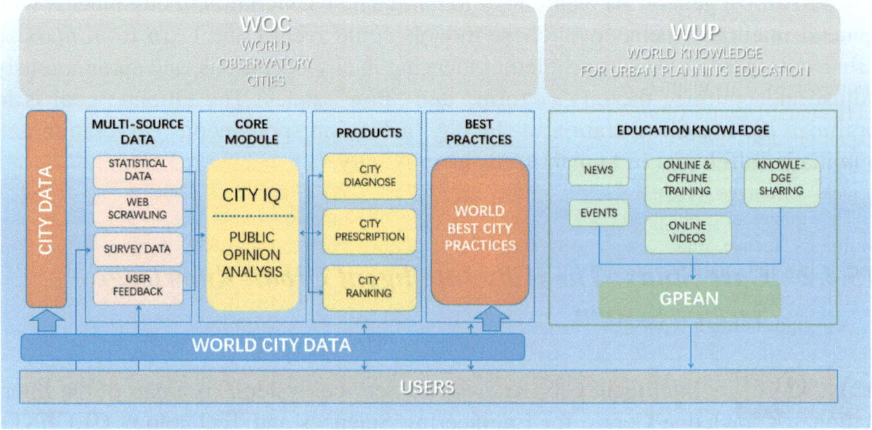

Fig. 15.2 The structure of iCity

The "World Observatory of Cities (WOC)" utilizes global city data (Citydata) and an intelligent city case library (World Best City Practices) as its foundation. Simultaneously, it develops functionalities represented by CityIQ, enabling recent capabilities such as city data queries and comparisons, with future goals of city simulation and diagnostics. Open to the public, it realizes fundamental features such as global city overviews and case studies, providing basic quantifiable queries, analysis, and comparison functions. Cities can learn from each other's successful development experiences and compensate for their own shortcomings. As the platform's influence expands, more cities will interact, actively participating in data construction and extending services to global cities.

The "World Knowledge for Urban Planning and Education" acts as a link to industry and academic cutting-edge information. It focuses on creating a shared knowledge platform for global planning education, tracking real-time updates, and providing lifelong learning and educational resources for scholars, practitioners, and related professionals. This platform aims to facilitate the exchange of achievements, promote collaborative development between academia and industry, and contribute more technology and talent to the research and construction of smart cities and planning education.

Representative expert	Opinions
WU Zhiqiang Academic of Chinese Academy of Engineering	All the smart cities in the world are like intelligent seeds scattered across the Earth. These seeds of intelligence need us to jointly maintain, nurture, and provide them with sunlight and rain. iCity, this website, serves as a platform that enables global smart cities to unite and achieve sustainable development goals in the future

Index

Z. WU, *The AI City*, The Urban Book Series,
https://doi.org/10.1007/978-981-96-2560-4

T

U

GPSR Compliance

The European Union's (EU) General Product Safety Regulation (GPSR) is a set of rules that requires consumer products to be safe and our obligations to ensure this.

If you have any concerns about our products, you can contact us on ProductSafety@springernature.com

In case Publisher is established outside the EU, the EU authorized representative is:

Springer Nature Customer Service Center GmbH
Europaplatz 3
69115 Heidelberg, Germany

Batch number: 08479043

Printed by Printforce, the Netherlands